Walking the Munster Blackwater

'There are few localities in the British Isles so rich in picturesque scenery,
historical associations and monumental remains,
as the valley of the Blackwater.'
(19TH CENTURY GUIDEBOOK)

✿

This book is dedicated to Frank O'Malley, Sean DeLacour
and Timmy Flavin

Walking the Munster Blackwater

Ó Thriopall go Caoin Eochaill

JIM O'MALLEY

ashfield
PRESS

Published in 2015 by

ASHFIELD PRESS · DUBLIN · IRELAND

© Jim O'Malley, 2015
Photographs (except where stated) © Jim O'Malley, 2015
Maps compiled by Ashfield Press

ISBN 978 1 901658 96 5

British Library Cataloguing in Publication Data.
A catalogue record for this book is available from the British Library.

The walk, described in this book, is not intended for others to follow.
Accordingly, the author and publisher do not accept responsibility for any mishap or injury
that may occur if some person (or persons) attempts (attempt) to follow the described route.
It is our wish that reading this book will motivate readers to enjoy and experience the wonders
of the Munster Blackwater in a safe and healthy manner but as this publication does not
purport to serve/act as a guidebook additional advice/information should be sought.

Designed and typeset in 11 on 13.5 point Quadraat by
SUSAN WAINE

Contents

Introduction

THE FIRST BOOK on the Blackwater, *The Blackwater in Munster*, written by J. R. O'Flanagan, was published in 1844. O'Flanagan travelled up river from the town of Youghal in a boat belonging to Sir Richard Musgrave of Tourin House. From the comfort and security of a cabin, he observed the scenery, the castles, monasteries and 'seats' of the numerous gentlemen who resided along the course of the river.

The outcome of his travels resulted in volume of finely-tuned writing in which he recorded a great range of impressions and detailed historical events along with an inventory of the great houses in the river valley. O'Flanagan's primary aim was to cultivate an awareness of the scenery and the cultural heritage of the area. In conjunction with his supporters, the gentlemen who subscribed to the publication, he aimed his writing at tourists and other visitors to the Blackwater valley. His attachment and love of the Blackwater shine through the pages of his writing.

The passage of time has, however, lessened the appeal of his work – the formal literary style and, perhaps an over-emphasis on the great houses built in the Blackwater valley.

One hundred and eighteen years elapsed before the second written account of the Blackwater was delivered from the printing press. Annraoi Ó Liatháin walked the full length of the river from source to sea in 1959 and recorded his impressions in *Cois Móire*, published in 1962 by 'Sairséal agus Dill.'

Ó Liatháin grew up in Glendine, close to Youghal Harbour where the Blackwater meets the sea. An ardent nationalist, a dedicated angler, and an energetic walker, he undertook the task of painting a picture of the river and the countryside with an engaging enthusiasm. His writing, *as Gaeilge*, never earned the recognition it deserved or reached the wider reading audience that would have relished his lyrical version of life along the river valley.

Fourteen years later (1976) Liam Milner penned, *From the Kingdom to the Sea*, a detailed and systematic account that focused especially on the tributaries of the river, the castles, great historic events as well as the illustrious individuals associated with the catchment of the Blackwater.

The magic and lure of the great water course has continued to fascinate writers and readers. The most recent work on the Blackwater is Niall O Brien's, *Blackwater and Bride: Navigation and Trade, 7000BC to 2007.*' O'Brien, a keen historian from west Waterford, has unearthed and made available to the public a wealth of archival material relating to trade and navigation on the Blackwater through the ages.

The present writer was born and grew up in the hinterland of Youghal where he developed an attachment and fascination for the natural heritage of the area. He has absorbed 'green values' and, consequently, holds the firm belief that our community has a responsibility to protect and to conserve the natural features that enrich and support our lives.

While the story that unfolds within the pages of this book can be regarded as an interesting adventure, the author aims to reconnect readers to local places and to the fascinating array of life that manifests itself along the Blackwater from source to sea.

Dedication

THIS BOOK is dedicated to the memory of my brother Frank (1943-2011), to my classmate and GAA friend, Sean DeLacour (1947-2010) and to my 'Blackwater' friend, Timmy Flavin (1957-2015).

A short time before I undertook the Blackwater Walk, I asked my brother Frank a very direct question, 'What do you think of my plan?' His brief and even more direct answer startled me, 'I think it's mighty.'

Walking for Frank involved moving from field to field to check livestock, erect and repair fences, move animals to new pastures, free drains and clear scrub. Being a countryman, he was utterly aware of the challenges I faced and framed his response with the explanation, 'If you went into Flynns' at Park creamery and followed the Tourig down through the inches, into Motherway's and Gibbons' land, you'd have a tough job.'

A silence descended over the kitchen as the stark reality sank home. He then referred to the formidable fence and drain between the Flynns' and Motherways'.

During his life as a farmer, Frank developed an affection for the flora and fauna on the farm and along connecting roads. He knew that the rare yellowhammers perched on the whitethorns of Clasheel Hill and that they flew from bush to bush as he approached on his tractor. On one occasion, a family member remarked that a hilly part of the Glen should be cleared. His direct answer finished all further discussion – 'Where would the birds go then?'

In later years he told me that while topping thistles and rushes in a rough pasture, he saw a hen pheasant nesting ahead of the mower. Instead of continuing and, in the process, destroying the pheasant and its chicks, he turned the tractor around and headed for home. 'I couldn't do it; I know others do but I couldn't do it.'

Frank left school at the age of sixteen and from that time worked our family farm for an unbroken period of fifty-two years. Physically demanding labour and long hours never affected his good humour and his readiness to help out his neighbours. He faced his premature death, at the age of sixty-eight, with a quiet acceptance.

Sean, in contrast to Frank, was very much a townsman. Born and reared in Youghal, he knew and loved all the old streets, the climbing lanes and connecting alleys of the town.

His quiet but ready laugh, the good-humoured twinkle of his eye and his pleasant banter along with his love of sport distinguished him especially. From a young age, Sean displayed an athletic prowess on the playing field in both hurling and football. In 1965 Sean and his good friend Frank Cooper were selected for the Cork minor hurling team.

We played together at all the underage levels in both codes for the Youghal Hurling and Football Club. By 1968 we had graduated to the intermediate squad. We travelled in the same car and tended to sit together in the dressing rooms before and after games. Our sporting companionship was, however, tested during a school league in 1962 when we found ourselves on opposing sides and marking one another at midfield.

Sean proved to be a veritable ball of fire, dashing away for the breaking *sliotar* a vital split-second before his opponent. Most opponents only saw a flash of blond hair in his wake as he raced up and down the playing pitch.

Timmy Flavin lived the first nine years of his live in Clondulane close to the Blackwater. His family then moved to Ardsallagh and later to the town of Youghal where he attended Youghal CBS.

Instead of football and hurling, Timmy discovered the river and harbour of Youghal. Leaving east Cork behind, he kayaked around Ireland, off Scotland and the Faroes and down uncharted rivers in Borneo and Patagonia.

When I confided my walking plans to him, his eyes lit up and he immediately offered to provide all the relevant maps to facilitate my walk. Within a short time, he returned bearing enlarged sheets that showed distances, tributaries, bridges, towns and villages in great detail. From that time, we discussed every aspect of the plan – the length of the daily walk, access to certain areas, ridges and inlets that could slow down progress.

Subsequently, sharing and reliving the experience of walking the Blackwater distilled deeper insights into the experience and pleasure of exploration for both of us.

Acknowledgements

ARLY CONTACTS I am most grateful to my brother Joe for liaising with me during the walk and supplying me with the necessary sustenance. I thank my UCC colleagues, Denis Burns and Hannah Joyce, for accompanying me along stretches of the river. I wish to express my thanks to the Mulcahy family, Conna, for their interest and support. A special word of thanks is due to John Lane and Tadhg (surname withheld), Mallow, for helping me to negotiate around troublesome obstacles.

I appreciated the warm welcome, cup of tea and conversation with Mary O'Farrell in Keale, Millstreet where my water supply needed replenishing. The hospitality of all my B&B hosts was greatly appreciated. Thanks to Eily Buckley (Millstreet), Joan & Steve Roche (Banteer, Rosnalee), Pat Walsh (Mallow) and Joe & Noreen Willoughby (Ballyrafter).

My son, Eanna, dropped me off at sunrise to begin my long walk. Nelius Mulcahy, Ned Miller (Kilbarry) and Martin Trusler (Mocollop) guided me around the area where General Lucas was kidnapped. Kieran Heffernan lent me a copy of *History of Strancally Castle*. Mike Hackett gave me a copy of his book *Echoes over the Blackwater*. Pat Fennessy and Ed Ward provided other interesting books. Niall O'Brien's book, *Blackwater & Bride: Navigation and Trade*, was inspirational. *The Claymen of Youghal* by potter Tony Breslin helped to round off my narrative. The documentary by RTE journalist Liam O Brien, 'Fishing in the Blackwater', opened up a dramatic window on the issue of fishing rights. Ace angler, Johnny Guerin, shared his fishing secrets with me. Dr Jim O'Sullivan, classical scholar, helped to clarify the older names of the Blackwater.

I owe a huge debt of gratitude to my good friend, Timmy Flavin, who mapped the route for me, calculated the distances of the seven stages of my journey and was constantly prepared to discuss the challenges I faced in writing this account.

While researching and writing this book, I returned to various locations along the river: Con Houlihan guided me to Duarrigle Castle and related how his father bought and sold the castle. His neighbour, Leo O'Leary, was similarly helpful. Sean Radley supplied me with suitable photos of the Millstreet area.Subsequent encounters with landowners and farmers, such as Michael Daly (Dysert) and Dan Kelleher (Dromaneen) have enriched this account. Timmy O'Keeffe gave me details of his father's boatbuilding in Ballinaclash. Thanks to the management of Ballynatray Estate for permission to walk through the estate.

The DeLacour family, Youghal, came to greet me on my arrival at Green's Quay, Youghal, where I concluded my trek.

Michael Fewer, author of a multitude of walking and local history books, read and offered me a helpful critique of my first draft. His advice and tips have been heeded. The lure of Immrama, Lismore Travel Writing Festival, attracted me to the writing workshop organised by the author, Paul Clements. His guidelines have been implemented. I regard myself as a graduate of the Lismore school of travel writing. Paul subsequently read 'Day 5' and suggested relevant changes in that section of my account.

Having produced a completed narrative, I turned to a teaching colleague and close friend, Pascal Mac Gabhann, to correct and rewrite sections of my account. Gabhaim buíochas ó chroí leis. Eve Burhenne, Connecticut, read and gave me a most insightful and encouraging response. Charley Hayes, colleague and walking companion, explained why the Blackwater turns south at Cappoquin. The relevant pages (170-172) are based on his detailed notes. Kevin McCarthy, Cappoquin Heritage Group, sent me local history books and photos. Richard Pardi, cousin and ally, gave me belief and confidence in my own writing.

Permission from the following publishers is gratefully acknowledged: Irish Academic Press; Four Courts Press; Picador & Cannongate; Oxford University Press & Cork University Press; Faber & Faber; Sairséal & Dill; Woulfhound & Ballinakilla Press; Geography Publications; Grafton Books & Routledge & Kegan Paul (London); details taken from *The Irish Times* & *Examiner* are similarly acknowledged.

During the course of writing this book I used a considerable range of material from the journals of Cumann Luachra, the Duhallow Historical Society, Aubane Historical Society and Mallow Field Club. The research of the numerous contributors to their journals has been greatly appreciated. Historian and genealogist, Turtle Bunbury, has been generous in granting me approval to quote details from his research into the Holyroyd-Smyths and the Hare family, Convamore.

My publisher Susan Waine, Ashfield Press, took on the challenge of turning my raw manuscript into a colourful and attractive book.

While every effort has been made to acknowledge material quoted in this work, the author asks for due allowance if acknowledgement has been inadvertently omitted.

All weary walkers return home – their true destination. Kathleen has listened to all my Blackwater stories and countless musings at the kitchen table where we talk and eat together.

AN ABHAINN MHÓR
Watershed at source

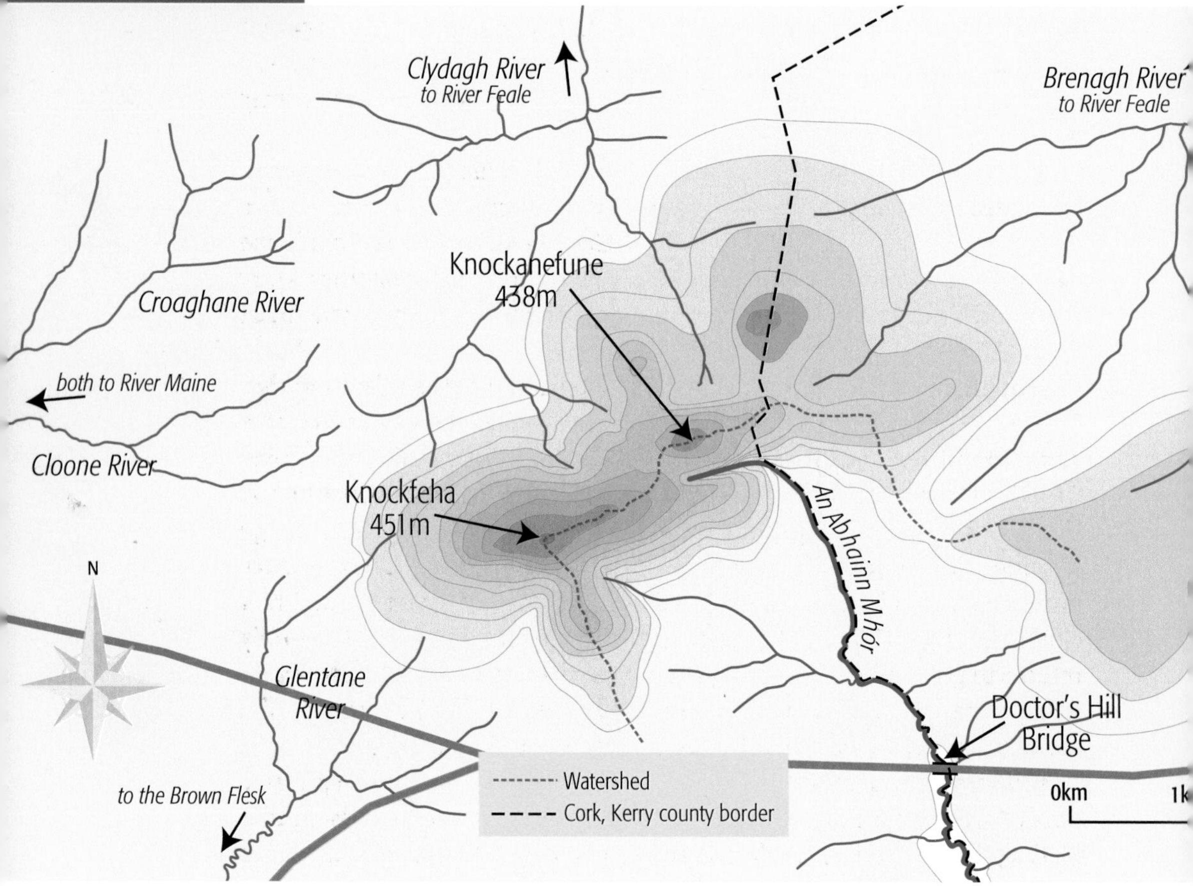

Clydagh River
to River Feale

Brenagh River
to River Feale

Croaghane River

both to River Maine

Cloone River

Knockanefune
438m

Knockfeha
451m

An Abhainn Mhór

N

Glentane
River

Doctor's Hill
Bridge

to the Brown Flesk

Watershed
Cork, Kerry county border

0km   1k

Adapted from a map by Timmy Flavin

Beginning

'Who that beheld the broad river bearing tall ships into Youghal bay would recognise this tiny rivulet as the commencement of that truly noble stream, the Blackwater?'[1]

I T IS TIME TO RECONNECT. After a decade of scandals, political corruption and ineptitude (2000-2010), it is time to return to another Ireland, not to a nostalgic reductionist past but to the bedrock, the physical landscape and to the cultural contours out of which our country has evolved and grown.

My search for the source, for the 'pot' from which the Blackwater rises has ended in failure. The early maps show the source of the Blackwater as a dividing rivulet between the townlands of Coom and Glanowen, both in the county of Kerry. It then becomes the boundary for part of another Kerry townland Knocknacurragh before meeting the rebel county townland of Muinganine.

Hoping to locate a spring from which water could be seen clearly to rise, I follow the tiny trickle backwards until eventually it is absorbed and lost in a mass of saturated sphagnum vegetation. Muinganine (*Muing an Oighinn*, 'The Cauldron of the Morass') is accepted as being the source of the great river, a placename suggestive of upland habitations and Bronze Age feasting. The south-west wind blows quietly but insistently, sending a series of ripples through the masses of purple moor grass (*Molinia caerulea*) that clothe the upper slopes of Knockanefune (1442'). Today, nature stubbornly refuses to give up her secrets. I must be satisfied with the bare sights, with wind, water and soil. An unsettled lonely place, inhabited only by the mountain hare, the hovering kestrel and the scarce hen harrier.

Climbing upwards to the highest point, known as the 'Steeple,' I gaze north to the Shannon, north-west to Tralee Bay, west to Iveragh and McGillycuddy's Reeks, south to Mangerton and the Paps, and lastly, I turn my gaze eastwards to the Galtees and the Knockmealdowns. From this vantage point, an amorphous mass, resulting from the Armorican folding,

---

1   O'Flanagan, J.R., *Historical and Picturesque Guide to the River Blackwater in Munster*, 19441

was thrust upwards to form the Mullaghareirk Mountains that follow an east-west grain, dividing county Limerick from county Cork. From the flanks of these sprawling mountains, a triad of rivers radiates to the coast with the river Feale entering the sea between Kerry Head and Loop Head in Clare, the river Maine flowing into Castlemaine Harbour and the Blackwater begins its long journey to the Celtic Sea off the south of Ireland. A watershed that determines the drainage of 13% of the physical landmass of Ireland, but equally significant as a territory where grim historical events were played out.

The name 'Blackwater' fails to reflect the true character of the river that struggles to escape from the slopes of these desolate uplands. In contrast, the Gaelic name *Abhainn Mhór na Mumhan* ('The Great River of Munster') implies rank, history and character. Ptolmey, the Greek geographer, named it 'Daurona' in his second-century geography of the then discovered world. Another ancient name for the Blackwater is *Nem/Neimh*, cognate of the modern Gaelic word *Neamh* ('Heaven').

My journey of rediscovery along the course of the Blackwater will allow me time to reflect on the naming of the river. A river is much more than a mass of water that falls and flows with the gradient: a river becomes a boundary; a life-line to the sea and a great artery on the face of the landscape that throbs and subsides in accordance with the mood of the weather.

My first steps are tentative, testing the marshy and rushy ground where masses of withered vegetation lie undisturbed. Here and there between the rushes, I can glimpse a tiny trickle of brown bog water – the embryo phase of this great river, – emerging from the soggy hillside of Knockanefune. Masses of tussock sedge abound, later little groves of eared willow which I walk around, and, terrier-like, I follow the trickle sousing underneath my feet.

A new information board informs me that the Blackwater is 104 miles long, has 148 main tributaries and is crossed by twenty-two bridges before it reaches the sea in Youghal harbour. Two signposts – one in red and white points to the east, while the other, in green and gold, points west to Kerry.

After a short distance, the incipient river forms a pool that then flows into a channel carved out of the bedrock. Here the Blackwater becomes a recognisable stream which I can follow, and at times walk along the river bed in order to avoid the briars, furze and other vegetation that cover both banks. The slope on both

… the Blackwatwer, a recognisable stream.

banks steepens with the course of the river turning into a groove. The Sitka spruce afforestation towers over me on either side. Occasionally, I stoop beneath its overhanging branches and make my way along the channels left by the deep ploughing tractor that invaded Muinganine some thirty years ago. Today, a harvester is at work here, felling trees and leaving great swathes of ground pillaged, ransacked and desolate.

I am not the first, and hopefully not the last adventurer, to follow the Blackwater from its source here in Duhallow to where it joins the Celtic Sea. Annraoi Ó Liatháin (AOL), a civil servant, writer and a man of learning, achieved this feat in 1959 and recorded his adventure in a very readable account, *Cois Móire*.[2] Today, I retrace his footsteps and step into the path already trodden by him but, perhaps, viewing the environs from a different perspective and a different mindset because, in the fifty-one intervening

2   Ó Liatháin, Annraoi, *Cois Móire*, Sáirséal agus Dill, Baile Átha Cliath, 1964

years, this landscape has been transformed beyond recognition.

About 400 yards downhill, I pause to examine the reputed site of the hut where Gerald, the fifteenth Earl of Desmond took refuge after four years of warfare (1579-83). Occupying a level niche on the sheer slope, the foundation of *Reidhtheach an Iarla* ('The Earl's House') can still be seen through the furze and briars that have enveloped this ground. Here in July 1583, the once powerful Earl sheltered from the English commander Pelham whose forces were rapidly closing in on this lonely haven. The fugitive Earl and his followers escaped by the skin of their teeth across the hills to Glanageenty, a wooded townland between Castleisland and Tralee where they sheltered until November of that year.[3]

Early on the morning of 11November, his pursuers, led by Owen MacDonnell Moriarty, closed in on the small cabin where Gerald and his depleted garrison had taken refuge. The previous day the Earl's men had

Reidhtheach an Iarla ('The Earl's House'), indicated by stake.

stolen cattle and a horse from a local farmer. With a bounty on his head, his plight was truly a desperate one. 'I am the Earl of Desmond. Save my life,'

---

3   Ó Ríordáin, John J., *where Araglen so Gently Flows: A story of Munster and Ireland through life around Kiskeam in Duhallow, Co. Cork,* 2007

he pleaded with his captors who hauled him mercilessly from his last hiding place. Fearing that the Earl's supporters in the area would quickly regroup and attempt to rescue their leader, Moriarty ordered one of his men, Daniel Kelly, to execute the wounded Earl whose injuries were slowing their progress. Kelly drew his sword and, with a single blow, beheaded the Earl whose head was then brought to Castlemaine and later sent to London where it was displayed on London Bridge on 13 December, 1583.[4] This final act of barbarity brought the Munster rebellion, 1579-83, to a conclusion.

The Desmond rebellion devastated a great part of Munster. Up to one third of the population perished in the rebellion, either slain in the conflict or ravaged by famine and disease. Though there were pitched battles, much of the conflict occurred in the form of raids or ambushes particularly on the part of the Desmond supporters who sheltered in the then extant great woods of Kilmore and Cleanglass from where they sallied forth to attack passing bands of armed troops. The English retaliated by engaging in a scorched earth policy, leaving large tracts of land devoid of livestock and crops. The authors of the Four Masters wrote that the lowing of a cow or the whistle of a plough-boy could scarcely be heard from Dún Caoin [West Kerry] to Cashel. Elizabeth Tudor and her officials, having routed their opponents from a great part of Munster, declared the land of the Desmond and of their allies confiscated. The victors then began the process of carving up the spoils of war and of imposing English law along with the beliefs and practices of the reformed religion. [5]

Paradoxically, I'm beginning my unearthing of history with the end rather than the beginning. I will follow the frayed and tangled threads of this story from the mountain to the river valley beneath and from there to the sea. I take my stance and my *imprimatur* from the great poet, Aogán Ó Rathaille (1670-1726), who, a century later, in his last poem, *Cabhair Ní Ghairfead*, lamented the downfall of the Gaelic aristocracy and the death-knell of Gaelic poetry. Perhaps, in his despair, he besought this lonely place, Glentripple, where he envisaged that his grief would flood the infant river that flows from '*Truipeall to pleasant Youghal.*'

> Fán dtromlot d'imigh ar chine na rí mórga
> Treabhann óm uisceannaibh usice go scímghlórach;
> Is lonnmhar chuirid mo shrutha-sa foinseoga

4   McCormack, Anthony M., *The Earldom of Desmond 1463-1583: The Decline and Crisis of a Feudal Lordship,* Four Courts Press, Dublin, 2005, p. 17

5   McCormack, *The Earldom of Desmond,* p. 17-18

Glentripple – 'the water ploughs in grief ...'

San abhainn do shileas ó Thruipill go caoin-Eochaill[6]

(Our proud royal line is wrecked; on that account
the water ploughs in grief down from my temples,
sources sending their streams out angrily
to the river that flows from Truipeall to pleasant Eochaill.)

As I follow the course of the river downhill and plunging through thickets of briar and bush, I am at one with the nascent river. The gradient drops sharply and the infant river hurtles onwards. Escaping into the Sitka plantations offers a respite until a rusty barb wire fence forces me to crawl over the dead needles. The towering conifers sieve the afternoon sun, filtering a diluted light to the dead woodland floor. If 'walking the Blackwater' involves such hardship, then I am prepared to endure what the rugged terrain can inflict. AOL had an easier passage, observing the teams of turf cutters at work on the mountain side as he strode with the fall of ground. Here and there I catch sight of some long-abandoned turf banks where the *sleán* ('turf-cutting instrument') once cut deeply and where a *meitheal* ('a working group') of neighbours spread and footed their winter fuel. Large turf-cutting machines have replaced the culture of manual

---

6   Ó Tuama, Seán & Kinsella, Thomas (ed), *An Duanaire 1600- 1900: Poems of the Dispossessed,* The Dolmen Press i gcomhair le Bord na Gaeilge, 1981, p. 164-167

The depths of despair, *in umar na haimléise*

labour in Irish bogs. Days of toil combined with story-telling, the bog breeze, the swaying *ceannabhán* ('bog cotton'), the turning and, in due course, the footing of the sods are now recalled by older men to remind the younger generation of the hardship they endured in times past.

Enclosed in the woodlands, I find myself beset by an anxious impatience and long to re-emerge into the open moorland. The first tributary from Baraveha (*Barr a' Bheithe*, 'The Peak of the Birch') joins and enlarges its sister stream from the higher ground. Stooping under over-hanging branches, planting each footfall deliberately between stones and tufts, the prospect of sunlight and unimpeded movement motivate me to persist. Then, at last, I emerge into a rough pasture which leads into a succession of fields where a suckler herd and a young Charolais bull are grazing until they sight me. The bull becomes fretful, snorts and paws the ground; I calculate the distance between us and, to my relief, he retreats, followed by his attendant herd though, unfortunately, in the very direction that I have plotted. Eventually, I am forced to cross the river to the Cork bank and, in that way, I manage to avoid the retreating animal.

Reaching Doctor's Hill Bridge and the road, I look backwards at the first stage of the river which will be my companion for the coming week. The evening has been a tough trial that exceeded, in no small measure, my expectation of the difficulties, obstacles and challenges that the river will throw in my path for the coming week.

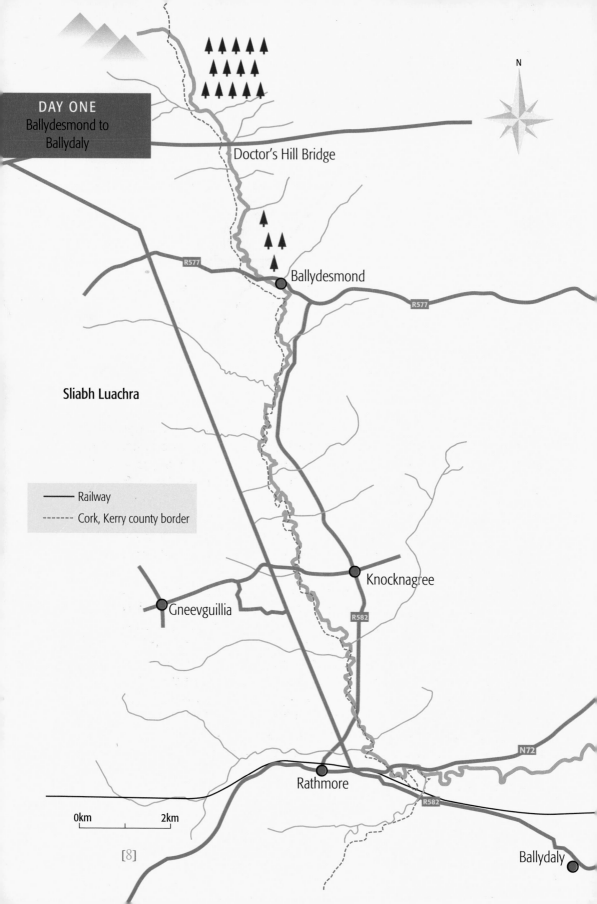

DAY ONE
Ballydesmond to
Ballydaly

N

Doctor's Hill Bridge

R577

Ballydesmond

R577

Sliabh Luachra

——— Railway
- - - - Cork, Kerry county border

Knocknagree

Gneevguillia

R582

N72

Rathmore

R582

0km   2km

Ballydaly

[8]

Ballydesmond to Ballydaly

'The countryside is argumentative. It wants to pick a fight with you. It wants to dish out scars and bruises. It wants to give you roughened palms and gritty eyes. It likes to snag and tear your arms and legs on briars and on brambles every time you presume to leave the path.'[1]

IT'S 7.15 a.m. My son Eanna has dropped me off at Doctor's Hill Bridge (OS 6", 1832). This is the first bridge on the Blackwater, a double-arched structure under which the peat-stained waters from Muinganine flow southwards through difficult terrain. Situated about three miles north of the village of Ballydesmond – border country where sporting loyalties have to be declared with the green and gold of Kerry being hoisted west of the Blackwater and the red and white of Cork on its eastern side. Curiously, one householder has dared to fly the 'red and white' about 100 yards from the bridge on the Kerry side.

Having climbed over the first tubular-iron gate into an ungrazed field, I get my knapsack entangled in the electric fence. Agitated and frustrated by my misfortune, I wonder to myself what eccentric trait in my make-up is driving me to undertake this seven-day walk from the source of the Blackwater to the sea in Youghal. The morning is bright though somewhat chilly and the grass is laden with a heavy fall of dew. I haven't asked permission from the landowners but knowing that they are still tucked up in their warm beds, I press ahead through field one and field two while keeping close to the river or, more fittingly, the stream. Before long, I find the path more difficult than I had expected while pouring over maps and

---

1 Crace, Jim, *Harvest,* Picador, 2013, p.63

Doctor's Hill Bridge | Carriganes

conducting some reconnaissance. Very soon I am forced to cross to the Cork side into Carriganes (*Carraig*, 'Rock, Carraigeán) where formidable earthen fences with tight rows of wire on top and a not inconsequential dyke test my mettle to the full. Contrary briars and knotted tufts of bracken add insult to ignominy. And then the solution occurs to me to walk along the river bed. Fr Anthony Culloty in his history of Ballydesmond writes,

> There are some still living who can remember having seen men and women from Carriganes, Knocknaboul and Glounawadra, coming to Mass on horseback with no other road other than the bed of the Blackwater.[2]

Following in the footsteps of the mass-goers, I make progress into the townland of Knocknaboul (*Cnoc na bPoll*, 'The Hill of the Bog Holes or Pits.') where I notice, to my dismay, the tell-tale signs of pollution, probably, caused by rainwater washing artificial fertiliser and slurry into the river. The growth of strips of ugly brownish algae, attached to stones, indicates enrichment due to excess levels of nitrates in the water. The Department of Agriculture, aiming to reduce the problem, have instructed landowners to spread fertilizer and slurry during periods of dry weather when the ground will absorb the chemical content. Annual rainfall levels tend to be high here

---

2 Culloty, Anthony T., *Ballydesmond/Baile Deasmhumhain: A Rural Parish in its Historical Setting,* Elo Press, 1960,. The name may refer to either Dr Towhill, the first person to buy the area, or 'Dr Francis Crump who held1,415 acres of Glanawaddra and Glanowen.'p.300

in this part of north-east Kerry and north-west Cork and the soils less absorbent. The presence of such material in the river ecosystem reduces the number of aquatic insects, invertebrates and fish in the water. The heavy rainfall of the area combined with regular spate floods from the uplands in the Mullaghareirk Mountains most likely flushes the river bed and prevents harmful substances from accumulating.

The angle of the rising sun catches the dewdrops on the blades of grass. Then, I notice a silvery covering of light frost where the poplars and birches cast their shadows. 'Frost in the end of August,' I exclaim to myself. Forced to look closer, I observe the patches where the frost has formed overnight, spread in a linear pattern alongside the river.

Scanning the fields uphill from the river, my eye rests on a figure leaning on a gate and gazing in my direction. An early-morning farmer has spotted the 'stranger with the black and red knapsack,' walking through his land. He has just driven his herd of dairy cows into the modern milking parlour where a machine soon kicks into action. Coming from a farming background, I know that farmers develop a watchfulness that enables them not only to observe the movements of their livestock but also anyone who rambles through their lands. In fact, it is not easy to walk through the countryside without one's movements being monitored. The Irish proverb, 'Bíonn súile ag na machairí agus cluasa ag na sceacha,' ('The plains have eyes and the bushes have ears') aptly represents the situation.

It is almost 8.00 a.m. I had expected that I would have reached Ballydesmond by this time but I still have in the region of one mile left. Reaching lower and wetter ground, great stands of rushes (*Luachra / Juncus* spp) force me to zigzag around their dense mass. This extended part of Kerry along with the adjoining part of Cork is best known as *Sliabh Luachra*, famous for its traditional Irish music played by Padraig O'Keeffe, Denis Murphy, Julia Clifford, Paddy Cronin, Johnny O'Leary and at the present time by stalwarts such as Jackie Daly and Matt Cranitch. The name *Sliabh Luachra* seems to raise expectation among all music lovers. One could justifiably ask what gave rise to such a unique heritage especially in an area that lacked the resources available elsewhere. Straining my ears, I listen to the soft wind and the trickle of the water in the hope that, perhaps, some air, reel, slide or polka will materialise out of the hillside and boggy fields around me. Perhaps, like the Blasket Islanders, I could catch some lost long-ago tune.

Much debate takes place among Irish music enthusiast as to the precise area included in the placename *Sliabh Luachra*. As the argument rages in dimly lit pubs, one is tempted to imagine that the name denotes a state of mind, a heightened mood brought on by excessive foot-tapping to the slides and polkas of this boggy rushy land. The scholarly lexicographer, An tAth. Pádraig Ó Duinnín (1860-1934) noted that the district of Sliabh Luachra lies within a triangle extending from Millstreet to Killarney and from there north to Castleisland. The occurrence of the placename *Sliabh Luachra* in the Fenian tale, *Bodach an Chóta Lachna*, offers us clear evidence of the ancient character of the name.[3] The name *Sliabh* here does not stand for a 'mountain' or even for a 'tall hill' but for a 'moor, oft. low-lying.'[4] In the eighteenth century, dispossessed landowners from fertile lands along the Blackwater were forced to take flight into this barren and unoccupied district where they eked out a frugal living from the harsh landscape. Surnames such as O'Keeffe, O'Callaghan and McCarthy, descendants of the proud Gaelic chieftains, are common in Rathmore, Gneevgullia, Knocknagree and elsewhere at the present time. The village of Ballydesmond was built as a model village, 1830-33, and named Kingwilliamstown in honour of King William IV (1765-1837) A century later in 1932 the village was renamed to commemorate the last days of the Earl of Desmond in the area.

At 8.30 a.m., I cross the bridge over the Blackwater but before proceeding downhill to the Centra Supermarket, I hide my knapsack in a clump of bracken. However, I have only taken a few steps when my attention is drawn to a large modern building a short distance from the bridge – the Nora Herlihy Memorial Centre, dedicated to the memory of a local woman who became the driving-force in the setting up of the Credit Union movement throughout Ireland. Born in 1910, Nora qualified as a national school teacher and spent her career teaching with the Sisters of Charity in inner-city Dublin where she witnessed social deprivation on a disturbing scale.

Despite the early hour, the village is showing ample signs of life with cars, vans and lorries bringing people to work or elsewhere. The supermarket is open and a few early customers are buying their copy of the Irish Examiner to read all about their local football hero, Donncha O'Connor, who rescued the Cork football team from imminent defeat at the hands of their Dublin rivals on the previous Saturday evening. With time running out and Dublin leading by five points, Donncha scored a penalty and three points to give Cork victory by a single point and passage into the All-Ireland on the third Sunday in September. No wonder the red and white

---

3 Ó Conluain, Proinsias agus Ó Céilleachair, Donncha, *An Duinníneach,* Sáirséal agus Dill, Baile Átha Cliath, 1958, p. 41-42

4 Ó Conluain & Ó Céilleachair, *An Duinníneach,* ‚citing the definition of 'sliabh' as defined in *Focloir Gaeilge agus Béarla/Irish-English Dictionary,* p. 41

Ballydesmond

Nora Herlihy Memorial Centre, Ballydesmond

flags are still hanging proudly after the excitement of the previous weekend. All Ireland fever is in the air.

I help myself to a large cappuccino from the machine at the back of the supermarket. Settling down at a table, I jot a few notes about my walk so far and look at my walking schedule for the rest of the day.

Before leaving the village, I would like to recount the story of Nora Sheehan, a young graduate from Tureencahill, who opened Scoil Mhuire, a co-educational secondary school here in Ballydesmond, September 1942, to provide secondary education for boys and girls whose parents did not have sufficient resources to send them to boarding school. Having bought a small two-room cottage on the Newmarket road, she had the dividing wall between the two rooms knocked and began teaching a mixed group of 26 pupils (5 boys and 22 girls) in September. Within a year, however, Bishop O'Brien of the Kerry diocese wrote to her requesting that she discontinue the policy of educating boys and girls in her school. Miss Sheehan complied with the Bishop's request and the five male pupils did not return to school the following year. Three years prior to that, Pope Pius XI in his encyclical *Divini Illius Magistri*, 1939, had labelled co-education as 'the promiscuous herding together of the sexes.' Her single sex school, however, proved to be a success and after ten years she transferred it to the nearby village of Boherbue where she later reintroduced dual-gender education.[5] At the present time, the local

5   O'Malley, James, 'The Catholic Lay Secondary Schools of Rural Ireland, 1922-75,' Ph.D. thesis, 2012

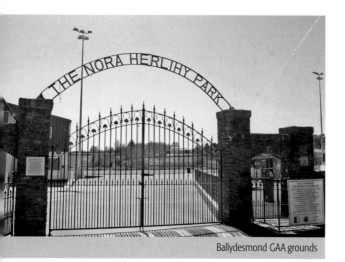

Ballydesmond GAA grounds

Kingwilliamstown renamed Ballydesmond, 1938

boys and girls attend either Boherbue Comprehensive School or Pobalscoil Sliabh Luachra in Rathmore.

Back at the bridge and re-united with my knapsack, I take a moment to read the plaque on the bridge to commemorate the 150th anniversary of the founding of the village, 1833-1983.[6] I set out again on the Kerry side of the Blackwater through the townland of Ballynahulla (*Baile na hÚla*, 'Homestead of the Altar.')' The river runs along the western boundary of the Nora Herlihy Park, the grounds of Ballydesmond GAA Football Club. Founded in 1964, this progressive club has installed floodlights to facilitate night-time training, opened a gym, built concrete steps for spectators as well as developing a riverside walk as an amenity for local people. Enough to make this ageing GAA man pause in his tracks. It is noteworthy that their playing field is named after a woman – a distinction that Ballydesmond shares with Markievicz Park, Sligo.

Before the building of the model village of Kingwilliamstown in the 1830s, life for the tenant farmers and cottiers of the area was unrelentingly harsh. Without roads to facilitate travel and access for the military, the region had become a haven for the dispossessed after the wars of the seventeenth century. From here outlaws and whiteboys could launch punitive raids on the English settlers who occupied the more fertile lower land. Having carried out their raids, they would then retreat to the uplands

---

6   Culloty, p. 125

of Pobal Uí Chaoimh. A report commissioned in 1834 by the government recommended the building of a new road, running from Castleisland through the mountain at Knocknaboul to the coalfields of Clonbanin, Dromagh and Coolclough to join the new road to Cork at Clonmeen Bridge.'[7] The site of the present village was deemed by the authorities as a convenient point where travellers and carriers could break their journey for the night. With stone from a newly opened quarry, an inn with stables for travellers (the 'Nora Herlihy Memorial Centre'), cottages for labourers and tradesmen and a chapel and school (the present Centra supermarket) were built. Other improvements included land reclamation and the development of a model farm in the assumed hope that farming practices could be improved.[8]

The birth of this new village, the building of roads and the draining of land helped to improve the lives of the native people though the great famine, 1845-47, undermined the progress that had been made. Culloty, the local historian, concludes that military and political considerations were the real reasons for such work.

> It was neither compassion nor the promptings of conscience that now sparked the renewed interest in the improvements of the locality...For the security of the empire this district had to be developed and then displayed as it commanded all the great roads to and from the south western corner of Ireland.[9]

Richard Griffiths and his assistant, James Weale, were responsible for the Report and for the successful implementation of the plans. Griffiths personally supervised the construction of the planned road that enabled hundreds of men to earn a good wage as well as bringing some hope of a better future to the area. He realised the necessity for good industrial relations and even paid the work- men during periods of bad weather to ensure their loyalty to the project. I imagine that Griffiths and Weale would be pleased to visit and inspect how their concept of a 'model village' has endured to the twenty-first century.

Within a short time, an embarrassing mishap occurs when the seat of my trousers is ripped from my right buttock down to my knee while negotiating a passage through a dense maze of brambles. Having assessed the extent of the damage, I resolve to continue, reassured by the fact that my

---

7   Ibid, p. 97
8   Ibid.
9   Ibid.

lack of modesty is unlikely to prove a problem along the Blackwater with only suckler herds and a few horses likely to take the least notice of a solitary wanderer. However, my problems were only beginning and more and more difficult challenges had to be overcome as the day progressed.

After a respite of a few fields, I come face-to-face with a stark notice which unambiguously tells me, 'Hazardous Waste Site.' A considerable quantity of earthen spoil has been deposited here, some of which may have been excavated from a large pond which is now full of rainwater. Being completely at a loss as to what hazardous waste could be here, I determine to slip through the site as quickly as possible. I depart from the waste site without delay and continue along the Kerry side of the Blackwater. My progress, however, is interrupted when patches of rampant briars and bushes compel me to cross to the Cork side. A sheep wire fence with a row of barb wire provides a stiff test into a plantation of ash, sycamore and alder trees. The respite is only short-lived and after a short walk through the plantation I am left with no option but to rescale the fence and continue along the river bed.

Describing these problems to a man from Ballynahulla later, he explained to me,

> You see...it's like this...a lot of the landowners in the Blackwater valley have gone into REPS [Rural Environment Protection Scheme], and they have to fence off the river.

Developing this explanation, he comments,

> That was the source of your problems, why you had all those fences... the REPS. It's a [European Union] scheme to protect the environment. You have to keep livestock out of the streams, maintain fences, reduce the amount of fertiliser you spread and you're also supposed to plant more fruiting trees and bushes for the wild birds.

Raising my eyes upwards, I catch sight of two gigantic wind turbines whose enormous blades rotate with a whirring sound and cast a fleeting shadow over the river banks. I am approaching Munster Joinery which is situated about 4k from Ballydesmond. Manufacturers of PVC windows, doors, fascias and soffits and other accessories, this thriving business was founded here at Lacka Cross in 1973 by two brothers, Paddy and Donal Ring, in a shed next to their family home. Today their thriving enterprise fills a sprawling site of several acres. At the peak of the boom over 1,000 employees worked here, drawn mainly from Duhallow as well as east Kerry, south west Limerick plus a large contingent of immigrants from Poland

Joinery wind turbine   Munster Joinery

and other east European countries. From such small beginnings, the Ring family have seen their project expand and prosper. Munster Joinery is now the largest manufacturer of windows and doors in Ireland. And then the chime I heard earlier resounds loudly followed by a brief announcement.

The collapse of the building industry has affected orders, consequently, the workforce has been reduced and the working week shortened to a four-day week as business slackens. In recent years the Rings have taken steps to reduce the carbon emissions from their plant by erecting two wind turbines with an output of 4.2 megawatts. In addition to the use of wind energy, they have commissioned a biomass CHP plant fuelled by sawdust and off-cuts of timber. The owners claim that they 'have optimised the thermal performance of all their products.' These energy-efficient innovations have seen their business win the Green-Product award in 2013.

Leaving Munster Joinery behind me, I proceed through an extended inch where four piebald horses graze contentedly. That is until they are alarmed by my presence. Aware of the intruder, they become skittish and break into a gallop. They race to the end of the field and anxiously anticipate my arrival there. At which point they take off again at full speed.

The sun rises steadily higher, giving off a pleasant heat through the white clouds that float overhead. The river here flows along the floor of a valley that slopes gradually to the west but more steeply to the east. A dipper (*Cinclus cinclus*) scuds low along the water surface following the course of the river. Here the Blackwater begins to meander through a series of curves. Cognisant that the shortest distance between two points is a straight line, I take the direct route without having to slavishly follow every turn and twist of the river. Gradually I slip into an easier rhythm and succeed in solving the challenges of fences and vegetation more easily until confronted by a high earthen bank towering up from the river bed. Managing to find a foothold, I grasp at a sod. Just as I am hauling myself up, the muscles of my right thigh cramp painfully. In desperation, I manage to complete the climb, depending solely on my left leg. But just as I reach safety, that leg cramps even more viciously, leaving me lying helplessly on the ground. In response, I draw a deep breath and exhale slowly which helps to relax the muscles. Back on my feet, I feel increasingly vulnerable, and begin to wonder whether I can cope with the challenges ahead or not. Later, I text a friend, remarking that Moses must have had an easier time crossing the Red Sea. Though shaken by the experience, I am not unduly alarmed, knowing that a good dose of tonic water will supply the necessary intake of quinine to prevent a repeat of such a painful experience.

Reaching Lisheen Bridge, I debate with myself whether I should walk the one mile off-route to the shop in the village of Knocknagree (*Cnoc na Graí*, 'The Hill of the Stud) or persist despite my diminished water supply.

I opt for another solution by walking to the nearest house where I explain my mission and lack of water to a smiling young lady who, in response, hands me a litre bottle of distilled water. The quiet village of Knocknagree has a fair green of two acres where huge fairs were formerly held. Along with the open area, the village had, at one stage in its recent history, the unenviable boast of having a total of twenty-two licensed premises where farmers slaked their thirst. The last fair was held in the nineteen fifties and the number of licensed premises is now in single figures. Near the church, the Cumann Luachra Historical Society has erected a memorial stone to the poet, Eoghan Rua Ó Súileabháin (1848-1872) with the poignant inscription, 'Sin é an file go fann nuair/a thiteann an peann as a láimh.' More about this anon.

Somehow, I feel that the terrain to Nohoval Bridge will be easier. Later events, however, were to confirm my unshakeable naivety. In negotiating a fence and unaware that the tear in my trousers had become entangled in briars I ripped the damaged garment down to my ankle. But being a former GAA player and used to togging out at the base of ditches, I pull on a strong pair of unrippable shorts with deep pockets front and aft, and resume my wandering along the Blackwater.

Scholars of Irish poetry have noted the frequency of references to bushes, bogs, rivers and streams in the poetry of Aogán Ó Rathaille. Born in Scrahanveal (*Screachán na bhFídheal*, 'The Rough Place of the Calves),about two miles west of the Blackwater, his family moved to Stagmount (*Cnoc an Charrfhiadh*, 'The Hill of the Stag') after the death of his father. The Battle of Kinsale (1601) dealt a lethal blow to the old Gaelic order under which poetry was valued and the bardic poets were generously recompensed for the poems they composed to honour their patrons. Ó Rathaille voiced the anguished sense of loss and displacement that affected him and his fellow poets as guardians of an ancient tradition. In one of his poems Ó Rathaille imagines that the loud flooded waters of all the rivers of Munster give voice to the sorrow of Ireland and its people under the yoke of a foreign invader. Curiously, he omitted any reference to *Abhainn Mhór na Mumhan*, most likely due to its long descriptive name as opposed to the Lee, Maine, Flesk, Roughty and other rivers.

Sliabh Luachra – a land of music and poetry. Directly to the south stand the twin peaks of *Dhá Chíoch Anna* ('The Paps'), the breasts of the goddess Anú, beneath which lies the stone fort, *Cathair Crobh Dearg*. This was originally a place of pagan worship and later a site of Christian devotion where people came in great numbers for the annual pattern on May Sunday. My route along the Blackwater, however, veers eastward near Rathmore. Ó Duinnín regarded the 'Paps' as the Irish Mount Olympus beneath which poetry flourished and great poets such as Ó Rathaille, Eoghan Rua, Geofraidh Ó Donnchadha and Edward Walsh gave voice to the joys and sorrows of their people.

While poetry and music have flourished for generations here in Sliabh Luachra, tragedy struck in the nearby townland of Knocknageeha (*Cnoc na Gaoithe*, 'The Hill of the Wind') on Sunday, 28 December, 1896, when, after days of heavy rain the bog known as *Bogach na Mine* ('The Bog of the Meal') began to move downhill in the direction of Killarney. Following the course of the Owenacree River, a two-acre mass of peat and vegetation obliterated the landscape and engulfed the house in which the Donnelly family lived.

Cornelius Donnelly, Lord Kenmare's quarry steward, his wife and six children perished in this appalling tragedy that shocked the entire country. The 'Moving Bog' continued to shift and slide towards the Flesk River, carrying trees, furze bushes and livestock.

THE MOVING BOG
December 28th, 1896

Tharla maidhm mhór phortaigh anseo ar Chnoc na Gaoithe oíche i dtrátha na Nollag in 1896. Cailleadh Con Donnelly, Johanna, a bhean chéile, agus seisear dá seachtar clainne nuair a slogadh a dteach agus iad ina gcodladh. Anseo ar láthair an tí cuireadh leacht mar chomóradh céad bliain na tubaiste. Tháinig Kate Donnelly (15 bliana) slán mar bhí sí ar cuairt chuig gaolta i gCnoc Uí Shéana, Cnoc na Grai, nuair a sciob an portach a tuismitheoirí agus Daniel, Humphrey, Hannah, Margaret, James agus Eliza.

The Moving Bog disaster resulted in the deaths of quarry worker Con Donnelly, his wife, Johanna, and six of their seven children whose abode was submerged while they slept, on December 28th, 1896. The memorial, erected on the centenary of the tragedy, stands on the site of their home. One child, Kate, then aged 15 years, survived as she was staying with relatives near Knocknagree on the fateful night.

A large section of bog slipped, releasing a massive volume of water and peat which flowed westwards along the valley of the Owenacree River. Some item of furniture from the Donnelly home were found in the Lakes of Killarney, about 14 miles away.

Poor drainage and little or no management of turf-cutting resulted in a huge build-up of trapped water which eventually burst and, according to a report on the tragedy by the Royal Dublin Society (RDS), millions of cubic metres of material were discharged, covering hundreds of acres along the valley through which it ran.

Kate Donnelly later married Paddy O'Donoghue and they settled down and raised a family close to this spot. Kate died in 1964.

Numerous bog slides have been recorded in Ireland, but none with the same human consequences. This monument is erected in memory of the Donnelly family and also is a tribute to all who took part, sometimes at personal risk, in the search for the and to all who helped in any way.

Erected by Cumann Luachra, December 1996

Bog bursts or landslides are natural phenomena that occur when masses of peat or clay become saturated and, consequently, their stability is undermined. Older people regarded 28 December as the unluckiest day of the year since the massacre of the holy infants was perpetrated by Herod on that fateful day. The Royal Dublin Society (RDS) appointed a committee consisting of Prof. W.J. Sollas, Dr A. F. Dixon, Mr A.D. Delap and Dr Llyod Praeger to investigate and report on the phenomenon.' These scientists travelled to Kerry 2 Jan,1897 and spent three days viewing the scene and the extent of the disaster. In their view, 'The bog gave way along the line of a turf-cutting from four to ten feet deep.' They speculated that it may have been linked to an earth tremor that had occurred in Gloucester earlier that day.

Bearing in mind the proverb, 'It's an ill wind...' a group of local people regarded the disaster as a potential tourist attraction. Accordingly, Joseph Dinneen, a 'brother of the Dictionary man,' wrote 'A Guide to the Moving Bog,' containing a summary of the disaster along with a minute description of the surroundings, a map of the district, railway and ocean time-tables; details of fairs and markets and all information necessary for tourists were also included.[10] The aim of this rather insensitive publication was to persuade tourists on the train to Killarney to interrupt their journey at Rathmore railway station from where they could hire transport to visit the scene of the calamity, three and half miles to the north, close to the village of Gneevgullia. The extent of the advertising would seem to indicate a detailed level of business acumen as the reference to 'The Land Slip Hotel' in one such advertisement might indicate.

At Knocknaseed /Cnoc na Saighead / The Hill of the Arrows, 'the arrows of outrageous fortune' strike. I pause briefly at a picnic table where to my horror I discover that the borrowed digital camera and digital tape recorder that I had safely stowed away into a pocket are missing. Retracing my steps through a field, I frustratingly fail to find them. That loss combined with the torn trousers and the cramps revive the nagging doubt that I have bitten off more than I can chew.

Resuming with a heavy heart, I find that I have ventured into what looks like an abandoned gallops, covered with polythene and sand, but now somewhat overgrown with weeds and grasses. At the end of the gallops, I am quite surprised to discover an old abandoned metal footbridge, high over the Blackwater. Curiosity leads me to climb the steps on to the bridge where I gaze down through the alders at the water below, and then descend on the western side before returning across the bridge again. At this point I can only surmise that the old bridge may have been a route for local people to attend Mass in Knocknagree.

The respite from the travails of walking this uncharted course along the Blackwater proves to be a temporary one. A formidable bank, with a large drain at its base, now bars my passage. Grasping a cluster of ferns, I attempt to haul myself to the top but end up instead falling backwards into a muddy drain which leaves me and my knapsack besmeared all over. A torn trousers, excruciating cramps, a lost camera and now a mud-besmeared weary adventurer. What next I wonder? Having washed off as much of the soil as possible in the river, I set off again though the Blackwater throws more and more obstacles in my way.

Though my spirit is sinking and my legs weakening, I push on nevertheless. Up to this point I have not encountered a single landowner along the 7-8 miles I have walked today. I am about to face my first test. Though I wandered freely and unhindered through the neighbours' fields in east Cork where I grew up, the climate has changed especially since the

---

10   Dinneen, Joseph, *The Story of the Moving Bog*, republished by the Aubane Historical Society, 2009

last 'foot and mouth' scare in 2001 when walking, whether for leisure, fowling or angling, was strictly prohibited. Since then the sense of ownership of land as being a private entity has become much more pronounced than previously. Rights of Way, formerly, taken for granted, are increasingly being contested and, not infrequently, debarred. In my own present situation, I readily acknowledge that I am a trespasser who presumes the goodwill of the owners on whose land I have made myself an uninvited user.

The noise of a tractor grows steadily louder as I approach a large sloping field where tilling for reseeding is in full progress. A large John Deere tractor drags a broad harrow uphill, breaking and refining the soil to facilitate the germination of a new crop of grass. Just then I catch sight of a second tractor at the far end of this extensive field. The operators, enclosed in their cabs, work at speed while I pause in my track to allow them thunder past. Then I notice two men watching the operation from the roadside gap through which I will have to make my exit. I am beginning to feel uncertain, fearing that they may object to my walking through their land.

One of the onlookers is wearing a cap and looks grim though the other man looks more relaxed. Both of them are dressed in working mode with their shirt sleeves rolled above their elbows. Like myself they seem to have passed the three score mark. The wind and sun of the four seasons have browned their complexions, leaving them tough and sinewy. I guess that they have plenty more in store and will continue to farm full time for another decade or more.

I owe them an explanation which I proceed to relay to them...that I am a retired teacher, that I have wanted to walk the Blackwater for years, that I'm a Cork- man married and settled in Kerry for thirty years, that I started off this morning at 6.45 a.m. Their interest is aroused; the uncapped man asks me,

'What are you doing it for?

And quickly adds,

'Are you being sponsored?

Replying that I have not sought sponsorship, a momentary wave of regret hits me that, perhaps, I should have planned the walk as a fund-raiser for some charitable organisation. Then the man with the cap asks me the six-marker question,

'Who are you going to cheer for in the All-Ireland?'

A Corkman, married and domiciled in the Kingdom that has defeated the Rebels in the finals of 2007 and 2009, is bound to find himself in a tight corner when sporting loyalties have to be declared. I am fully aware that I am now standing on the Cork side of the boundary (the Blackwater) between the two counties. In a moment of inspiration, I reply,

'What colour is my blood?'

Whatever tension existed in this brief roadside encounter has been utterly dissolved, blown away. They wish me well and wave goodbye to the walker.

Walking a mile to Nohoval Bridge affords me the time to recollect myself after the tribulations of this terrain. Sauntering downhill, I glance through the hedgerow at the river flowing parallel to the road. The blackberries are beginning to ripen, offering me a few juicy morsels, and yellow leaves remind me that autumn has arrived. Nohoval (Nuachongbháil, 'The New Convocation') cemetery lies a short distance away to my right where the remains of the sweet-tongued poet, Eoghan [Rua Ó Súileabháin] an Bhéil Bhinn, may be buried though his memorial stone is in the fifteenth-century Muckross Abbey in Killarney National Park where he is interred along with the other great Kerry poets: Piaras Feirtéir; Aogán Ó Rathaille and Geofraidh Ó Donnchadha. The contrary view is that his funeral procession was halted by a torrential flood in the Blackwater and his corpse was taken instead to Nohoval Cemetery. Whether the poet lies there or in Muckross, his life as a poet, a scholar, a school teacher, as a sailor and a spailpín fánach ('A migratory labourer') was lived intensely with rhyming repartee pouring spontaneously from the spring well of his imagination.

His poem, A Chara Mo Chléibh, appeals especially to me as it describes his concern in having a 'a smooth clean shaft' made for his spade by the blacksmith, Séamus Mac Gearailt, his friend and drinking companion who kept a forge in nearby Rathmore. His hope is that the skill of the smith will enable him to earn sixpence a day as far afield as Galway where he will entertain his company with the legends of Troy, Samson, Alexander, Hector and Caitcheann Mac Tréin. But when his labouring has been finished, he will return home to Sliabh Luachra to spend his earnings with Séamus greannmhar gráigh, 'the light-hearted and loving friend of his breast.'[11]

Poor gifted Eoghan believed in living life to the full. After a term in the English navy, he returned home sore and battle-weary. Hoping that he could revive his fortune, he opened a short-lived school in Knocknagree. After the closure of his school he sought to gain some recognition by writing a poem

---

11   Séan Ó Tuama & Thomas Kinsella (eds), *An Duanaire, 1600-1900: Poems of the Dispossessed*, p. 182-185

praising his patron Colonel Daniel Cronin who failed to reward Ó Súileabháin for his poetic composition. Stung by this rebuke and mindful of the proud bardic tradition he had inherited, it is believed that Eoghan composed a searing satire about his former patron. In the summer of 1884 he encountered Cronin's servants in a tavern in Killarney. An argument broke out between them and heated words were exchanged that resulted in one of Cronin's servants striking Eoghan with a thongs. Badly shaken by the encounter, he managed to make his way home to Knockngree but, contracting a fever, his condition worsened and he died within a short time. Tradition (as narrated by an tAth. P. Ó Duinnín) has it that, knowing that death was nigh, he requested pen and ink to compose an *Aithrí* ('A poem of repentance') but, weakened by the fever, the pen slipped from his grasp leaving him to gasp his last words.

We need poetry to live, to save us from the horrors of consumerism that,

At Nohoval Bridge

combined with the invasive media, threaten to engulf us in a spate of hyper virtual reality. But no sooner has the solace of poetry faded than consumerism jolts me back to the twenty-first century. Glancing over the parapet of Nohoval Bridge, I find, to my horror, that someone has dumped three black polythene bags of disposable nappies into the river. The contents have been saturated by the river water, and I can see what appears to be a residue of urine trickling into the mass of river crowfoot (*Ranunculus aquaticus,*) that dangles wavingly in the current. Disposable nappies take from 600 to 800 years to biodegrade; an infant requires an average of 5,000 during his infancy which amounts to a total of five tons.

It is after three o'clock. I had planned to reach Shamrock Bridge in Ballydaly by 4.00.p.m. From this juncture the Blackwater begins a manoeuvre to shift from its north-south course into a west-east channel. The next stretch to Duncannon Bridge is a relatively short walk of 1.35k which I manage to walk in about thirty minutes. A succession of carefully managed green fields, where calves and a herd of Friesian cows graze, speed up my progress. At Duncannon Bridge, named after Lord Duncannon and built by the engineer and surveyor, Richard Griffith in 1834, I pause briefly to admire the solid workmanship of this limestone bridge. The village of Rathmore is less than a half-mile away. Caherbarnagh (*Cathair Bhearnach,*'Gapped Mountain'), a dark purple mountain with its broad, almost flat peak, lies to the south, close to the Paps. Cadbury's Chocolate Crumb Factory occupies a site a short distance downriver. Opened in 1948, Cadburys brought industrial employ-ment to the languishing village of Rathmore and the surrounding countryside. Their decision benefitted not only the village community but also the small farmers of the area from whom they purchased their quota of milk for the manufacture of chocolate crumb. Their sugar requirements came from the Sugar Factory in Mallow until that industry closed down in recent years. A faint aroma of hot chocolate hangs in the air; or, perhaps, my imagination is tantalising me.

Johnny O'Leary, the great Sliabh Luachra accordionist, worked here until his retirement. A warm-hearted individual who radiated his love of music as his fingers danced deftly over the keys to entertain and delight his audience with tunes such as the 'Meentogues Lad,' 'Green Grow the Rushes,' 'The Hare in the Corn,' 'The Cat in the Corner' and other tunes. With the work of the day over, Johnny could then devote himself to his true vocation.[12]

---

12 Donal Hickey, 'Death of Johnny O'Leary' in *Sliabh Luachra: Journal of Cumann Luachra,* Vol 1, No. 12, Nov. 2006, p 55-57; Moylan, Terry (ed.), *Johnny O'Leary of Sliabh Luachra: Dance Music from the Cork-Kerry Border,* Lilliput Press,

A short distance beyond the factory, the River Aunaskirtaun flowing down from Caherbarnagh mountain, joins the Blackwater. 'Abha na Sciortán, the 'River of Ticks,' earned its strange name as cattle grazing along its course tended to become infested with ticks that gave them the troublesome problem of 'Redwater,' a form of anaemia, characterised by loss of appetite and red-brownish urine. [13] A good farmer will keep a close eye on his cattle and visit them every day to detect the early warning signs. Keeping the pastures short will also help reduce the habitat available for the ticks that carry the *Babesia*, a single-cell parasite that infects animals and can, if neglected, lead to death. Memories of our carefree childhood come flooding back when we too picked up 'sciortáns' ('ticks') that could prove difficult to dislodge once hooked on some part of your body. Nevertheless, we ran our 'heedless ways' through the fields, over fences, down bóithríns and across streams until exhaustion called us home.

After Cadbury's factory, I continue to walk on feet and legs increasingly feeling the strain of the journey. From here I am following a geological Fault Zone that extends from Dingle to Dungarvan and beyond there to Germany. In the language of the layman, two tectonic plates collided along this stretch. The theory of tectonic plates was posited in 1963 by J. Tuzo Wilson, a Canadian geologist, creating a new understanding of the formation of continents and islands as well as providing a new explanation for earthquakes, tsunamis and other physical phenomena relating to the crust of the earth. This Fault Zone, referred to as the Variscan Orogeny, has been much investigated by geologists in recent years. South of the fault line is an area of Old Red Sandstone (ORS) while on its north side limestone is the predominant rock type. From here the Blackwater valley is overshadowed by parallel ridges (low mountain ranges) with the Boggeragh and Nagle Mountains to the south while the more distant Ballhoura Hills and Knockmealdown Mountains flank the Blackwater on its northern side. I have entered what the geologists have labelled 'the ridge and valley' upland of Munster, features that define the livelihood of the farmers with 'an enduring human contrast' between the lives of the 'mountainy men' and the 'comfortable lowland farmers' who inhabit the Blackwater valley. Edmund Spenser (1552-1599), the Elizabethan poet who settled in north Cork, described this striking contrast in *The Faerie Queen*. as 'the breathing fields and mountain hore.' [14]

---

13 Kathleen Moynihan, 'Remembering the Aunaskartaun River in *Sliabh Luachra*, Vol. 1, No. 12, p. 84-87
14 F.H.A. Aalen, 'The Making of the Irish Landscape' in *Atlas of the Irish Rural Landscape*, Cork University Press, 1997, p. 16

Within ten minutes, I slip back into the fields to rejoin the river. A young farmer with a quad is erecting a fence on the far side of the field, probably to section off grazing paddocks and in that way to ensure a more managed grazing regime. I wave to him and he acknowledges me in turn though he must be still wondering who, in heaven's name, came walking through his land here in Nohovaldaly (*Nuachobháil Uí Dhálaigh*, 'The New Convocation of Daly'), Monday, 30 August 2012. Here the river buckles and flows in a horseshoe, forcing me to loop around with it until I lose patience, wade across and take a shortcut to where it straightens out. From Carrigaline to Lyredaowen, I keep up a relentless trek, mostly along the north bank though, at intervals, I am forced to wade across and walk the south side until a fence or drain forces me to re-cross.

Meanwhile, my UCC colleague, Denis Burns, calling me on his mobile, has arrived at Shamrock Bridge. He is anxious for a walk and tells me he will set out to meet me along the north bank. But, finding my way barred by formidable fences, I revert to the south side again where, to my pleasant surprise, I find a narrow road along which the roadside fences have been bulldozed and flattened. Now it's only a canter to Shamrock Bridge where transport awaits to whisk me into Millstreet until a massive New Holland T7 206, hauling a full load of silage and occupying the entire breath of road, forces me to step back to allow the mechanical monster roar past.

A smiling Denis soon appears and looking me up and down comments, 'Jim, what has happened to you? You're wrecked.'

I make a token effort to brush off the spattered mud but he continues to scan me and to express concern about the deplorable state I am in.

Having heard a summary of the day's events, Denis proffers me a can of Coke which is gratefully accepted. I have walked 26k (16 miles) over a period of twelve hours - too long and too tiring to maintain for the rest of the week. Denis is wearing a daffodil-bright yellow t-shirt, and turning around, he points out the word CREW emblazoned on the reverse side - a relic of a walk from Cork to Dublin that he and some friends undertook a few years previously.

Like myself, Denis qualified as a national school teacher in 1970 and taught in Cork and Dublin. Having worked as a curriculum facilitator with the Department of Education in the 1990s, he then took up a lectureship in University College Cork (UCC) where he teaches in the education department with specific responsibility for the 'Diploma for Learning Difficulty for Primary and Secondary teachers.' During the early 1970s we met in hurling and football games with Denis playing for the famed city

Boing Crossing where O'Sullivan Beare forded in 1602

club, St Finbarr's and myself togging out for Youghal. His roots, however, are here in Duhallow and Sliabh Luachra as his mother was born in Millstreet and his father, Con, came from nearby Rathmore.

Driving me to Millstreet, Denis explains that he has arranged for us to meet with his friend, Sean Radley and a camera man, Brendan Murphy, at the Boing Crossing, four miles from Shamrock Bridge. He adds that he and Sean were in St Patrick's Training College, 1968-70, and that they have remained close friends since that time. Sean had telephoned a week earlier and suggested that he would like to interview me about my Blackwater walk for Local Community Television (LTV2). With a mike directed towards me and a camera focused, Sean asks his opening question which is to explain my plan for the week along with my reasons for walking the Blackwater.

Sean, having asked a series of pleasant questions, suggests that I might walk across the river to give the viewers a realistic image of what is involved. Trudging across, the brownish water washes my shins up to the knees. Three local boys, sitting on large stones mid-river, probably on the last day of their summer holidays, stare in amazement at the aged wader struggling to reach the opposite bank where having reached the dry ground, he proceeds to turn and to re-cross the ford.

The soft glow of the declining sun casts a gentle and balmy light over the river and midges and flies swarm in their thousands under the overhanging alder branches. Four centuries ago an army of foot soldiers and horsemen crossed at this very point on their expedition south to join with their Spanish allies at Kinsale. Here too Donal O'Sullivan Beare led his desperate followers northwards to a presumed haven in Leitrim.

Having completed the filming of my Blackwater walk, Sean drives me to his hometown of Millstreet where he has spent the last thirty years teaching in the Presentation National School. Tomorrow, Tuesday, 31 August will be his last day in the classroom after a career that has spanned forty years: teaching in Dublin, Mallow and later here in Millstreet where he concentrated on learning support in the latter part of his career. His only comment about retirement is that he has set up a texting programme for the school principal to enable her to contact parents at work in the case of a pupil being unwell or any other emergency occuring. Sean, in his enthusiasm, tells me that his reading *Cois Móire*, Ó Liatháin's account of his Blackwater walk, delighted him especially as it contained a sketch of his uncle's forge with the name 'T Radley' clearly evident. From a humble forge,

Denis Burns, the author and Brendan Murphy at Boing Crossing

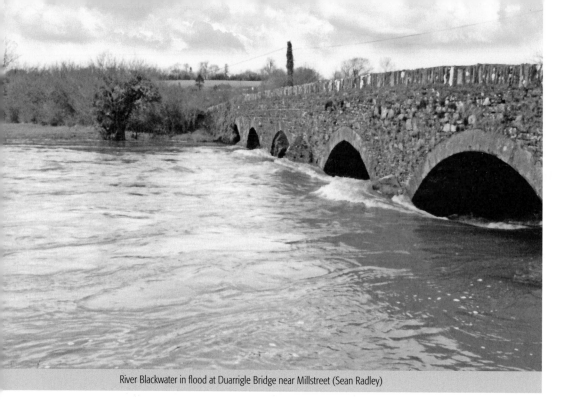

River Blackwater in flood at Duarrigle Bridge near Millstreet (Sean Radley)

the next generation of Radleys, John and Thomas, founded Radley Engineering in Dungarvan in 1972. Their achievement in fabricating and erecting the Spire in O'Connell Street, Dublin, January 2003, offers clear evidence of their business success. Sean, the retiring NT, refers to them as 'my cousins in Dungarvan.'

Ó Liatháin stayed in Millstreet on Easter Saturday night, 1959. As a strong nationalist, he expressed his dismay that the local community had failed to organise a fitting commemoration of the Easter Rising and were far more concerned about a dance in the local hall which he labelled, *a scioból mór gránna*, ('an ugly barn') from which he could hear the blaring of a trumpet and saxophone, accompanying the smarmy and amplified singing of the vocalist. What would Ó Liatháin think of the staging of the Eurovision Song Contest in the Green Glens Equestrian Arena in 1993 or the world super-middleweight fight between Steve Collins and Chris Eubank in 1995?

Sean drives me to Eily Buckley's, B&B, on the Macroom Rd, where I wash and refresh myself. Later he returns and drives me to Christy's Family Restaurant in the West End of the town. The fare is simple but fresh and cooked with due care. The other clients are nearly all teenagers who smile across the tables at Sean who has taught many of them down through the years. His deep roots in the locality have motivated him to establish a

Radley Engineering Dungarvan, Co. Waterford

Kilmeedy Castle Millstreet (Sean Radley)

Noel C.Duggan with European Winners 2014

museum in the local library that now houses a large collection of documents, artefacts and other items pertaining to the area. Along with his interest in local history, Sean is active in the community, and is currently planning to build extra storage space for the museum.

Green Glens Arena, Millstreet (Sean Radley)

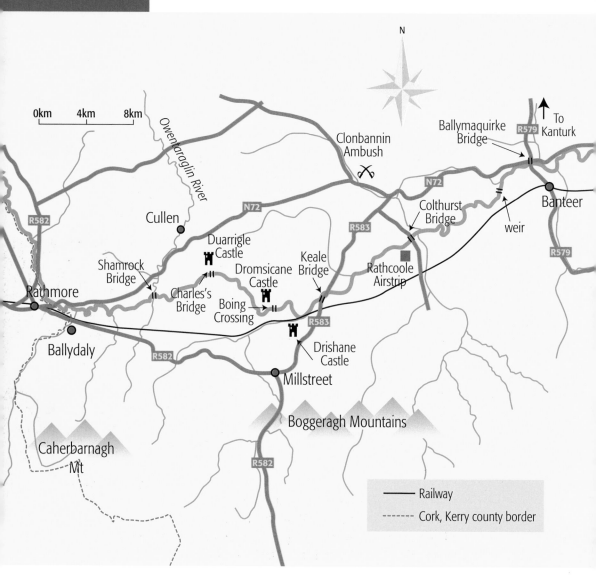

DAY TWO
Ballydaly to Banteer

N

0km 4km 8km

Owenaraglin River

Clonbannin
Ambush

Ballymaquirke
Bridge

R579

To
Kanturk

N72

Colthurst
Bridge

Banteer

R582

Cullen

N72

R583

weir

Duarrigle
Castle

Keale
Bridge

Rathcoole
Airstrip

R579

Shamrock
Bridge

Dromsicane
Castle

Rathmore

Charles's
Bridge

Boing
Crossing

R583

Ballydaly

R582

Drishane
Castle

Millstreet

Boggeragh Mountains

Caherbarnagh
Mt

R582

Railway

Cork, Kerry county border

Ballydaly to Banteer

'I love the sweet smell of the countryside in the morning.'[1]

THE SOLES OF MY FEET are tender. I walk gingerly to the bathroom, wondering how they will hold up to another demanding day along the Blackwater. Eily has tumble-dried my sodden walking boots, and with new socks, the vigour that drove me to undertake this walk begins to seep back into my legs and limbs.

A hearty Irish breakfast completes the process. Hoisting my knapsack and bearing my hazel walking stick in my right hand, we set off in Eily's Fiesta to Shamrock Bridge where I finished my first day. A traffic hold-up on the main road into Millstreet causes her to divert through Kilmeedy, otherwise, she might miss her 9.00 a.m. slot on C103 on which she reads the local news. This delay, however, turns out to be a windfall for *Walking Man* as Eily points out the houses where her married daughters live and relates how O'Sullivan Beare sent the women and children of his band along this side road in order to avoid any possible skirmish that might develop between his force and the garrison of the town. 'This road has been called Bóthar na mBan ever since,' Eily informs me.

Eily Buckley (Sean Radley)

Having forgotten to restock my water supplies, at 8.45 a.m., I nab a plastic half-litre of milk outside the still unopened Top Shop in Ballydaly for which I leave €1.50. With the half-litre in my left hand and the hazel rod in the other, I am beginning to look an eccentric, though, harmless figure, plodding along the banks of the Blackwater.

Before I say goodbye, Eily, spontaneously, comments, 'I love the sweet smell of the countryside in the morning.' Few people nowadays utter such sentiments. Before the heat of the day develops, the faint scent of the woodbine, dog rose and vetches along the roadside wafts through the air – a scent that we seldom notice and tend to pine for in smoke-ridden cities. Country air reeks of freshness; however, this morning, I am in dairying country where the Friesian cow is king (queen?) and all I can detect is the earthy odour of cow dung or, more likely, that of a recent slurry spread.

As Eily drives back to attend to her news reading duties, I compose myself for the challenge ahead. Organising my walk from bridge to bridge, has given me apt reference points for dividing up the journey. This morning I plan to walk from Shamrock Bridge to Charles's Bridge, a distance of 3.37k which I hope to complete within one hour. Bridges provide a convenient vantage from which I can view the flowing water, judge the mood of the river as well as admire the architecture of the bridge structure. Built of concrete and without the ashlar stone, featured in Duncannon Bridge, Shamrock Bridge has remained undistinguished apart from the openings, resembling shamrocks, left in the concrete. A sign, nailed to an ash tree, tells me that the fishing is reserved for the 'Upper Blackwater Anglers' and that fishing licences can be obtained from Cahill's Bar in Rathmore.

Immediately on the east side of Shamrock Bridge, the River Araglin (Owentaraglin) joins the Blackwater after a journey of seventeen miles from Garraunbaun Mountain. The townland west of the Araglin is known as Lyredaowen (Ladhar dá abhainn, *the fork of the two rivers*), and to the east lies Ahane (Áthmheáin or *the middle ford*). I enter the field, and walk parallel to the Blackwater that seems not to have been noticeably augmented by the waters of the Owentaraglin. Soon I reach a small tributary, Rathhduane stream that flows from Caherbarnagh Mountain. The recent spell of dry weather has reduced it to the status of a drain more than that of a stream though the tangled mass of grass and sedges, dangling from the strands of the wire fence, indicate the height the river reached in its last flood. The Blackwater between these two bridges is confined by higher ground on the north bank

Having easily crossed the stream and bounding fence, I veer away to my left, back to the Blackwater where I find, to my delight, that the river has swollen into an enormous pool – the deep water beloved by anglers. Perched on a high clay bank, I gaze over the dark undisturbed surface of the water and wonder what trout or salmon may be lurking in the depths.

Up to this point, Abhainn Mhór na Mumhain has been more prosaic than poetic, but it has now declared a clear statement of its awesome potential. Leaving the great pool behind, I saunter off, hoping that more wonders will unfold. After two or three fields, the north bank rears up into a cliff of dull brown shale, bedecked with ash and beech trees, and hangs dramatically over the quiet river. Shale is classified as a sedimentary rock that is easily fractured. Consequently, its use is limited to trunking passageways and farmyards.

Kayakers at Shamrock Bridge: Timmy Flavin and Bernard Forde

A herd of Friesian calves frolic towards me. Having grown up on a farm, I know and appreciate that livestock should remain as undisturbed as possible. Despite my lack of interest, they persist and tail me to the next fence where I manage to crawl under the electric wire into the next field which has been recently reseeded. Progressive farming requires that pastures are reseeded on a 5-6 year cycle otherwise the quality of the grass deteriorates with the coarser varieties invading the more nutritious sward of Italian rye. While the regular regime of reseeding improves the quality and weight of livestock, we lose the diversity of weeds, insects and bumble bees that formed the rich and varied pattern of wildlife during my childhood in the 1950s and 1960s. Approaching the fence at the end of the field, I notice the outer fringe of leaves on the trees has been burnt. A glance on either side shows the damage continuing right around the field perimeter. To my dismay, I realise that a Glyphosate-based herbicide has been sprayed all over the old sward of grass to kill off scutch grass, creeping fescues, dogtail and other less nutritious grasses for a new beginning with Italian rye. The trees will undoubtedly recover from the effects of the spray that a breeze seems to have blown towards them but what is not calculable is the loss of insect-life with a knock-on effect on bird life. From the farming point of view, there is no calculated aim to eradicate wildlife but the effect of this intensive regime of grass management has resulted in the disappearance of the corncrake, the yellowhammer, the skylark and the meadow pipit.

Nevertheless, the sprouting grass is tender and easily damaged, so, in order to avoid trampling the grass, I head for the river bank where I can observe the rippling Blackwater, now anxious to speed up on its journey to Youghal Harbour. Reaching the corner of the field, I pause for a moment and gaze at the river. I then nose my way through a hidden opening made by the local anglers through the fence into the next field. While the anglers facilitate me, the electric fences pose a constant problem.

After a few more fields of steady, though not rigorous walking, I come to a field of Miscanthus, more popularly known as Elephant Grass. At first glance I assumed that it was a crop of maize but soon noticed that it lacked the swelling cobs of grain, arranged along the stem, and that the typical maize rows were not evident. Elephant grass is now grown around the country as an alternative crop for farmers from which organic fuel can be processed.

Across the river, on the northern side, I observe two large dairy herds, browsing contentedly after the early morning milking. Field after field slide by until I have passed through about eighteen fields while trying to stay as close as possible to the hurrying river and gazing through the alders and sallies that grow along the bank. Two or three mallard fly off in alarm, followed by a solitary heron. Apart from the hassle of the electric fences and the difficulty of finding a way through boundary fences, the tranquillity of the surroundings, the gentle breeze and the quiet flow of the river play a soothing music to guide me on my way.

Charles's Bridge

Duarrigle Castle

My progress, however, has been slower than anticipated. I remind myself that this is not a competitive event but a journey to be savoured from which I hope to wring a sense of place, an intimate experience of landscape along with contact and insight into its history and people.

Arriving at Charles's Bridge, a half-hour behind schedule, I glimpse the ruined Duarrigle Castle a short distance downstream overlooking the Blackwater from a high ridge. Time for a break, and conveniently I find two ESB poles on the open space close to the bridge. Cars, especially people carriers and delivery vans, travel to and fro along this road that connects Millstreet to the nearby village of Cullen. Here the townland of Coalpits borders the Blackwater on the north side, and as the name so picturesquely suggests, a low grade coal was mined here and elsewhere in Duhallow from the eighteenth century to the 1840s. The three types of Duhallow coal were divided according to their quality – culm, pindy and anthracite. Culm and

pindy were suitable for forge fires and limekilns while the anthracite, a rather slow fuel to burn, sufficed in local homes though never of any commercial worth. The Justice family, owners of Duarrigle Castle for nearly two hundred years, operated colleries here.

Duarrigle Castle, a medieval tower house, was built by the O'Keeffes in the sixteenth century, destroyed in the Cromwellian wars and fell to ruin until Thomas Holmes Justice restored it as a Gothic revival castellated house in 1806. Local people can still recall having tea there.[1] This morning the historic ruin stands gaunt on the high ground over the Blackwater. The castle, gate house and twenty-five acres were sold for £1,400 in 1955 to Tim Houlihan. His son Con takes up the story of how his father came to own a castle.

> My father returned home from America in the 1930s and bought a large farm of 119 acres in the next townland of Lisnashearshane (*Lios na Seirseán,* 'The Ring-Fort of the Archers or Mercanaries?'). He married and settled down to life as a hard-working and ambitious farmer. Unfortunately, he suffered a nearly fatal accident and could have bled to death. Though he recovered, he no longer had the robust health required to manage such a large farm, and was, consequently forced to sell. Within a short time, the nearby Duarrigle Castle was offered for sale. He decided to purchase the entire holding – the castle and all its contents along with twenty-five

---

1   Diarmuid Ó Cadhla, 'Duarrigle Castle' in *Seanchas Duthalla 1976-77*, p. 16-17

acres of land. He then had the choice of moving his family either into the spacious three-storey castle or, alternatively, into the gate lodge. They opted for the gate lodge.

Con pauses for a moment as the poignant memories come flooding back. He explains that the rateable valuation on the castle would have placed an unbearable burden on his father's limited resources. The only realistic option open to him was to remove the roof and to auction off the antique furniture and all the accoutrements that went with the residence.

> I was only four and a half years of age at the time. I remember the day of the auction – 1955. That day it became a ruin, and it's a ruin ever since. I did nothing with it. We had three children to educate and we couldn't afford to lay out the huge sum of money it would take.

II. CHARLES'S BRIDGE – BOING CROSSING – KEALE BRIDGE, 6.876K

Time for *Walking Man* to resume his trek, his quest for insight into the past, his search for bedrock values and to find his own contentment and peace in retirement. Having earlier scanned the OS Discovery map, I've decided to take the northern bank for the next phase of my walk from Charles's Bridge to the Boing Crossing. Gazing over the bridge parapet, I watch the growing river rushing onwards in a manner that suggests it will brook no delay or obstacle.

Once again, the local anglers have made a convenient entrance through the hedge into a pleasant inch running parallel to the river. On the left side of the inch the landowner has planted ash and oak saplings that are now firmly rooted and pointing strongly to the sky in the race for light and air. After 250m I come to a formidable drain; moving away from the river, I negotiate my way across and enter the wooded lower reaches of the eminence on which Duarrigle Castle was built. History calls, but rather than clamber up the almost vertical slope, a challenging task, I move diagonally to more gentle ground east of the castle site. Emerging out of the wood, a large modern two-storey house stands directly before me. The owner is busy adjusting the wrought iron gate at the head of the avenue. Experience has taught me the benefits of approaching people rather than shying away; only the locals can give the walker/traveller the colourful tale of local memories. And on this occasion, my curiosity was more than rewarded.

Leo O'Leary smiling broadly, bespectacled and sporting a ponytail, tells me that the castle was built up here to enable the occupants to keep an eye on everything that happened. Extending his arm to indicate the great stretch of countryside visible from this height,

They could plainly see who was approaching and could take appropriate action if necessary.

Warming to the story of the castle and its inhabitants, Leo adds,

> Madame Halikiopulo lived in the castle when my mother was working as as servant girl for a local farmer, and she would come down to keep Julia, the housekeeper, company at night when the Madame was visiting friends in London or elsewhere. My mother and Julia had to sleep in the basement.

Leo explains that Madame Halikiopulo's maiden name was O'Callaghan and that she grew up in Killeenlea, Kanturk. She emigrated to England where, having acquired property, she married a Greek shipping merchant who later became invalided after an accident. After her husband's death, she returned to live in Duarrigle and negotiated a lease of the castle from the Land Commission who had acquired the property and land from the previous owners The Duhallow historian, Diarmaid Ua Cadhla, described her lifestyle as follow, 'She had a constant stream of guests and was noted for her tea parties. She was a very gracious hostess and once completely disarmed a parish priest who came to admonish.'[2]

Having said goodbye to Leo, I follow again the faint path trodden by the local anglers and make my way back to where a giant beech tree has fallen across the river. There is just about enough space for kayakers to paddle downstream. Its great rootstock rises above the water; amazingly, its branches still bear leaves and an otter has deposited his spraints (droppings) along the now horizontal bole.

A few fields farther on, a large dairy herd choose to ignore me. The electric fences are everywhere, delimiting grazing paddocks and keeping the livestock from the boundary fence. They present challenges, forcing me to unstrap my knapsack and crawl underneath to avoid the jolting charge from a mains line. Here in the townland of Gorteenafinnoge (*Goirtín na Feannóige*, 'the little ploughed field of the grey crow'), a crescent-shaped oak wood runs along the northern fence of a large tract of land until it converges with the Blackwater at its eastern corner. A Sitka spruce plantation merges with and almost overwhelms the oaks. The leaf canopy provides a cool shade and relaxation after the exertions of the morning. The acorns have formed though not filled to maturity. A visit to a corner coffee shop can hardly compare to the tranquillity I enjoy under the overhanging boughs.

---

2   O Cadhla, *Seanchas Duthalla*, p. 16-17

A large farmhouse, with a complex of farm buildings to its rear, overlooks the land ahead. I feel uncomfortable and glance frequently to the house, wondering if I have been observed and what could be the outcome. I envisage a revved-up quad accelerating towards me with an irate farmer telling me to clear off his land. However, I promptly dismiss such feelings, knowing that busy farmers have more important business than chasing harmless strollers off their land. The second cut of silage (or possibly the third?) has just been harvested from this paddocked section. Probably, the greatest worry of the average dairy farmer is that he will have insufficient fodder for his cows in the spring especially if the winter prolongs into April. Farm land is now almost totally devoid of people as a result of the modern mechanised approach to managing the land and rearing livestock.

The river bends to the south before flowing past the historic ford, locally referred to as the 'Boing Crossing.' My visit to this location the previous evening was arranged to facilitate an interview with Sean Radley. The placename 'Boing' sounds exotic to our ears though its derivation can be traced to *buan*, meaning 'eternal, enduring, permanent' *et cetera*. To support such an explanation, the name Boyne (as in Boyne river) has a similar source. Some historians claim that O'Neill and O'Donnell forded the Blackwater at Lombardstown rather than here. On the other hand, the crossing of O'Sullivan Beare and his followers is regarded as a historical fact. Pádraig Ó Súileabháin from Rathmore informed me that the river names in Irish are all regarded as feminine nouns with the Sullane being the only masculine exception.

The veteran local historian, Patsy Moynihan N.T., informed me that local farmers used this Crossing on their way to Millstreet creamery up to twenty-five years ago. A planning notice has been posted on the south bank to notify Cork County Council of a proposal by the Beara-Breifne Committee to erect a footbridge over the Blackwater at this point. The purpose of the proposed development is to commemorate the journey of O'Sullivan Beare along with facilitating walkers retracing his epic journey to Leitrim. Personally, I would prefer to see such a historic location being left undisturbed as it was 410 years ago. The river is quite broad at this point and the proposed structure could entail significant disturbance to the river bed and banks.

An information board, put in place by the Duhallow Development Group on the north bank, details the history and prominence of the O'Keeffe clan in Duhallow. Having been displaced by the Normans in the twelfth century, they moved westwards into Duhallow where they became so entrenched and numerous that the district was called Pobal Uí Chaoimh, atrociously anglicised as Popple O'Keeffe. Their motto, *forti et fideli nihil difficile*, ('to the brave and faithful man, nothing is difficult'), sustained them in their castles at Dromach and Duarrigle until being dispossessed and driven into the poorer lands of Sliabh Luachra in the eighteenth century.

The arrival of a tractor hauling a large slurry tank awakens me from my reverie about times past. The driver enters the water and proceeds to turn his tractor in mid-river. Having exited the cab, he detaches the hose which he lays down in the flowing river where he secures it with a large stone. I stand aghast, fearing that he intends to release a large volume of slurry into the Blackwater. The power drive of the tractor is then engaged and the engine is throttled for the purpose of filling the tank and transporting a supply of water to a farmyard or, possibly, to water a suckler herd on an outlying farm. In fairness, I did not witness a discharge of slurry or effluent of any kind. The driver climbs back into the cab and drives away after a job that has scarcely taken five minutes.

So here I am at a historic location having witnessed such a questionable practice. My intuitive sense tells me to keep calm and to understand it from the farmer's point of view. Even now, writing this account, I am reluctant to jump to quick conclusions. However, the incident has highlighted for me the demands made on the great river. Discussing the scale and the large vehicles used in silage making and in harvesting maize with my farmer brother, Frank, he wryly comments, 'Your cow is an expensive animal to feed and manage.'

The road from the Crossing runs north-east past Dromsicane Castle. All I can glimpse of the castle is a long extensive wall. Realising that my footsteps are now treading the very ground that O'Sullivan Beare trod, a deep and poignant emotions awakens in my Gaelic soul. Cardinal Rinucini enjoyed hospitality here from the McDonagh McCarthys in 1645 but the doors remained shut against O'Sullivan Beare.

After a short distance, I leave the road that leads north-east to Clonbannin Cross where Sean Moylan and his men ambushed a party of auxiliaries in 1921. Another dairy herd of Friesian cows, and again I am unsure about trespassing on farm land though tolerance has always been shown to anglers and others who follow the course of the river. Luckily, the cows have no interest whatsoever in me; their daily routine of being twice milked has accustomed them to human contact. The simile of the poet, Thomas Kinsella, comes to mind, 'Domestic autumn, like an animal/Long used to handling by those countrymen/rubs her kind hide against the bedroom walls/Sensing a fragrant child come back again.' Rivers and poetry have a natural affinity as great rivers give rise to poetic thoughts though the theme may be more about water and its might than the specific river. Excepting Spencer's brief reference to the Blackwater and its tributaries, I am not aware of any poem of worth that relates to the Blackwater apart from some local ballads. The pleasures of poetry sustain us through strife and grief. I set off once again striding through the well-managed farmland of Duhallow along the northern bank of the 'Great River of Munster.'

The drone of traffic from the town of Millstreet drifts over the tall beech trees of Drishane where Dermot Mór McCarthy built his medieval tower house in the fifteenth century. After Kinsale (1601) and the Cromwellian wars the Planters confiscated his land and home. But the millwheel of history revolved and the Planters left the lands they had occupied for two hundred years. Another Irish poet, Austin Clarke, penned the memorable line, 'The house of the Planter is known by the trees.' And here in Drishane, just across the Blackwater, the lordly beeches recall for us the age of the planter as do the crumbling walls that bound the estate. The house of the Planter may be recalled by the trees but the story of evictions, rack-renting and moonlighting has been recorded in history. While the conflict over the ownership of land has now been assuaged, the tyranny inflicted on the tenants should not be forgotten.

Field after field pass by until I come to a small cottage acre where the overgrown grass has been mowed and now waits to be baled. The occupied cottage stands in the corner of the field with a gate nearby. I walk away from the river to the gate over which I can join a small bye-road that will lead me in a short time to Keale Bridge. I haven't spoken to a single person since I left Shamrock Bridge. Solitude allows one to experience the landscape in more depth. I don't wish to disturb anyone's security but a quick chat and introduction would break the effort of walking; stories of angling, otter hunting, who knows what might be recounted to this solitary walker who has just drunk the last drop of his half-litre of Centra milk and needs replenishment to continue on his pilgrimage to Youghal Harbour. And then for a moment, seeing the water, the trees and the mowed acre, I imagine that this scene could be Gainsborough country without the wainright.

With the last drop of milk drained, I decide to pay a brief visit to a good friend who has already invited me to drop in. Her Yorkshire terrier senses my approach and proceeds to let its kind owner know that a caller has arrived. Mary greets me warmly, and recalling her mother's phrase from a bygone age, welcomes me to join her for a cup of tea, 'As my mother used to say, the kettle's always on in our house.' And then she adds that Miley [Michael Lally], the popular actor from *Glenroe*, passed away that very morning. We discuss the charm that Miley had for so many people with his strong Mayo accent and his ability to portray the quintessential roguish Irish countryman. Time passes pleasantly as Mary talks about her family, garden and house. Her son and grandson arrive. Before I take my leave, I replenish my water supply and say goodbye to Mary and her family.

Reading the plaque on the new Keale Bridge, I learn that Cork County Council demolished the old stone-arched bridge and replaced it with a mass concrete structure in 1985. The demolition of the old bridge was necessary to remove a bottleneck on the road between Millstreet and Mallow. Pausing for a moment and glancing over the iron railings, I observe the flowing waters of the Blackwater underneath on its unceasing journey to the sea. Pale autumn sunshine filters through the alder, ash and willow trees that line both banks of the river. I sense that the flowing water is inviting me to follow, to resume my trek in search of adventure, knowledge and insight. Karl Jung believed that the individual human experiences a journey of the soul. Something deeper is driving me onwards, and for this episode, I have the reliable and constant company of *Abhainn Mhór na Mumhan*. Hopefully, the walk will yield to some deeper awareness of my life's path and, possibly, dovetail my own insights into a greater awareness of history and culture.

Jim up to his neck in Himalayan Balsam

Descending the steep slope close to the bridge and surmounting a taut sheep wire fence, I make my way through a succession of small fields. The river has been deepened along this stretch to prevent flooding. I watch the sparkling ripples and look up at the overhanging ash and beech whose leaves have begun to turn yellow with the advancing season of autumn. A solitary heron flaps away to safety, finding his stand being encroached on by an uninvited intruder. My involvement in nature conservation has led me to conclude that we humans are intruders into the world of nature who leave our damaging footprints everywhere. Today, I am a passerby, a witness, who wants to leave the flora and fauna unspoilt and safe. No human hand could design such a subtle blend of water, trees and plants; perhaps, disordered and almost rakish but still manifesting a unique face to the world. Recalling Gerard Manley Hopkins's (1844-89) poem *Inversnaid*, I silently recite his lines,

What would the world be, once bereft
Of wet and of wilderness? Let them be left,
O let them be left. Wilderness and wet;
Long live the weeds and the wilderness yet.

Hemmed-in between the water and the high bank, I fear that I am heading down a cul-de-sac from which I may have to turn and retrace my footsteps. And that's exactly what transpires with briars and bushes barring my way. However, rather than return to where I started, I decide to claw my way up the earthen bank that offers few gripping points or footholds. My first effort fails dismally. My second attempt proves to be more successful as I just about drag myself and knapsack back to open ground over the river.

After the scramble to higher ground, I plod onwards under the shade of mature beech and oak trees under which a herd of calves are feeding. The arrival of a walker distracts them totally from their foraging. I am surrounded, whooshing them from my path, then beating a hasty retreat to the next fence I manage to escape these pesky animals.

The pattern of field-after-field is disrupted when I enter a farm where the fences have been cleared and replaced with a network of electric fences. About 500m away, I see two men herding cattle towards a corralled space where they can drink at the water's edge. The cattleman, accompanied by his son, explains that they have rented the grazing here in Prohus from a retired farmer. I introduce myself and explain that I am walking the Blackwater from source to sea, adding that I grew up in the Killeagh-Youghal area. On hearing the reference to Killeagh, the cattleman asks me if I knew his cousin the late Margaret Browne – the well-known cook who passed away in March. He warns me that Friesian bulls are the most dangerous, that they will chase and attack people quicker than other breeds. Eyeing my hazel walking stick, he enquires what kind of stick I like to carry. His own preferred option is a good sally switch. In answer to my query whether the land here is affected by flooding or not, he describes the aftermath of a storm a few years previously when three of his bullocks were carried downriver for a half-mile or more. Luckily, his animals were washed ashore and survived. Later when the unlucky cattle were sent to the meat factory, tests revealed that they had been infected by liver fluke though the rest of the herd were unaffected. Casting my eye around this grazing land, I can see a series of low hillocks divided by interlocking channels through which the river waters had coursed and swept away the unsuspecting graziers.

Leaving the cattlemen to complete their task, and anxious to press ahead, I resume my trudge. Soon I enter the Rathcoole Airstrip – a large area of 25-30 acres or more with a closely mown strip, extending for 300-400 metres, that serves as a take-off and landing space for the light aircraft that use this facility. On the far side stands a low building where equipment is housed. Nearer the river, the tall and dense grass impedes my progress, forcing me to lift my tiring feet an extra inch or two.

At Colthurst's Bridge, I climb over the style onto the Rathcoole road. I like bridges: they allow time for a pause and a survey of the water flowing underneath. Here the Blackwater divides the townlands of Rathcoole and Drumahoe, and once formed the boundary between the estates of Captain Niocholas Leader of Rosnalee and that of Sir George Colthurst on the Rathcoole side. This is a magnificent structure, built in 1859 with stones from the nearby Prohus quarry 'where the quarry workers were paid four pence a day and the stone cutters sixpence.' Con Fitzpatrick adds other colourful details in his account of the *Bridge* which is 'known by various names,' such as 'The Blackwater Bridge, The Big Bridge and Forrest's Bridge.' He also tells us that the Dromtarriffe football club held their meetings on the bridge in the 1930s, and that the bridge was also 'a romantic spot where boy met girl.' The Dromtarriffe football team were nicknamed 'the rough and tumble men.'

Dromtarriffe parish is very much a rural parish without a village or any definite meeting point apart from the local church that lies north of the Blackwater off the Killarney-Mallow road. A notice proclaiming the fishing as strictly private deters me initially from continuing; however, I have no choice only to press ahead and hope that the owners will not be unduly annoyed. The bank has been strongly fenced off from the rest of the land where sheep quietly graze. After a few footsteps, I meet an Englishman from Bristol, seated at the water edge, absorbed in the tranquil flow of the water while his companion fishes a short distance away. I weave my way past clumps of nettles and wet ground until the fence curves to the river bank and closes off my route. A double row of barb wire at the top presents a formidable challenge for *Walking Man*. Looking around for a solution, I see cut sections of ash and sycamore trees. Placing one on top of the other to make a platform and balancing precariously, I leap over the fence. If necessity is the mother of invention then ingenuity must be its off-spring!

The planting and harvesting of sugar beet, once an important crop in this area, has been discontinued since 2008 though a few farmers continue to grown fodder beet for their livestock. However, with its high sugar content, some farmers still grow fodder beet, a variety more suited as an animal feed than for sugar production.

Rathcoole Airstrip (Sean Radley)

With briars, nettles and other plants growing profusely along the margin, I am forced to walk between two furrows of fodder beet. The mature leaves flap against my shins and slow my progress though there is the compensation of scentless mayweed, sun spurge and other flowering species. A study of the OS map has shown me that below Colthurst's Bridge, the Blackwater curves away to the south only to curve back northwards after a short distance, resulting in a great horseshoe of land in-between. Rather than following the southward flow and then returning with the north-bound river, I pick a point where the water's depth allows me to ford the river conveniently. Escaping from the beet field, I emerge into a rough pasture where horses have been grazing though I see no sign of them at this moment. Having taken off my sodden boots, I drain away the bilge and wring my walking socks. To give my white and spongy toes some relief from their imprisonment, I decide to walk barefooted across this rough pasture of thistles and coarse grasses. Progress is slow as my sensitive and soaked feet object to the tough fibrous plants of the horse shoe-shaped field.

Seated on the bank, I pull on my wrung socks and tie up my boots to complete the last part of my walk to Banteer. At this point, the flow of the river is halted by a solid wall of limestone in a manner that suggests confrontation between the river and land. Remaining on the northern bank and climbing the higher ground, I skirt around the rock face that redirects the course of the river eastwards again. Having climbed over a tubular gate, four handsome fillies approach me at a fast trot, all eager to make acquaintance with the uninvited stranger who has just arrived among them. They sweep past me at gallop pace, complete a u-turn and reassemble to face me from the ground ahead. Trying to minimise the effect of my presence, I stay close to the fence and soon reach a closed gate that bars the horses from pursuing me further. Safely over, I feel relieved to walk away with the thoroughbreds behind me.

A low-lying meadow or inch stretches unbroken for approximately half a mile or more. Stands of rushes grow here and there with the toxic ragwort, displaying its array of yellow flowers on which military beetles crawl around along with the caterpillars of the cinnabar moth. Midway across the inch, I reach a long thin pool of water. The low-lying terrain is obviously subjected to regular flooding in periods of heavy rain. A Limousin suckler herd grazes at the far end of this old pasture. My plan is to stay close to the river in the hope that I can circle around the livestock to avoid a stampede in my direction. Back by the river bank, I scan the herd to see if a bull is still running with the cows. Reassured, I persist along the bank, keeping a close eye on the livestock that are beginning to face ominously in my direction. And then, to my horror, I see the missing bull - calmly drinking from the river though oblivious to the passing stranger. But, I am far too close to him for comfort, and, more importantly, for safety. I walk on determinedly, while glancing over my shoulder in case this young bull decides to chase me away from his herd. Step after step increases the distance between me and danger. Young bulls pose an extra threat that should never be underestimated. If I had realised beforehand that there was a bull here, I might have forded the river to keep a safe barrier between myself and the menace. Anyway, all's well, that ends well. I've learned a lesson that I intend to keep in mind.

Walking Man resumes his tiring trek. My energy levels are flagging. Once again another limestone outcrop dictates and redirects the course of the river. The Blackwater swells into a dark pool beneath the calcareous barrier as if pausing in homage, or, perhaps, a declaration that the question of who rules this land will be settled some other time. Rather than skirt around the looming outcrop, I wade across as the river is easily fordable at a point close to the great pool. Safely across, I take time to gaze into the dark depths that reflect the blue sky and the white clouds slowly drifting across the late August sky.

Back on the north side of the river, I notice that the bank has been strongly reinforced with slabs of concrete, salvaged from a demolished building somewhere; not an aesthetic way for containing the river during floods, but, nevertheless, an effective solution. After a short walk of two minutes along the bare bank, I reach another pool over which a large gathering of swallows and house martins have congregated. They dive and twirl as they skim mere mouthfuls from the water with only the slightest contact with the surface of the river. Occasionally, some let a drop or two fall as they fly away. It is late autumn and their time for departure to their winter homes is fast approaching. Adults and fledgling birds disport themselves in an intricately woven pattern, using their time to savour the mellow rays of August sunshine, 'And gathering swallows twitter in the sky.' It's almost 5.00 p.m., I am quite spent and my tired legs demand more rest.

Over the years, I have frequently driven along this section of the Mallow –Killarney road, unaware of the appealing landscape through which the Blackwater languidly flows without realising that the roadside fences hide scenes of great appeal. Walking through the land, allows one to experience the delights of rural Ireland that remain hidden from speeding tourists.

Over the brow of the field, I can see the rooftops of modern farm buildings from which the low but steady sound of a milking machine is plainly audible. Rather than wander into a busy farmyard, I re-cross the river into fields where silage has been cut some time previously. A few months after my walk, I availed of an opportunity to return to this area, Dysert (*Díseart*, 'A Hermitage.') where I introduced myself to Michael Daly whose farmyard and residence I had skirted around during the evening milking of his cows. Michael, having turned off the engine of his tractor, descended from the cab and welcomed me to Dysert. He explained that his grandfather bought the farm from the large Leader Estate in 1918. Almost a century later, he is the third generation of his family to farm these low-lying fields that stretch along the banks of the Blackwater. Turning the conversation to the topic of floods in the area, Michael tells me a frightening account of the huge flood that engulfed this region of the Blackwater Valley in November, 1980.

It had rained heavily during the night and when we woke up in the morning these lower fields were a sea of water. The water from the steeper slope of the south bank had washed straw and bales of hay into the river where the debris soon blocked the flow of water under the arches of the bridges. Ten of our cows were drowned off land we had rented in Drumcummer about half a mile below Ballymaquirke Bridge. In fact, one of them was washed up in Youghal harbour.

Michael, probably, noticed the disbelief spreading across my countenance, and hastened to add,

I am not exaggerating. An official from Youghal UDC rang me and gave me the registration number on her ear tag.

Nowadays, he takes the precaution of housing his stock if the weather begins to deteriorate and water levels to rise ominously. As a tillage and dairy farmer, he leads a busy but satisfying life in this part of Dromtarriffe which he claims to be the lowest lying area of the extensive barony of Duhallow. We say goodbye to one and another. He bounds back into the tractor cab with a large trailer attached and drives away to the N72.

Having skirted around the Daly's farm, I ford the river and emerge into a fully-grown field of maize where I manage to walk, totally concealed, between the rows. A series of small fields, sloping to the river, follow which have deep scooped drains with high fences that present a serious challenge. After three or four of these maize fields, I find myself in lower, wetter ground with scattered pools of water under the low growing branches of sallies and alders. Here I manage to duck and dodge from strong branches to light limbs that could swish back and lash me across the face. Later, I discovered that this area, by the Blackwater was designated as an 'Area of Scientific Interest' (ASI) by an Forás Forbartha in 1981, '...the series of semi-permanent ponds and marshes that occurs on poorly drained soils in the Blackwater Valley, west of Banteer presents a sequence of vegetation types from open water to fen.'[3] Unfortunately, a legal challenge to this scientific evaluation was successful as such areas had been designated without the owners being informed. However, within a few years and after a full process of consultation with the landowners, the area was redesignated as a 'Natural Heritage Area (NHA).

Plunging underneath the sallies, alder and ash, I re-emerge on to the river bank to the dramatic sight of water cascading over Ballymaquirke

---

3 'Report on Areas of Scientific Interest in County Cork, An Foras Forbartha (Dublin, 1981)

Ballymaquirke Weir

Weir – a drop of five feet with the splendid sight of foaming water hurtling through the air into the tar black pool. For the first time on this walk, the delight of seeing a great quantity of water moving out of its own element thrills me. Weirs are constructed, not only to slow and break a mass of water from wrecking havoc farther downriver, but to trap salmon returning from the sea. I can envisage gentlemen and ghillies with amply stocked food baskets, casting their lines to hook the king of fish.

Later research revealed that the Leader family constructed the weir in 1806 during the Napoleonic wars. With a raised water level, they then developed a millrace to draw water to power the millwheel at Gurteen Mill about a kilometre from the weir.

Reluctantly, I turn my back on the falling water. I have, approximately, a mile to walk through long fields of clover to Ballymaquirke Bridge but, rather, than describe vegetation and farming again, lets diverge into local history. Having previously spoken to Con Tarrant, a local historian with a passionate interest in the history of Duhallow, I knew that the barony had been ruled by four great Gaelic clans: the McDonagh McCarthys; the O'Callaghans; the McAuliffes and the O'Keeffes. These strong patrimonies held sway until the Cromwellian era when they were displaced and ordered to 'Hell or to Connaught.'

Seated in the waiting area of Tarrants' Garage in the nearby village of Banteer, Con grants listening time to those of us who have an interest in the history of the Duhallow area. Oblivious to the resplendent new Superba, Octavia and Fabia marques that stand on display in their modern showroom, eighty-five year old Con recounts with delight tales and episodes of the battles, killings, old monasteries, fishing and former pastimes of the locality.

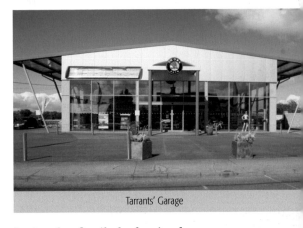

Tarrants' Garage

By the end of the seventeenth century, the Leader family had gained ownership of 9,000 acres in Duhallow. Later they acquired Nashville, the home of Andrew Nash, through marriage. This imposing residence with its manicured grounds, leisure walks and flower gardens stood scarcely a mile north from Ballymaquirke weir where I now pause with all the upheavals inflicted by the Cromwellian forces and the after-trauma of banishment, enforced by the Williamites, 1690-1693, resounding to me over the Blackwater. The Leader family built the New Line, which is now part of the Killarney-Mallow road and opened a millrace, close to the weir, that powered their flour mill in Gurteen. Their great mansion, Rosnalee, was abandoned in 1906 and, eventually, was demolished to leave the laurels and trees over-run the manicured gardens, leisure walks and ornamental statuary. To further complete the destruction, the IRA burned Gurteen Mill in 1921, leaving only the perimeter walls standing. Incredibly, an American woman built a modern bungalow within these walls. The present owner is constrained from lowering or demolishing the walls by a county council conservation order. Despite all that, trying to extract a comment about the vanished landlords and their exploitation of their tenants from another local man later that day, all I could coax was the cautious response, 'I suppose, they gave employment.'

Mixing history and folklore, Con told me the story of the Black Dog that was often seen at the Dead Woman's Gate just beyond Gurteen Mill, 'Coady, the herdsman of the Leaders, was driving out their cows when they refused to enter the pasture close to the mill. Wondering what the problem was, Coady looked around and saw a dead woman, wearing a hooded cloak, at the oak tree. This particular spot has been known ever since as 'The Dead Woman's Gate.' A black dog with donkey hooves appears and accompanies

Lush, green farmland along the River Blackwater valley

people as far as the Dead Woman's Gate and then disappears.

Con told me that he loved fishing for salmon and trout along this stretch of the Blackwater that I am now walking,

> The weather dictated fishing. You'd want to know the flies,' Con explained, '...you'd catch a fly with your hand out of the air, and then use that fly.

Warming to his topic, he described the old custom of fishing for freshwater pearl mussels,

> We did shell fishing, using a sweet gallon with a glass bottom, and, wearing a scarf around your head, you used a forked stick. You stuck your stick over the shell.

He added that finding pearls was a long shot, and that some pearls were deformed but, on the rare occasion, when fortune favoured the pearl-hunter, a young man's thoughts turned to romance,

> If you found a pearl, you'd give it as a present to some pretty young lady you had your eye on.

And with a roguish smile, spreading across his face, Con told me that he was fishing late one night, at 1.00 a.m. in the morning, when he heard a noise that chilled him to the marrow of his bones. Fearing that the Black Dog with the donkey hooves was approaching, but, to his great relief, he discovered that, 'It was only a courting couple.'

And relishing the memory, he good humouredly commented,
'Sure, only for that none of us would be here.'

Remnants of the Banteer to Kanturk and Newmarket railway line

Leaving the long field of clover and passing into a field where silage has just recently been harvested, the solid structure of Ballymaquirke bridge looms into view to signal the imminent end of a long day's walk. Away to my right, a Land Rover is driven through a gap out of which a young couple emerge with a frolicsome sheepdog that immediately begins a vigorous but fruitless search for disappeared rabbits. The young man walks ahead of his girlfriend, inspects a parked tractor and eyes the silo wrap bales that litter the field. Back at the river, *Walking Man* stops to gaze at the last surviving remnants of the railway bridge over the Blackwater across which the branch line from Banteer to Kanturk and Newmarket ran, This iron bridge had five steel spans, each of 63 feet. The spur line, 8.75 miles, was opened in 1889 and closed on Saturday, 2 February, 1963.

By now all traces of the track have been erased and the entire steel structure has been removed for scrap, leaving the abutments on either side and two pillars in midstream. The line was never profitable though popular for annual excursions to the seaside, pilgrimages to Knock and the annual exodus to Banteer Sports in June. Poignant also to recall that limestone for St Coleman's Cathedral in Cobh, quarried in Meelin, was transported on this line to Cobh when the great neo-classical structure was being built.

A glance at my wrist watch reveals that it's now 7.15 p.m., and time for *Walking Man* to find shelter for the night. With weary footsteps, I head south to Banteer village where I hope I can find B&B accommodation. Luckily, the county council have developed a convenient footpath closer to the village. Nursing my weary feet and a raging thirst, I plod to the village, past O'Leary's stoneyard and Tarrant's garage to the White Country Inn where I cast off my knapsack and call for a pint of beer. In response to my query about 'a bed for the night,' the lady behind the counter informs me that there's no one in the village providing accommodation; however, she opens the local directory of businesses, and with the aid of two of her customers, peruses the entries. Within a short time, she tells me that Joan and Steve Roche, Rosnalee, have a vacant room, adding that I can ring them from the bar phone which she immediately points to inside the counter and, raising a section of the counter, she gestures me to come inside to talk to the B&B lady. A few quick words, with the lady at the other end of the line, follow who offers to pick me up within ten minutes.

Naturally, there's little privacy in an Irish rural public house. The men drinkers have a fair idea of what I am up to, so to break the ice, I tell them that I am walking the Blackwater from source to sea, adding a few more details about my background and other points of information. They're quite

interested and want to know if I am doing the walk for some charity. Having explained that I am fulfilling a long-standing ambition, I tell them that I plan to walk from Ballymaquirke to Mallow the following day.

'You're going to have a few problems,' one of them comments, 'You'll have to cross the Glen River,' and, after a pause, adds, 'It'll, probably be low at this time of year, so, you'll be alright.'

I then explain that I've come down by Ballymaquirke Weir, adding 'There seems to be great land around here.'

The older man nods and comments, 'Sure, land in the Blackwater Valley makes a good price whenever a farm comes up for auction.'

And then after a short pause, he adds, 'You'll be passing through one of my fields tomorrow, the second last one before Roskeen Bridge.'

He reassures me that I have his blessing to walk away and to enjoy myself. And now for a bit of friendly local banter (which, of course, one always expects in Banteer),

'God, you'd think a man of your age would have more sense, now wouldn't you?

Pub 'slagging' calls for a quick reply – removing my baseball cap to let them see the state of the hairline, I retort,

'I am only about the same age as yourself.'

At that point, the proprietor interrupts the good humour to let me know that Joan has just arrived. Saying goodbye to the men and thanking them for their help and good-humoured interest, I walk out to a Mitsubishi, parked across the road. Joan welcomes me and reassures me that there is absolutely no rush.

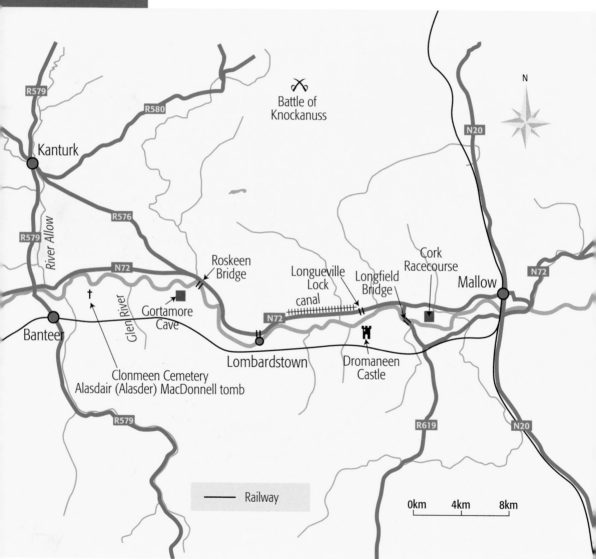

R579

R580

Battle of
Knockanuss

N20

N

Kanturk

R579

River Allow

R576

N72

Roskeen
Bridge

Longueville
Lock
canal

Longfield
Bridge

Cork
Racecourse

Mallow

N72

Gortamore
Cave

Glen River

Banteer

Lombardstown

Dromaneen
Castle

Clonmeen Cemetery
Alasdair (Alasder) MacDonnell tomb

R579

R619

N20

Railway

0km   4km   8km

Banteer
to
Mallow

Ballymaquirke – Mallow
Ballymaquirke to Roskeen bridge, 7.87k

'If a walker is indeed an individualist, there is nowhere he can't go at dawn and not many places he can't go at noon.' (EDWARD HOAGLAND)

B Y NOW, I have settled into a pattern that gives me reassurance. After a good night's sleep in Joan and Steve Roche's B&B I am provided with a hearty breakfast and this lays the foundation for a solid day of walking. Assessing the more than adequate complement of sausages, rashers, fried egg, black pudding and fried tomatoes, I ask Joan to make a sandwich for me with these fine samples of Irish bacon.

With my knapsack safely aboard the Roches' Mitsubishi, Steve drives me two miles back to Ballymaquirke Bridge to resume my trek along the 'Great River of Munster' (Abhainn Mhór na Mumhan). I am eager to begin, to get back to the river bank, to see how the river is expanding with more and more tributaries joining it from the north and from the south. Just as I am about to wave goodbye to Steve, I realise that I have forgotten my hazel walking stick which has become, not only my companion, but my probe through muddy places, my support over fences and my shield against over-enthusiastic guard dogs. Steve promptly wheels his car around and we head back to Rosnalee to collect the hazel that I've cut and trimmed from our own garden.

After my initial false start, I am back where I finished yesterday. I step over the style on the north side of the bridge and walk along a frequently used fishing stretch where two notices, at intervals, warn me that the fishing here is strictly reserved. Within a short distance the River Allow joins the Blackwater. The River Allow itself joins the Dalua in Island Wood and later the Allow + Dalua receives the Owenare and, after that, the Brogeen in Bluepool, Kanturk. My walk is brought to an abrupt halt for though the Allow can be easily forded at this point, my socks and walking boots are comfortably dry, and, the thought of soaked and spongy feet for the rest of the day makes me shudder uneasily.

I follow the Allow north to where it crosses the Killarney-Mallow road under the nearby Leader's bridge. Tucking in carefully, on the grass margin of the right hand side of this busy road, I round the bend past Lehane's corner and enter a paddocked field where this year's Friesian calves are quietly grazing. Calves are curious by nature and so as not to arouse their curiosity I crawl beneath the electric fence into an ungrazed paddock. A short walk brings me to the river but the electric fence, running right along the course of the river, debars me from a closer view. I manage to glimpse the flowing river rushing in a lively mood down a slightly increased gradient. The Blackwater is now an energetic young man with a swagger in his progress, declaring to all that *he* means business and intends to make an impact on our world.

Here in Dromcummer Beg (Drom Comair Beag, *The ridge/hill of the little confluence*), the invasive Himalayan Balsam/Policeman's Helmet (*Impatiens glandulifera*) has established itself along the river banks and has spread up the course of its tributary, the Allow. A recent EU-project, involving the Department of the Environment, the Inland Fisheries Ireland and IRD Duhallow has been established for the purpose of eradicating this pretty but invasive plant. If this exotic species is left to grow unhindered, it will proliferate and outcompete the native flora. The newcomer dies back in winter, leaving patches of the river bank bare, and, consequently, subject to erosion. In such a scenario silt is then washed downstream causing harm to salmon eggs in their spawning beds. A sum of one million Euro has been granted for work to rid the area of this threat. I had already observed the plant upriver beyond Knocknagree. 'Balsam Bashing' has been used as a method of control on the Dartry, Lee, Barrow and other rivers.[1] Personally, I am not at all sure that this colourful alien can be so easily repelled; I will return to this topic when I reach the stretch of river below Cappoquin.

It's an ideal day for walking, warm and sunny, with cumulus clouds drifting leisurely across the over-arching sky. I am into my stride, relishing the freedom and anticipating the walk ahead as the expanding Blackwater flows on to Mallow. The first field, an amalgamation of several fields where

---

1   See www.irishfisheries.ie

the original hedges, ditches and fences have being bulldozed and leveled, follows the bend of the river to the south-east and then back to the north-east. The second field is even more promising with old oak and ash trees growing here and there, suggesting eighteenth-century landscape planting. But within a short time, I find myself walking into a tapering corner where the electric fence has been very strongly secured. In all likelihood, the power has been switched off, but, such is my fear that I crawl underneath to avoid the jarring voltage. Here the vegetation forms a solid barrier that brings my progress to a sudden halt. For ten minutes, I slash with my walking stick, seeking to open a path to the open road through the dense entangled mesh of vegetation. Eventually, I am forced to admit defeat and to accept that a retreat to a gate, about 200 metres away, is a more prudent and practical solution.

Somewhat crestfallen, I re-emerge onto the Mallow-Killarney road which at this time of mid-morning carries a sizeable volume of heavy vehicular traffic. *Walking Man,* facing the oncoming juggernauts and hurrying cars, tucks himself into the left hand side of the thoroughfare, hoping that he will soon find a re-entry point back to the river bank. Over a fearful stretch of one kilometre, I tread carefully, mostly along the grassy margin until I find an old wrought iron gate hung on two bulky piers that plainly belong to the vernacular architecture of rural Ireland.

Studying the Ordnance Survey map later, I realise that the course of this busy, modern road has been determined by the meandering path of the Blackwater. Locked in a sensual embrace, river and road flow onto Mallow and beyond. Prior to the opening of the Mallow-Killarney railway line in 1853, the Bianconi carriages transported travellers along this route while poorer people trod along the dusty and pot-holed margins. In earlier times the migrant labourers, the Duhallow *Spailpíní Fánacha* (itinerant farm labourers), bearing their scythes and kit-bags, walked from farm to farm during the hay-cutting season and later for the corn harvest. The equipment in their kit bags consisted of 'two edging stones, *cláiríní* ('small flat boards'), hammer, *duirníní* ('handles'), piece of tin, leather horse shoe stubs and two laths.'[2] Older Duhallow people have referred to the 'charm' or *ortha an fhaobhair*, that the *Spailpín* recited as he drew his scythe through a furze bush to ensure that it kept its sharp edge for the day. The folklorist, Kevin Danagher, failed to obtain an actual example of such verses.[3]

2   Dan S. O'Keeffe, 'The Duhallow Spailpín Fánach' in Seanchas Duthalla, (1991), p. 98-99
3   Dan S. O'Keeffe, p. 98-99

While the *Spailpín* has been romanticised by cultural nationalists and commemorated in ballads, the harsh reality was that their way of life was one of dire deprivation that required them to work in the fields from dawn to dusk. The *Spailpíní* worked in a *meitheal* ('team') of four to six men. 'The average mower could cut half an acre of hay in a day and a *meitheal* would cut a field of four to five acres in one day.'[4] The introduction of the horse-drawn mower brought to an end this old labour-intensive mode of mowing hay.

The thought, that I am walking the paths and the roads, that the *Spailpíní* followed, stirs a poignant memory from my school days. In the 1950s migrant labourers from county Mayo worked in east Cork where they thinned the beet seedlings – tedious work that the local farmers left to the 'Mayo Men.' These hard-working men did not respond to our calls as we walked to Kyle N.S. in the early morning.

The poet Eoghan Rua Ó Suileabháin journeyed into the heart of the prosperous Blackwater valley as a *Spailpín*, as a poet, a minstrel, a tutor, and indeed, as a philandering young man who loved company and entertainment (See Day 1, p.23). We know from his poetry that he worked for various families near the Mallow area.[5] Picture the young poet with his shock of flaming red hair, a glint in his roving eye and rhyming verses flowing from his imagination as natural as the flow of the Blackwater. The working day over the eloquent poet could release his flow of poetry to captivate the Nagles and other farming families.

> Rua a bhí tú
> Rua is aerach
> Is lámha briste spíonta
> Rábach, gréagach
> Lámha an Spailpín,
> Lámha a chothaigh cloig
> Is donndó na gréine
> Ag saothrú leathanghort
> Nár bhain leat féinig[6]

Unfortunately for Eoghan, he was press-ganged into the English navy and served under Admiral Rodney in the Carribean where he witnessed Rodney's triumph over the French fleet in April 1782. Hoping to secure his release from the navy, Eoghan composed a ballad commemorating

---

4   Ibid
5   Ó Conchúir, Breandán (Ed), *Eoghan Rua Ó Súileabháin,* Field Day Publications, Baile Átha Cliath 2009
6   Michael Davitt, INNTI, Uimhir a haon, Márta 1970

'Rodney's Glory.' The Admiral, though pleased, saw through Eoghan's poetic scheme and refused to grant his wish to be returned home to Sliabh Luachra. Subsequently, we know that he was confined to barracks in England, having contracted fever. From there he made his way to Knocknagree where he hoped to revive his fortunes by teaching,

> '...bookkeeping and mensuration
> Euclid's elements and navigation
> With trigonometry and sound gauging
> And English grammar with rhyme and reason.'

However, as Robert Burns put it 'the best laid schemes o' mice an' men', can go awry and come to naught and Eoghan's untimely death at the age of thirty-five put paid to all those dreams and plans.

My drooping spirits lift when I see a convenient style adjacent to the wrought iron gate. Climbing over, I walk down a passage overgrown with oxe-eye daisies, hogweed and angelica into a field of tall maize plants. And, once again, the Blackwater surges past with the cumulus clouds and golden gorse reflected from its glassy surface. However, despite the presence of long stretches of limestone along the Blackwater valley, the lime-loving species are largely absent. The naturalist, Robert Llyod Praeger (1865-1953), attributed the scarcity of calcareous species to the presence of large quantities of 'non-calcareous drift from the Old Red Sandstone hills on either side' that effectively suppress the limestone-loving flora. [7]

Walking between the rows of maize stalks, droplets of dew spatter across my tee shirt and smudges of yellow pollen fall on my shorts. After five minutes, I emerge from the maize into a meadow where black silo wrap bales bestrew the mowed ground like great black beetles curled into protective discs. Glancing across the river, I observe a row of sand martin burrows from which the parent birds emerge in pursuit of flies for their fledging young. Suddenly I see an angel with folded wings. No, my eyes are not deceiving me. Adjacent to the Blackwater at this juncture is Clonmeen cemetery. It was here that the fatally wounded Alasdair (Alasder) MacDonnell was laid to rest on the 13 November 1647 after the Battle of Knockanuss. *Cnoc na nOs*, 'The Hill of Sighs').

Gazing across the river, I recall another story that Con Tarrant told me some months previously about his visit to the O'Callaghan crypt in the same cemetery. Accompanied by some friends, Con made his way down the steps and entered the burial chamber where they saw the lead-lining of a coffin that contained exceptionally long bones. They assumed that, in all likelihood, these are the remains of the fallen warrior. Looking closely at the skull, they observed what seems to have been a bullet wound that he suffered during the retreat from Knockanuss.

Born in the Western Isles, 1612, Alasdair was a man of gigantic frame, 7'2" in height, who inflicted fear and death on his enemies. In battle he wielded an enormous claymore (A Scottish two-edged broadsword) that had 'a ball of ten pounds weight' at its base. This ball would run along the back of his sword, causing the edge of his weapon to inflict deeper and more fatal wounds. Forced to flee from Islay in 1639, he sought refuge with the MacDonnells in Antrim. By 1647 he had allied himself with the

---

7   Praeger, Robert Llyod, *Irish Topographical Botany,* Dublin, Proceedings of the Royal Irish Academy, Dublin, 1901, p. xvi; cited by Tony O'Mahony, *Wildflowers of Cork City and County,* Collins Press, 2009, p. 208

confederate cause and was second in command to Lord Taffee who led 7,464 foot and 1,076 cavalry to the battle field in Knockanuss, about five kilometres north of the Blackwater from where I now stand. The Royalists, led by Lord Inchaquin, confronted them with 4000 foot and 1,200 horse. By evening, the confederates were in disarray. A total of 3,500 men lay dead in the blood-soaked fields where to this day cannon balls and other items of warfare are still unearthed 363 years after a truly awful bloodbath.[8]

And as if to recall me from my musings about the violent events of the seventeenth century, the traffic drones continually in the background. In contrast to the lush crop of maize, I enter a field of oats and then a field of ripening barley where the ears of grain swish back and forth in the gentle breeze. Suddenly I am all agog among this field of ripening barley. It is over fifty years ago and I am with my own father, Ned O' Malley (1903 - 1988). We are together strolling through these 'fields of gold'. As we pace through the ripening barley my father plucks some heads of grain and crushes them in the palm of his hand. Then he raises his tilted palm close to his lips and with a delicate but deft puff of breath winnows the chaff away. He then feels and examines the texture of the grain to ascertain if the crop is ready for harvesting. In fond memory of my father, I pluck and crush two heads of barley and winnow away the separated chaff with a puff of my breath. The mindful re-enactment of small meaningful acts of ritual is essential therapy for our wellbeing. Sting's beautiful song, 'Fields of Gold', captures the mood perfectly:

> Many years have passed since those summer days,
> Among the fields of barley.
> See the children run as the sun goes down,
> Among the fields of gold.

Walking through fields of ripening corn for the first time on this journey, it occurs to me that I am leaving dairying country behind me and I have now entered the region where limestone holds sway. After the shales, coal measures and red sandstone of Duhallow, I've crossed a geological timeline, passing from the Devonian to the Carboniferous period. Here the ground is firm and well drained with a distinct flora where the ash replaces the alder and rushes and wild irises disappear. I notice that large limestone boulders have been laid to reinforce the fraying bank. Bloodstock, such as breeding mares and foals, destined for racing or for show jumping thrive on limestone land which also produces better crops of cereals or fodder crops.

---

8   Con Tarrant, 'Alasdair MacDonnell' in *Seanchas Duthalla*

And as if reaffirming my own belief that farming prosperity and limestone land are intermeshed I see a country mansion with stables, horseboxes and 4x4 vehicles on the opposite side of the river.

Times passes pleasantly until I cross a fence into another farm and another townland named Gurteenbeha (*Goirtín Beathach/Goirtín na Beithe*). Here the reference to the birch tree in the placename, *Little Field of the Birch*, indicates that I am back again on sandstone/shale soil. Looking around, I notice a large Limousin suckler herd with some store cattle in the adjoining field. 'Please God, they won't bother me, and I can continue my walk undisturbed.' My silent prayer goes unheeded as a vigilant bullock has observed me and has begun to trot, ominously, in my direction. Within seconds the entire herd of matronly cows with their udders swaying, frolicsome calves and mature two-year olds bullocks career in full flight towards me. I am surrounded by a snorting herd who resent the presence of this intruder into their peaceful fields where they are left to graze undisturbed before being housed for the winter months in the slatted units of a farm a few fields away. Shooing them back with the cattle driving call of 'HOW,' I walk nervously towards the electric fence, though turning back constantly, to ensure a safe distance between my slight and less than lithesome self and the great mass of livestock. Pressed on by the pursuers, I crawl beneath the electric fence into the sanctuary of the ungrazed strip where I exhale a sigh of relief. The older cattle circle and charge once more towards the single strand of charged wire that separates me from them. For one disquieting second, it appears as if they will break through; luckily, within an inch or two of the electric fence they veer away. I am free to ramble again unhindered in the company of my fickle and moody friend, Abhainn Mhór na Mumhan.

Land owners seek to contain the flooded rivers with reinforced banks. A river has a mind of its own and who are we to set limits to its boundaries? Just here the river, obviously, overflows its banks, judging by the wetter ground, the dried-up pools, stands of willow and clumps of yellow flag. To my mind, T.S. Eliot's description of the river as being, '...a strong brown god – sullen, untamed and intractable,' expresses most vividly the latent threat of the flooded river that cannot be contained between two frayed banks of clay and stone. Landowners, try as they may, can never fully subdue or contain the rise and fall of a great river, such as the Munster Blackwater. The river, acquiescent at this quiet time of the year, reasserts itself when the storms blow and the rain falls day after day in the dark hours of winter.

Stooping low, as if in subjugation, I dodge the overhanging branches that always threaten to lash back. As I emerge out of this frequently flooded area, two duck shooters approach, accompanied by four frisky cocker spaniels that are utterly absorbed in their hunt for bird scent. The two fowlers are fitted out from head to toe with the latest in camouflage dress. Their double barrel guns are similarly coated with a soft camouflage material to prevent reflected sunlight from casting a glint that might disturb wary mallards. With their eyes and ears focused keenly on the water, the two men are quiet surprised as they hear a loud 'Hallo' from the approaching walker. They tell me that they're both from Lombardstown and that, so far, they've had no luck with their shooting. *Walking Man* also informs *Man the Hunter Gatherer* of his own eccentric mission. The younger of the two fowlers informs me that Roskeen bridge is about one mile distant from where we stand, and then, as an afterthought, he tells me,

> When you get to the end of the next field, you'd be better off turning away from the river. Follow the steam that joins the Blackwater down there, and you'll find a little footbridge. Otherwise, you'll have trouble getting through that dense cover.

Having said goodbye to the fowlers, I smile a contented smile to myself and trudge off again, keeping an eye out for the stream. Luckily, I succeed in finding the footbridge, and, within a short time, I am back on the Mallow road just where the fowlers have parked their car with a mobile kennel attached. From here I saunter a short distance to Roskeen Bridge where I gaze into the large fields in Gortmore on the opposite river bank, wondering if I can see the limestone cave where the outlaw *Dónal na Cásca* hid with his lover *Máiréad Ní Cheallaigh*. According to Con Tarrant, *Dónall* was an O'Keeffe who refused to bow to the threat of 'To Hell or to Conaught.' He sought sanctuary in a cave here in Gortmore with his fair lady.

Con told me that he had visited the cave which extends for a considerable distance underground but, unfortunately, the mouth has been blocked and access is no longer possible. Passion held sway between Donall and Máiréad, until she was lured by a tempting bribe from an English army officer, and agreed to betray him. The wily and furious *Dónal*, detecting the hidden dagger in her bosom, thrust the blade through her heart. To commemorate the tragic tale, the Knocknagree poet and balladeer, Ned Walsh, composed a lament for the fair but false lady who rejected love for gain. Sitting in the customer waiting room of their family's Skoda garage in Banteer, Con recited a verse for me in a rousing declamatory style,

The moss couch I bought thee
Today from the mountain
Has drank the last drop
Of thy young heart's red fountain –
For this good *skian* [scian-knife]beside me
Stuck deep and rung hollow
In thy bosom of treason
Young Máiréad Ní Cheallaigh.

Another local historian, Donie O'Sullivan informed me that the Blackwater had changed its course and no longer skirts the mouth of the ancient cave. It is possible that rivers in limestone regions can alter their courses due to the underground drainage and the effects of a torrential flood. The Gortmore cave is well known to speleologists who have explored and mapped its hollow caverns.

Roskeen Bridge

ROSKEEN BRIDGE TO LOMBARDSTOWN BRIDGE, 3.74K

My reliable OS map tells me that the distance from Roskeen Bridge to Lombardstown Bridge is 3.74 k. However *Walking Man* decides to take a well earned rest at this stage and lays his aching frame on the ground with his back to the trunk of a spreading horse chestnut tree. For twenty minutes, I pour over the OS map, checking details of the route, hoping to anticipate difficulties that may lie ahead. Here, the Blackwater curves in a south easterly direction as it skirts the inviting field of stubble that now awaits me from which the barley has recently been harvested. Striding on, the air is heavy with the smell of grain and straw as the stubble crackles under my walking boots. I am enjoying this stretch immensely; however, a tree-lined fence of tall sycamores converges obliquely to the river and abruptly halts my progress. Having reached the fence, I realise that it obscures a large drain. Instead of plunging through a depth of water and suffering briar scratches and nettle burns, I follow the drain back along the line of sycamores until I come to a strong wooden platform which was, probably, placed in position for the local anglers. Back into my stride, I cross fence and drain and follow them back to the river bank from which the trees and vegetation have been cleared. The river readjusts its orientation once more as it tacks to the east.

Following the anglers' path along by the river, I push ahead while keeping close to the river until I reach a boundary fence where a warning sign has been erected to discourage would-be trespassers from entering what clearly seems to be an intensive dairy farm where a large herd of Friesian cows are grazing.

A public notice nailed to the tree trunk stares down at me. I read it carefully. 'You are now on a working farm,', 'if you cross this boundary, the owner disclaims all responsibility.' I should have anticipated things like this but the honest truth is I didn't. And for a split second my mind goes blank and then my head is awash with stampeding herds of cattle and status-challenged young bulls pawing the ground and irate farmers with loaded guns. What had I let myself in for?

Either I turn back, forego my riverbank walk or accept the warning - the landowner has no responsibility towards me – and press ahead. I have no realistic option but to continue. Recognition must be given to landowners' concerns about the security of their property, liability and duty of care. We exist in a culture of insurance claim and blame: a child tripping in a

Flowing on to Pallas

schoolyard can now be a claim against the school management; an adult tripping on a path is now a claim against the local council. When are we going to acknowledge that we have a responsibility for ourselves? It is hard to blame the landowners.

The Latin phrase, *Solvitur ambulando*, recurs to me from the days and nights I spent studying Longman's Latin Grammar in Youghal CBS (1960-65). Previously, I assumed that the phrase broadly meant...*Let it work itself out*, but now in a moment of lucidity, it occurs to me that it could literally, and, in every sense mean...*Let it be resolved through walking*. I find this a fascinating idea that by walking you may solve you worries and problems. How often do we return from a walk with a clearer head and a limbered body? So there's more to walking than just the physical exercise of placing one foot before another and following that by letting the first foot outpace the second.

I follow the curves and twists of the river. Keeping an eye on the depth and flow of water, I can plainly see that fording is not a realistic option on this stretch. I reach a paddock where sixty or more cows graze contentedly. They cast an eye in my direction, whisk their tails and continue to graze or chew the cud in best bovine fashion. The entire grazing area can be clearly observed from the farmhouse that overlooks the ground through which I am now walking. Halted by a deep drain and forced to concede that dry feet and comfortable walking boots matter more than progress, I retreat along a surfaced farm track that leads directly to the farm buildings. Unsure of the reception that may await me and realising that I've ignored the warning sign on the farm boundary, I scramble up through a grove of trees and briars to a higher field where a great pile of silo wrapped bales has been built. However, to my consternation, I see a formidable looking Aberdeen Angus bull with a copper ring in his nose, grazing with fifteen heifers of the same breed. Once again, I beat a hasty retreat through a gap into an adjacent field. My OS map shows that a minor country road runs adjacent to the southern boundary of this field. In sheer desperation and not a little panic I might add, and with the aid of my stout and trusty hazel walking stick I scramble and haul myself up to the top of the roadside perimeter fence from where I jump a distance of five feet to the road below.

The impact of my feet hitting the solid ground jars my body from toe to head and not for the first or last time on this walk I feel my age. However, my boot camp conditioning soon kicks in and I rejuvenate in next to no time. Though frustrated to find myself forced away from the river, I draw on a residue of patience from deep within and begin to take a more sanguine view. Knowing that 'road leads on to road,' I saunter downhill to the small village of Lombardstown. Like Bodach an Chóta Lachna / The Churl with the Drab Overcoat in the tales of Fionn Mac Cumhail and the Fianna I browse on the succulent blackberries on both sides of the road and even attempt to reach over a low orchard wall to draw a ripe apple into my grasp. It remains, tantalisingly, centimetres beyond my reach. Around the bend and into the townland of Gortavoher (*Gort an Bhóthair*, 'The Ploughed Field of the Road.') the Blackwater reappears below me on my left hand side. On seeing the river my body is flushed with rush of adrenalin and excitement. I realise that I have missed my travelling companion during the short time that we have been apart. Nearing the first houses of Lombardstown village, I pass a busy house owner, whirring around his garden, skimming millimetres from what looks more like a golfing green than a domestic lawn.

Nearing the outlying housing estate of the village, two young women approach, pushing buggies in which two toddlers sleep peacefully. Replying to my query as to where the local supermarket is situated, the red-haired woman replies, 'It's the Post Office, but they close at 1.00 p.m.,' and then she adds, 'You're probably too late.' My next query seeks details of the local public house (if any?), 'It's about a half-mile uphill from the village,' her companion informs me.

To my dismay, the P.O. is closed, and, despite a few ardent knocks, *Walking Man* is not granted the opportunity to plead for sustaining food. It's *siesta* time for young and old, hardly a dog stirs as the swallows swoop over the restful residents of Lombardstown which should now be renamed Slumberstown. The area took its name from merchants from Northern Italy who came to Ireland to engage in business in the middle ages. Rather than address them by their exotic Italian surnames, people began to refer to them as 'Le Lombards' or 'The Lombards.' Various individuals with their adapted name prospered and owned land and property especially in county Cork but also in Waterford and other regions. Sadly, Lombardstown House, built by James Lombard *circa* 1750, was burnt to the ground a short time after I walked through the village.

The ancient Irish name for the area was *Gort Mhaolúir/Gort Maoluidhre* (The Ploughed Field of Maoluir), Gortmolire. Regrettably, Cork County Council have substituted the more modern name *Baile Lombaird* for the ancient toponym which up to recently featured on the bilingual road signs that directed travellers to the village. Members of the local community, wishing to retain the ancient name for their village, protested and defeated the first attempt by the council to substitute the modern name in the 1980s. *Gort Maoluidhre* remained on the signposts until the N72 was upgraded in recent years and *Baile Lombaird* was hoisted on the community once again. The renaming seems to have been accepted as a *fait accompli*.

The air reeks of animal feedstuffs from the Dairygold Mill where 'quality animal feeds' are manufactured to supply the needs of the farming community in counties, Cork, Limerick, Tipperary and Clare. The village also contains a large agri-trading store that supplies an extensive range of farm requisites to farmers in the surrounding area. I learned later that Lombardstown had the second oldest creamery in Ireland which was opened in 1890.

Dispirited and uttering a quiet goodbye, I push off once again to complete the last leg of today's walk from Lombardstown to Mallow. But just as I am about to step over the level-crossing, a bespectacled young man peers over a garden hedge and identifies himself as one of the hunter gatherers that I had encountered earlier this morning. His camouflage hunting outfit has been stowed away. 'We had no luck at all, but it's our first day out this season.' He enquires how I have fared since we met. Having heard a brief summary of my tribulations, he issues some useful advice, 'When you cross over the [Lombardstown] bridge, don't go into the first field as you'll run into trouble down at the end. The best thing to do is to walk over the bridge, turn right for Mallow and continue along the road for a mile or so, and you'll find a way back to the river.'

Since his first piece of advice has already proved helpful, I listen attentively

Mural of Lombardstown Creamery

and intend to follow his recommended route. Then over the level-crossing of the Mallow-Killarney rail line. Lombardstown no longer has a train station, and locals have to travel to Mallow (10k) or to Banteer (8k) to avail of rail transport. In 1912, Monday, August 5, one of the worst disasters in Irish rail history occurred here when a Great Southern and Western Railways train 'missed the points...and crashed into a buffer at the end of the station.' Luckily, there was only one fatality though seventeen passengers suffered severe injuries and many more incurred injuries of a lesser degrees.

Years later, Count John McCormack, the celebrated Irish tenor had a holiday house in the locality. It is said that locals would often gather outside Count McCormack's house while the noted tenor practiced his repertoire of classical songs and especially his mesmerising tonic sol-fa routine within. What a privilege that must have been for those lucky enough to have been there?

Rambling down the road, I muse that everywhere, no matter how isolated or inconsequential, has its own echoes of the past, hanging in the air. Pausing on the elegant five-arch limestone bridge, I watch the swallows and sand martins engage in their unceasing pursuit of flies and other insects. The level of the water is exceptionally low today, but I try to envisage a great volume of water surging underneath. Built in 1820, 'it serves as a reminder of the engineering achievements and the quality of local craftsmanship in the early nineteenth century.'[9]

9   National Inventory of architectural heritage

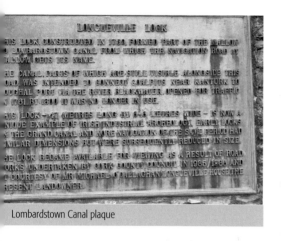

Lombardstown Canal plaque

The pedestrian now enjoys a safe haven from the stream of traffic along the hard shoulder of the upgraded N72. Despite the safety of the hard shoulder, the tar macadam surface offers no relief to my complaining feet. Despite the soreness, I have made good progress and ought to reach my next target, Longfield Bridge, in less than two hours.

The townland of Pallas lies to my north where the amazing story of the Lombardstown Canal began in 1756. White elephants cropped up willy-nilly during our recent building boom but, right here, on the northern barrier of the N72, one can still detect traces of an enterprise that should never have been sanctioned by the government of that period.

William Ockeneden, a Dutch entrepreneur, proposed that a canal should be constructed to link the Duhallow coalfields with Cappoquin. It was envisaged that barges could transport coal and other products on this inland waterway for export through the port of Youghal. A 5.6 kilometre-long section was cut between Lombardstown and Mallow before funding was withdrawn by the government. The total expenditure amounted to £11,000. Two locks were built: one close to the Lombardstown Bridge and the second in Longueville about three kilometres from where I now stand. The Lombardstown lock has been demolished but, luckily, the Longueville Lock has been preserved. Measuring 47 metres long and 6.6 metres in breadth, it constitutes a significant part of the industrial archaeology of eighteenth century Ireland. Apart from the two locks, all that remain of this industrial fiasco is a stagnant overgrown drain and a gate lodge leading to Longueville House.

The tendency of Walking Man to dwell too long on those interesting stretches of the river has put him under a certain pressure. As Robert Frost wrote in his poem *Stopping by Woods on a Snowy Evening*:

> The woods are lovely, dark, and deep,
> But I have promises to keep,
> And miles to go before I sleep,
> And miles to go before I sleep.

Leaving the busy thoroughfare and clambering over a great embankment of clay and stones, designed to prevent the Blackwater from flooding the road in times of heavy rainfall, I manage to return to the fields again. I sense that the landscape has taken on a new aspect as the flat and enlarged fields expand before me. A large flock of rooks forage for grains of barley among the prickly stubbles while a herd of contented Friesian cows lie still before being housed and milked for a second time this day. I notice, with interest, a cow track leading to a tunnel under the road through which the animals can safely pass to the farm buildings on the northern side of the road.

I have just entered the flood plain of the Blackwater. Here in Dromrastill and Woodpark, the river regularly overflows its banks as evidenced by the patches of sand and gravel strewn near the banks. Some understanding of the topography of north Cork helps to elucidate the factors that lead to the flooding of Mallow town. While the Irish translation of Mallow is now rendered (atrociously) as *Mala*, the older and more revealing name is *Mágh Ealla* which is translated as 'the Plain of Ealla/Ala.' The Blackwater, with the Boggeragh and the Nagle mountains on its southern side and the Mullaghareirk mountains and the Ballyhoura hills to the north, drains a quarter of the surface area of Kerry and Cork which constitutes 6% of Ireland as a whole.

Pushing on, I idly imagine stripping off for a swim in the water to cool down. But, regretfully, as a non-swimmer, I am forced to remain on *terra firma* from where I marvel at the enchantment of flowing water. Of all the substances of the physical world, water is the most mobile: shifting, transporting wood, boats and birds, it stirs our imagination to flow away with it. The lines from Tennyson's 'Lady of Shallot' play over and over in my head,

Cattle grazing on the flood plain of the Blackwater

> And down the river's dim expanse
> like some bold seer in a trance...

Wind, of course, is even more mobile than water but lacks the magic invoked when we stand to view a great body of glassy green water, ever flowing with beady bubbles bursting to the surface. If only I could immerse myself into the primal element that water is, and be part of it and with it. D.H. Lawrence, contemplating the mystery of water, 'It is hydrogen two parts, oxygen one, but there is also a third thing that makes it water and nobody knows what that is.' And then, as if to break the spell, a snow-white little egret espies me, takes to flight and emits a raucous call to notify his peers that their territory has been invaded. The little egret, a recent addition to our Irish avifauna, nested for the first time in Ireland on the Backwater close to Youghal in 1997 (12 pairs). Since then, exploiting a niche in slob lands and river margins, they have spread upriver to Mallow and beyond as well as establishing themselves on most rivers in the south of Ireland. Their pristine white plumes were much sought after for the decoration of ladies' hats in the Victorian era.

At 3.00 p.m., I reach the point opposite to where Dromaneen Castle stands silhouetted on a limestone cliff, eternally looking north over the Blackwater. Built by the O'Callaghans around 1600 the castle, or, more accurately, a fortified house, occupies an elevated site with a clear view over the surrounding countryside. Access requires a detour of 5-6k by road or wading across the river and climbing the ivy-covered face to the top.

Two months later, while driving home to Beaufort from Mallow, I succeeded in visiting the castle ruin. Dan Kelleher, a busy farmer, gave me permission to walk through the bawn to the castle ruin.

'No trouble, go right ahead, but, if it was last week I would have to refuse you as there were two young bulls grazing there.'

The bawn consists of two acres and is the largest in Ireland. 'We had to bring in a huge amount of topsoil and sand to cover the underlying cobble stones.'

A bawn is the defensive wall surrounding a tower house. The name possibly derived from Irish word for a cow *bó* and its plural *ba*. The original purpose of bawns was to protect cattle from attack. It was once a trench, and over time, these were replaced by walls. The name then began to be used for the walls that were built around tower houses.

Dan explained to me that the Office of Public Works (OPW) had laid down strict regulations concerning the conservation of the bawn wall. He then told me that he found a coin from the Williamite war on the ground a few years ago.

Dromaneen Castle

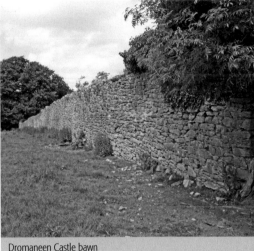

Dromaneen Castle bawn

A short walk on the western side of the bawn wall brought me to the castle which far and away exceeded my expectations. Entering the extensive ruins, I am immediately conscious of the towering chimneys and gables that overlook the entire scene. Continuing with my exploration, I pause before a very finely carved old fireplace around which the O'Callaghans and later residents feasted and socialised. A haunting eeriness pervades the location with pigeons and crows registering their protest over my intrusion.

Before saying goodbye to Dan, he told me that he and some American cousins had explored the cave directly underneath the ground where we stood.

'I was quite nervous about exploring the cave but the Americans wanted adventure during their holidays.'

Turning my back on Dromaneen castle and following the river as it curves north-east towards the N72, I walk between the massive round bales of barley straw. Trailing the palm of my opened hand over their corrugated surface, the bales of gold smell of harvest time, of ripeness and plenitude and of the kind earth. How inexcusable the folly of those farmers who regard straw and stubble as a nuisance that must be burnt to facilitate the sowing of the next crop After a short distance, I turn right in the direction of the now closed Sugar Factory and walk steadily to Longfield Bridge where my youngest brother, Joe, has been waiting for some time. He's blithely unconcerned and full of energy and bounce after a day's work as caretaker

A late lunch

in a national school in Cork city. He has brought sandwiches and fruit, and, even better – companionship and humour for the last section into Mallow.

However, before resuming the walk, we saunter onto the bridge where we observe the flowing water, the cattle herd on the south side and the loading of bales on the north side of the river. Next, I discard my knapsack and place it in Joe's car booth before heading off with him across one more large field strewn with bales. We bid the workers good evening, remarking that they're building a fine load that will safely reach its destination. After the corn field, we walk along the mown perimeter of the Mallow racecourse. While I have only a passing interest in the 'sport of kings,' Joe is a keen follower of national hunt racing and well informed about the breeding and training of race horses. We take time to examine the skilfully-crafted fences as Joe explains to me that the sharp ends of the birch twigs are placed deliberately at the top of the fence to train the race horses to avoid contact with the sharp birches.

This Wednesday evening, the viewing stand is empty, no flag flutters, the tote is shut and the bookies and punters are all at home. Mallow or, more correctly Cork Race Course, holds a total of thirteen race meetings during the year, their principal race being the Cork National in November. Inexplicably, County Cork, despite its status as the largest county in Ireland, has only one official racecourse. Nevertheless, there are numerous stud farms along the Blackwater valley where champion horses are bred.

The racecourse was overlooked by the Sugar Factory from its foundation in 1935 to its closure in 2006. The factory provided employment for generations of people from Mallow and the surrounding communities. The annual harvest saw lorries and railway wagons consigning huge quantities of beet from most parts of Munster. On arrival at the factory, a mechanical grab extracted a sample from the load that was then weighed, washed and pared of waste material such as roots and tops. The cleaned sample was re-weighed, minus the tare, and on this basis the weight and value of each load was calculated. The process of purification produced the sweet crystals, labelled, *Siúcra na hÉireann*, that were retailed in the small and large grocery shops throughout Ireland.

The growers had the option of purchasing the waste material, referred to as beet pulp, which was a valuable animal feedstuff. Out in the harvested beet fields, cattle and cows wintered on the tops with their high sugar content. The production of sugar beet was significantly subsidised by the government to guarantee a worthwhile profit for the producers. Entering the twenty-first century, world trade agreements compelled the Irish government to reduce and, gradually, to eliminate these subsidies. The rationale for the ending of support was to allow sugar cane producers equal access to the European and Irish market.

We stroll along light heartedly, exchanging yarns and stories about the Blackwater, the striking Cork hurling team and whatever else crops up. After the solitude of the long day's walk, it is wonderfully refreshing to talk and joke about growing-up together and the turns of fortune and misfortune that have been our lot. Then I recall, a comment the veteran republican, Ernie O'Malley, made about the town we're about to visit, 'Mallow is a very quiet town; nothing ever happens in Mallow.' Possibly, O'Malley was referring to the sickly tribe of valetudinarians who came 'to take the waters' at the spa from April to October. Perhaps, this weary walker, with his briar-scratched knees and 'measling' shins, should imbibe a draft of the curative waters before resuming tomorrow morn.

The growers had the option of purchasing the waste material, referred to as beet pulp, which was a valuable animal feedstuff. Out in the harvested beet fields, cattle and cows wintered on the tops with their high sugar content. The cessation of the beet industry in Ireland dealt a severe blow to farmers, to lorry owners and other stakeholders. No wonder that landowners feel that we are losing control over our economy. Policy decisions are now made in Brussels, New York,or Zurich where the G7 convene and draw up agreements that affect the lives of people on a global scale.

The modern town of Mallow originated as a Norman settlement in the late twelfth and early thirteenth century. Guarded by Castle Gearr or Short Castle at its western end and by Mallow Castle at its eastern end, its resident population of approximately 200 occupied one long street between these two castles. In 1282 the Desmond Geraldines gained ownership of the principal castle that guarded and controlled the vital ford over the Blackwater.

From the West End, we walk to Davis Street where the patriot Thomas Davis (1814-45) was born. Davis was very much to the fore in the founding of the Young Ireland movement. He and other activists aimed to revive the spirit of the Irish people after the calamity of the great famine. To promote the mission of the Young Irelanders, he founded 'The Nation' newspaper along with Charles Gavin Duffey and John Blake Dillon. He believed especially in using song and poetry to reawaken the pride of the Irish people in their own identity and heritage. To help achieve such a revival, he composed memorable ballads such as 'The West Awake' and 'A Nation Once Again.'

Born the son of a Protestant Welshman and of a Catholic Irish mother, a descendant of Donal O'Sullivan Beare, Davis strove to convince people of different religious beliefs that nationalism was not determined by one's background but rather by the commitment to believe in and to serve the nation of Ireland.

Other patriots whom Mallow can proudly claim are William O'Brien (1852-1928) and

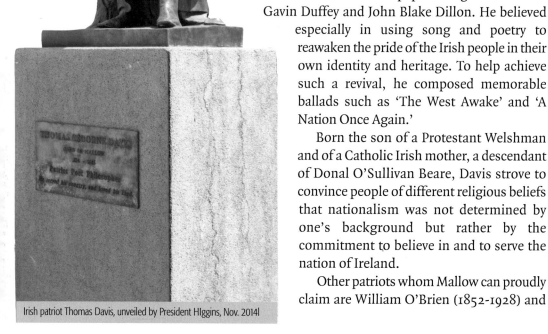

Irish patriot Thomas Davis, unveiled by President HIggins, Nov. 2014l

the novelist, Canon Patrick Augustine Sheehan (1852-1913). Born in the same year and in close proximity to one another, both served the cause of Irish nationalism – O'Brien as a journalist, agrarian agitator, social revolutionary and MP while Sheehan minded the spiritual and social welfare of his parishioners in Doneraile especially in their dealings with Lord Doneraile. They attended the same primary school though O'Brien's family was forced to move to Cork in 1868 due to financial misfortune. He was elected as MP for Mallow, 1883-85 and later for North Cork and Cork city. A deeply-felt sympathy for the plight of the tenant farmers motivated his political career and writings.

Sheehan became intensely involved at a parochial level in bettering the living conditions of his people. His novels, *Glenanaar, My New Curate, The Queen's Fillet, The Blindness of Dr Grey* and other works have been largely forgotten though the centenary of his death in 2013 has seen a revival of interest in his life and writings.

Our first stop is at O'Keeffe's Lounge Bar in Main Street where the nearest thing to a 'draft of the curative waters', two pints of Murphy's stout, go rattling down a-glug, a-glug. The atmosphere is pleasant as local workingmen enjoy an evening drink and exchange the news of the day with one another. Sitting at the back of the lounge, we mind our own business and study the black and white photographs of victorious Cork hurling teams. In answer to my query about accommodation for the night, the barwoman procures the local business directory and runs her index finger

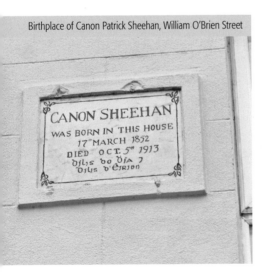

Birthplace of Canon Patrick Sheehan, William O'Brien Street

Greenfield Guesthouse, Navigation Road

over the list of guest houses and B&Bs in the town. After a short interval, she recommends Greenfield House B&B on the Navigation Road – a choice that turns out to be quite a fortunate co-incidence for me.

Across the street we pause for a moment outside a small second-hand bookshop selling a range of paperbacks: nevertheless, the patient bibliophile can uncover literary gems within. Then, in disbelief, I blink rapidly when my field of vision observes a paperback entitled, *Walking the Back Roads: a Journey from Donegal to Clonmacnoise*. So there is another of the species, a replica of *Walking Man*, out there, a Michael McMonagle, wandering from Gartan in Donegal to St Kieran's city fair in Clonmacnoise, another man who thinks 'the woods are lovely, dark, and deep,' but who has 'promises to keep, and miles to go before' he sleeps.

About an hour later, Joe drops me off at Greenfield B&B on the Navigation Road where the owner's land borders the Blackwater. Pat Walsh is most interested in my walk, informing me that he has campaigned successfully for the development of a pathway through townpark to the new Castle grounds, and that, he intends pressing the Urban District Council (UDC) to further develop this walk.

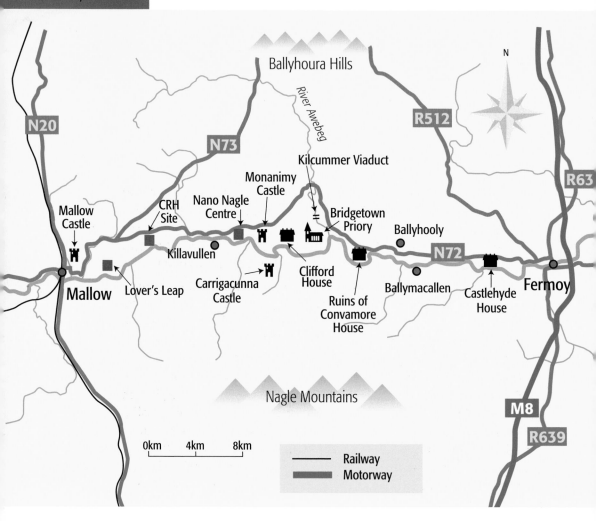

Ballyhoura Hills

River Awebeg

N20

N73

R512

R63

Kilcummer Viaduct

Monanimy
Castle

Mallow
Castle

CRH
Site

Nano Nagle
Centre

Bridgetown
Priory

Ballyhooly

Killavullen

N72

Mallow

Lover's Leap

Carrigacunna
Castle

Clifford
House

Ballymacallen

Castlehyde
House

Fermoy

Ruins of
Convamore
House

Nagle Mountains

M8

R639

0km   4km   8km

——— Railway
▬▬▬ Motorway

N

Mallow

to

Fermoy

Mallow, Killavullen, Ballyhooly to Fermoy

'There's great therapy in a flowing river.'[1]

THURSDAY MORNING dawns full of promise and bright rays of sunshine light up the dining room of Greenfield B&B. At the next table, a crew of Kildare men, currently surveying the route for the new Cork-Limerick road, tuck into a full Irish breakfast. *Walking Man*, too, avails of the full complement. After breakfast, Pat explains my route,

> Go around to the back of the house, pass through the opening and walk to a gate at the far left hand corner of the field by the river. Then turn right down the lane that runs with the steep railway embankment on your left. Cross under the railway viaduct and then under the new Mallow Bridge and follow the path through the public park to the old bridge.

Reassured by Pat's directions and bearing his blessings, I set off on what I hope will be a rewarding day-long walk to Fermoy. In a short time, I reach the lane that brings me directly under the viaduct that carries the Dublin-Cork train across the Blackwater. An imposing structure built in 1925 though not as imposing as the great limestone-arched viaduct that the Anti-Treaty forces blew up in 1922. Up to 150 stone masons had worked day and night, cutting and dressing the stone for the original structure that was completed in 1849,

> Nothing like Mallow viaduct had ever been seen in Munster. It excited the admiration of the building fraternity and the general public alike. It

---

1   Pat Walsh, B&B proprietor, in a letter to the author, 17 Nov., 2010

measured 515 feet across from buttress to buttress, the span of each arch being 45 feet.[2]

Not even the intervention of Michael Collins could dissuade the Republicans from their fanatical determination to disrupt lines of communication and supply for the forces of the *Saorstát*. The demolition of the 'ten arch bridge' disrupted transport severely and impinged greatly on people's working lives.

Standing underneath the replacement structure, grainy black and white scenes from old crackling celluloid film footage of the civil war flash before my eyes.

Today, however, I am not going to dwell on those harsh memories, especially as the morning sunshine lures me away from the viaduct along the Blackwater trail through the town park. I notice an abandoned Tesco shopping trolley washed up on the muddy margin of the river's course. I encounter dog owners with their 'best friends' and two joggers who cast a 'wonder where he is going' sort of glance in my direction. And like the frisky dogs, there's a joyful bounce in my step, feeling that the day ahead will bring its own share of sights and events for me.

Mallow town and environs are subjected to periodic floods that cause large scale damage to houses, shops and other buildings. The town park occupies the natural floodplain of the Blackwater and turns into a lake when

---

2   O Connor, *Ironing the land: the coming of the railways to Ireland* (Dublin , 1999), p. 64

Rial viaduct, Mallow 7626 W.L.

the swollen river overflows to reclaim the land that once constituted a natural part of its course. Mallow people classify the floods that affect their *locale* into three categories: the yearly floods that rise and fall without undue consequence; the ten-year floods that disrupt their lives and, lastly, the thirty-year floods that bring destruction and often death to the community.[3] Such disastrous floods occurred in 1853, 1875, 1916, 1946, 1948, 1969 and 1980.[4] After the most recent floods of 2008 and 2009, the Office of Public Works (OPW) have constructed a series of embankments that help to limit the effects of flooding in the lower lying parts of Mallow such as the Bridge Street area. Demountable barriers can now be erected within half an hour to halt the overflowing river on its destructive path. Today the Blackwater is low and sluggish, with scarcely a hint of the enormous mass and awesome power that lie within its potential.

The school-going traffic has halted on the old Mallow Bridge. Parents are dropping off their kids at the local schools. After forty years at the blackboard, I have bidden goodbye to the copies and text books, syllabi, tests, corrections and all the other encumbrances that make up the educational scene. The scholars and their parents catch a glimpse of *Walking Man* before he disappears through the dry arch of the old bridge. I bask in the sunshine of my new found freedom.

Incredible as it may seem to the present generation, no bridge was built

---

3 Conversation with Pat Walsh, Greenfield House, Navigation Road, Mallow.
4 Corcoran, 'Development and Examination of Flood Warning Systems for the Blackwater,' M.Eng thesis, UCC, p. 18

Mallow Bridge

across the Blackwater prior to the Elizabethan era. Lord Deputy Perrot, writing to the Privy Council in England in 1584 recommended that bridges ought to be built at key river crossings such as Mallow. English officials at the time were keenly aware of the vital importance of bridges in containing rebellion throughout Ireland, '...there was a faire forde in summer on the "broadwater", but in winter or in moist weather, there was no passage but in troughs or cots and even horses had to swim. Armies had to halt for three or four days or hazard attack or retreat.'[5] Shortly after 1588 the first bridge was erected at Mallow but was destroyed by the Williamites in 1690. A replacement bridge was constructed in 1712 and survived until the great flood of 1853 when it seems, according to contemporary sources, to have been destabilised though not demolished. The present bridge was built in 1856, and still continues to serve the area. The modern concrete structure, however, bears the bulk of vehicular traffic over the Blackwater today.

Passing through the dry arch, I recall having read in the Mallow Field Club Journal (MFCJ) that the IRA drilled holes in the bridge but were frustrated when local women and their children occupied the structure, forcing them to abandon their plan to blow it up. Without the convenience of the bridge, the lives of women and men would have become exceedingly difficult.

After the bridge, I pass through an unmanaged piece of ground that is, evidently, subjected to regular flooding. Striding across a new steel bridge, over the Spa Stream, I arrive into the new town park which formerly belonged to the Mallow Castle estate. Glancing across the river at the Bridge House [public house], I read the legend in large black letters on the gable: '1854/J.J. Murphy/Famous Porter.' All the blinds are drawn and, probably will remain drawn until evening time when the early locals and Blackwater anglers begin to ramble in for a quiet drink and pleasant banter about their fishing exploits up and down the river.

From here I catch an obscured view of the ruins of Mallow Castle. The building of the castle was commenced, sometime after the Desmond rebellion, by Sir Thomas Norreys (1556-1597) and completed by his daughter Lady Elizabeth Jephson, A loyal servant of the crown, Norreys was awarded a large grant of land for his role in defeating the Desmonds and their allies. His chosen site, previously, fortified by the Desmonds since the thirteenth century, empowered him to control this crucial crossing. The

---

5   O'Keeffe, Peter & Simington, Tom, *Irish Stone Bridges: History and Heritage*, Irish Academic Press, 1991, p. 77

grant of land required him to build a suitable dwelling in order to secure the dominance of the new order.

The architectural design of Mallow Castle expressed a new and less defensive approach that could be described as being a hybrid of a castle and a manor house. Though castellations and towers were still featured, the widows were broad to admit more light, and wood, rather than stone, was favoured in the interior. The emphasis had shifted from defensive occupation to a more comfortable mode of living. Nevertheless, the builder ensured a high degree of visibility for the occupants to enable them to observe all approaches to the castle. Norreys must have assumed that the time of conflict had passed and that peace would reign in the province of Munster. By 1690 his castle stood abandoned and his descendants, the Jephsons, had taken up residence in the modified stables and a servant's wing.

Today the ruins stand forlorn – a relic of the Elizabethan age as is the herd of white fallow deer, presented by Queen Elizabeth to Norreys for his service to the crown. Rambling along the newly laid path in Castlepark, I sight the white deer in the shade of the oak and beech trees. Their tails whisk back and forth to disturb the flies that bother them. They have, apparently, no lush pasture here but the dried out grass of late summer along with docks and yellow ragwort. I learned later that Cork County Council has reached agreement with the owners, the McGinn family, to purchase the modern castle along with the deer park. Check out 'Sale of Mallow Castle' on the internet, and the catalogue of furniture, paintings, porcelain, books and prints and all the other paraphernalia accumulated in the salons and halls of castellated mansions, cascade off the web page. The building stands empty, its walls and corridors bereft of ornaments. The age of castles has passed.

New Mallow Castle

I ramble through the newly landscaped park that was formerly part of the Manor, bidding 'Good Morning' to the lively local women and to the more leisurely strolling men with their Jack Russells on leads. Unsure of the route ahead, I request some information from an older gentleman who informs me that he has retired home to Mallow after thirty-four years in England.

> You'll have to walk uphill around the woodland. Walk over the rough ground to the top, and then keep right by the wood until you come to the wire fence.

We chat pleasantly for a few minutes. On hearing that I am walking the Blackwater all the way to Fermoy, he comments,

> An English colonel used come to Fermoy every year for the fishing over a period of thirty-five years. When he died his ashes were sprinkled on the Blackwater and local anglers erected a plaque in his honour.

After that pleasant interlude, I am feeling reassured for having figured out a way around Lover's Leap – the tall limestone outcrop that rises abruptly over the river. Nevertheless, I decide to investigate the nook under the projecting rock. Leaving the paved footpath and following the trodden trail to the very base of the overhanging limestone, I reach the point where young people congregate at weekends. Discarded cans of Dutch Gold, Magner's Cider and other brands of drink lie around the place with the charred remains of a fire. Naturally, I do not approve of such late-night gatherings but, who knows, perhaps, some hint of the Gothic past that invests the location, may be engrained in their sub-consciousness. A Lourdes–type cave provides shelter for the nocturnal party-goers. Much of the cave floor and the surrounding area are littered with splintered glass.

Having retraced my steps, I head uphill around the wooded Lover's Leap. Here I walk over ground from which the topsoil has been removed in preparation for the building of another housing estate. Evidently, the project has been abandoned with large piles of builder's rubble and other materials dumped here and there. Various weeds have begun to re-colonise this extensive area. Standing still, I muse on the phenomenon, or rather the mirage, of what was superficially labelled the Celtic Tiger... *We got it wrong, we messed up, we allowed the grey men to seduce us with their delusions, and here is the concrete evidence. What lunacy overtook Irish society?* Anyway, I am determined to push on and not to let the sordid building mess get me down. My knapsack is an ample weight to bear without burdening myself with the planning mess that now shackles our economy.

At the boundary of this abandoned site, I manage to climb over a chain-link fence into a large field where a crop of barley has been recently harvested. The spikes of stubble crackle from the pressure of my walking boots but soon rebound to their original position, dispersing sparkling drops of dew. My nose catches the wholesome smell of straw and grain as flocks of wood pigeons fly away to the nearby beech trees. Glancing towards Lovers' Leap, I wonder whether I should probe into its dark interior to see the rock from which the 'star-crossed lovers' hurtled to their death in the river below. Divesting myself of my bag, I find a track through the trees that leads to the pinnacle from where a young Protestant man and his Catholic fiancée plunged to their death after the refusal of their parents to approve of their relationship. Peering downward from the daunting height, I draw back from the edge of the awesome precipice that towers over the Blackwater. Nearby, I find the remains of what was once a viewing shelter or gazebo. Apparently, Lovers' Leap was a well known spot for romantic trysts or, to put it more colloquially... a well-known haunt for courting couples.

Having re-emerged out of the wood, I stride freely down the long slope to the river nestling snugly and slumbering in the valley below. The open expanse of corn land lures me onwards. *Walking Man* is at one with the countryside, his purpose and performance rhyming smoothly with one another. A faint mist lingers over the river that recalls apt lines from Keats's 'Ode to Autumn,'

> Seasons of mist and yellow fruitfulness.

Changing tack, I redirect myself diagonally across the sloping field past an abandoned farmhouse where the landowner has parked machinery near the windowless house. Rusty docks and ragworts abound outside the shut door. A gap directs me onward to the next harvested field which I quickly traverse. Within a short time, I reach a long inch where sally trees grow along the river bank while oak, ash and hazel trees stand aloof on the dry higher ground. It's time for a short break but just as I have removed my knapsack, the 'outdoor ring tone' of my mobile phone shatters the silence. Answering the call, I instantly recognise the familiar voice of an old school and sporting friend – Sean DeLacour.

Sean inquires as to what time I expect to arrive at Green's Quay in Youghal on Sunday. I explain that I hope to listen to the All Ireland hurling final between Kilkenny and Tipperary and that I should reach Green's Quay around 5.30p.m. after the final whistle. Unfortunately, Sean was having chemotherapy for cancer in his thyroid gland since November. He speaks rather hoarsely today but his good humour and optimism remain undimmed despite the serious illness that has afflicted him. Bidding him goodbye, we conclude our brief conversation until Sunday's hurling drama has unfolded. Sean and I were classmates in Youghal CBS, 1960-1963. We became friends, playing hurling and football on the underage teams. After the Intermediate Certificate examination, Sean left school to serve his apprecenticeship as a decorator and house painter with his father Johnny.

Resuming my trek, I emerge from the wooded fields into the headland of a fully-grown crop of maize, causing me to stop abruptly in my track. I have negotiated my way through the rows of maize stalks west of Mallow but, on this occasion, the planted rows are crossing my direction instead of following an east-west pattern. The landowner here explained to me later that the headlands are planted in a circular pattern whereas the rest of the field is planted in straight lines. So, I veer away from the tall stalks and follow the vehicular track around the crop on the northern side of the field. More than likely, this track will lead directly to the farmyard where *Walking Man* will have to explain his business to a busy farmer who may not be altogether pleased with an uninvited stranger rambling through his land at 10.00 a.m. in early September. Rounding a bend, I see the farm buildings about 150 yards away and the farm dwelling even closer. Up to this point, I have steered scrupulously away from farmhouses, fearing that my intrusion might not be approved of, and that I might be told to retrace my steps off the land.

A low whirring sound is emitted from the milking parlour where a young man is busy rinsing and cleaning after the morning milking. Inside the kitchen window, I notice the farmer sitting but faced away from the track along which I am approaching his home and workplace. Realising that his wife or another member of the household will see me, I wave in their direction and continue past the milking parlour towards the side entrance where I intend to knock and say 'Hello.' However, before I can approach the door, the farmer, who by now has been appraised of my arrival, walks towards me and, with a look of surprise written all over his face, bids me 'Good Morning.' In response, I inform him that I am walking the Blackwater 'from source to sea,' adding that I am a retired secondary school teacher, originally from Youghal but now living in the Killarney area. Having put my cards on the table, I feel unsure how he may react to a complete stranger, who has walked through his land without permission and who has now brazened his way uninvited to his door. But looking straight at me, he immediately concerns himself about the challenge facing me on his own doorstep.

You're going to have a problem. You won't get around the security fence on the perimeter of the John A. Wood quarry in Lackamona. But, if you want to, I'll drive you in the Jeep around the back almost to the point from which you left the river.

Without waiting for a reply from me, he adds,

If that is not against the rules? Can you take a lift or are you supposed to keep walking?

For a millisecond, I experience a crisis of conscience, wondering whether I should accept his generous offer that is clearly calculated to help me on my way.

'No, there are no rules. I'll be very happy to take a lift from you.'

Without further ado, I sit into the passenger seat of the Jeep but, before heading off, John enquires if I'd like a cup of tea and something to eat. I reassure him that Pat Walsh has already taken care of all my nutritional needs.

Having reversed the vehicle, we're soon out on a narrow road that leads us out on to the Mallow-Fermoy road. John points out the new state-of-the-art Mallow GAA complex. He further explains, as he enters the John A. Wood Quarry, owned by Cement Roadstone Holdings (CRH), that he knows his way through this sprawling site. The security man in the entrance hut waves to a neighbour whom he frequently sees on his way back and forth to

Roadstone quarry, Carrigoon

his fields by the river. Changing into a lower gear, John passes through an opening in the security fence into a passage way which leads exactly back to the boundary of the maize field.

> I intend to write a book about this walk. A Dublin-based civil servant, Annraoi Ó Liatháin walked the Blackwater in 1959, and subsequently wrote a very vivid account of his adventure as Gaeilge in a book entitled Cois Móire which was published in 1962.

Having informed John about the previous book, I add further details to make my intentions clear.

> Over fifty years have passed since then and the country has changed enormously in that period. So I'll be updating the picture, filling in all the changes that have occurred.

John is quite interested in my plans and asks me to send him a copy of the published work.

I really wondered how John felt about my brazen incursion on to his land and, therefore, I ask him if he has any reservations about my uninvited presence on his property. Is he ill at ease about the potential prospect that someone like me might lodge an insurance claim for an injury sustained while on his property? His reply is reassuring: he has absolutely no objection.

'People have a right to walk along the river bank.'

Hoisting myself out of the Jeep, he accompanies me to the fence that divides his land from the next farm. For about ten minutes or more, we chat pleasantly, exchanging stories and yarns about the GAA, the river and the locality. For my part, I describe an U-14 county hurling semi-final, played in Fermoy in 1961, when a physically more mature Mallow trounced Youghal CBS in a replay. John has played hurling but when we do a quick check on our respective dates of birth, it turns out that John is my junior by nine years. Pointing to a large rock in the river,

> That's known as 'Carraig Dhúin/The Rock of the Fort' from which this townland, Carrigoon, has taken its name. But Brother Fiachra in the [Patrician]Academy used to tells us, when I was going to school there, that it should be 'Carraig Abhann' rather than 'Carraig Dhúin.

Fascinating that a man, who has long left his secondary school days behind him, can still recall a casual comment from a teacher. He imparts a good deal more interesting information but warns me not to include any of it in my book. A pity! He then points out a nearby farm,

> That's Dick Griffin's place. His father Gerry played on the Cork hurling

team from 1946. He was such a skilful hurler that Christy Ring is supposed to have said to him on the first day that he played for Cork, 'Where were you up to now?'He came from Shanballymore originally. He bought the farm here which his son now works. There are old photos of him in the new Mallow clubhouse.

Reaching the fence, where we say goodbye to one another, John tells me that he enjoys walking and that he and his family often walk in the Killarney area. His final comment gives me an unexpected lift that sends energy shooting down into my feet and legs.

Only for the fact that we're going to Australia next Tuesday to visit our daughter who has just had a baby, I'd go as far as Killavullen with you.

Having climbed the fence, I glance back and watch John for a moment as he strides back to his Jeep and a day's work on the farm. Musing to myself, I can only say that I applaud his courage in taking time out from his work. Traditionally in this country farmers rarely took time off for holidays or travel. I am acutely aware of this from my own family circumstances. Modern farming has become a stressful occupation that involves the investment of considerable money to purchase labour-saving machinery and equipment. As production costs spiral profit margins dwindle. Farmers need to be in the full of their health to cope with and react to these trends. If John had walked further with me, we may have discussed these and other topics along the way.

Carrig Castle keep

Walking Man takes to the lonely trail once more but feels upbeat and buoyed by this recent encounter with another member of the species. Off again through these well-drained limestone fields, determined to reach Killavullen by 12.30. But as the poet Robbie Burns would say, 'The best laid plans of mice and men gang aft agley.' Within fifteen minutes, another limestone outcrop walls the river. Ascending to higher ground over the river, I sight the ruined keep of Carrig Castle. A stillness pervades the castle site with echoes of the past hanging in the air. The old name for the townland was Carrigleamleary (*Carraig Léim Laoire*/The rock of O'Leary's Leap). The castle and its lands belonged to generations of the Anglo-Norman family, the Roches, who gained possession of large tracts of land in this part of north Cork. Carrig was listed by the angler Joseph Adams, in his book. 'The Angler's Guide to the Irish Fisheries,' (1924) as one of the nine most prominent locations for fishing on the Blackwater.

I have become adept at squeezing through miniscule chinks but beyond the castle, a tongued-grooved partition has been placed on top of a garden wall. Consequently, with no way through or around, I am forced along a quiet country lane that soon leads me on to the Mallow–Fermoy road, N72.

The road here through Carriglemleary convolutes through a series of narrow curves. I tuck myself in carefully to the sloping margin which offers only the minimum of safety. High power tractors, with trailers attached, laden with round bales of straw, skim me with inches to spare. Artics and delivery vans add to the danger. In fact, I am at a standstill as frequently as I am walking, being forced on to a low ridge over the road. Then, as if in answer to an unspoken prayer, a hurrying young man approaches who, in response to my details about walking the Blackwater, tells me pointedly,

'If you value your life, get off this road. You'll be mowed down; it's deadly.'

And in order to keep me on this planet, he explains,

> I have a taxi, parked a short distance away, and I'll drive you to the Nano Nagle Centre. And you can get back to the river from there along the footpath by the river.

So, for a second time today, I sit into the passenger seat of a Toyota Corolla where to, my utter astonishment, I find a small glass aquarium with a full complement of goldfish, at my feet. Noticing my amazement, the driver offers an explanation,

'We're just back from holidays in Spain, and I am collecting the kids' fish from my in-laws who were minding them for the week.'

My guide and newly acquired chauffeur introduces himself as Tadhg from nearby Shonee. He informs me that a tragic accident occurred on this same stretch of road, pointing out where the tragedy occurred. He drops me off in the parking space adjacent to the Nano Nagle Centre. As with nearly all my casual acquaintanceship as I walked the Blackwater, it turns out that Tadhg is acquainted with at least one person whom I knew in times past. A run-of-the-mill Irish conversational ice-breaker nearly always does the trick. 'You wouldn't happen to know such a one?' As we exchange facts about mutual acquaintances, the goldfish eavesdrop and glide merrily round and round in their watery world. Before 'we separate and go our different ways', Tadhg and I touch on many disparate topics including the teaching of Irish in our primary schools.

I thank Tadhg for his guidance and help and set out in the direction of the Nano Nagle Centre. I feel revived and agile and I whisper to myself, 'Ah, Thursday, my favourite day of the week, you bring a full complement of

The Nano Nagle Centre for Heritage, Spirituality and Ecology

surprises and oddities before baleful Friday descends on us again!' A passerby at that stage may have glimpsed a wafer thin smile ripple across my features as I muse wryly to myself from where within me did that last reflection have its origin. The older we get the more eccentric we become and the child inside us all panders for our own attention.

The Nano Nagle Centre for Heritage, Spirituality and Ecology was opened by the Presentation Sisters to commemorate their founder, Nano Nagle. When Annraoi Ó Liatháin walked the Blackwater in 1959 he found no trace of the house here in Ballygriffin where Nano Nagle was born, the only remnant then being a stone barn. He rightly bemoaned our failure to commemorate her achievement in founding the Presentation Sisters for the education of impoverished children in our cities and towns.

> Tá an donas orainn in Eirinn gan aon amhras. Dá mba Shasanach í Nano Nagle, nó Spáinneach nó Afraiceach, bheimis á moladh agus á móradh de shíor, bheimis ag tuargaint na bhflaitheas den phaidreoireacht iar sin go dtí go naomhófái í.[6] (We, the Irish people are greatly at fault. If Nano Nagle were English, or Spanish or African, we would extol her praises, honour and commemorate her, and never cease to implore Heaven to have her canonised.)

---

6   Ó Liatháin, Annraoi, *Cois Móire*, Sáirséal agus Dill, 1962, p. 72

Their founder, Nano Nagle, born 1718, was the eldest of a family of seven children in the marriage of Garret Nagle and Ann Matthews. The Nagles had been prosperous Anglo-Norman landowners in the Blackwater valley since the thirteenth century. The Nagles, Hennessys and Cotters had managed to retain their estates through a combination of adroit politics and astute marriages to other great Catholic families in Tipperary, Galway and Dublin.[7] Despite being hemmed in by 'the largest Protestant gentry presence in the country,' they had managed to survive 'as an island of Catholic hegemony in a sea of Protestant ascendancy.[8]

Nano, christened Hanora, was educated in France as education for Catholic families was prohibited under the penal laws imposed by the English government 1700-1782. Having returned home, she witnessed the plight and degradation suffered by poor families in her native parish of Killavullen (*Cill an Mhuilinn*, 'The Church of the Mill'). Profoundly affected by such poverty and deprivation, she returned to Paris where she took vows as a member of the Ursuline order. Gradually, she became convinced that her vocation in life was to serve the poor of her own country. Consequently, she returned to Ireland and lived in Cork city where she opened schools for children.

With contributions from their worldwide communities as well as a generous sum from the local community, the Presentation Sisters purchased part of the land and site of the Nagles' home in 1972 for the sum of Ir£36,000. Development commenced in 1983 and was completed with an official opening in July 2007.

I had visited the Centre previously and was particularly impressed by the air of calm, tranquillity and peacefulness that pervades the place. I am not surprised by this. We are after all 'bundles of energy and our static emissions inform our surroundings.

How amazed Ó Liatháin, would be if he returned today to witness this meaningful commemoration of a woman who achieved so much in her lifetime. As a community,

---

7   L.M. Cullen, 'Blackwater Catholics' in *Cork: History and Society,* O'Flanagan, Patrick and Buttimer, Cornelius (Eds), Geography Publications, Dublin, 6W, 1993, p. 541-543

8   Breandán O Buachalla in 'Blackwater Catholics in Cork: History and Society,' cited by Katherine O'Donnell in 'To Love the little Platoon: Edmund Burke's Jacobite Heritage,'Ph.D, UCD

we have found appropriate means to honour and commemorate the work of great men and women such as Nano Nagle, Edmund Rice and others.

I stroll past the entrance, saying hallo to a young man quietly absorbed in weeding the ornamental plots of herbs around the front door. I would dearly love to talk to the Sisters but having already spent time with two local men, I am anxious to press on. A fenced path leads me directly back to the river, and from there I stroll contentedly to Killavullen, glancing over the hedge at the flowing river.

Arriving at the bridge in Killavullen, I discard and hide my knapsack in a shallow cave at the base of the limestone outcrop on which Ballymacmoy House is built. This Hennessy residence was built here in 1818 when their older home, a short distance upriver, collapsed. Described as a Regency house, it overlooks the bridge and a good stretch of river that has attracts visiting anglers from far and near.

Richard Hennessy left Killavullen to join the Clare Dragoons, a regiment of Wild Geese (exile soldiers) formed after the Treaty of Limerick in 1690. According to the most-up-to-date research, Richard had a brief career in

Richard Hennessy (Mediatheque, Maison Hennessy)

the army of Louis XV, joining in 1748 and leaving in 1754. Earlier claims that he participated in the bloody battle of Fontenoy in 1745, have not been substantiated. However, the best known portrait shows him attired in the scarlet uniform and regalia of that regiment, trimmed with gold braid, silver epaulettes and decorated cuffs.

In 1765 he founded Maison Hennessy to market and export the quality *eaux de vie* of the region. Two hundred and fifty years later, his enterprise continues to dominate the world cognac market. Having visited the Hennessy HQ in 2012 on the banks of the Charente River and sampled a modicum of the Very Old Special Pale (VSOP) Cognac, comparisons between Killavullen and the premier grape-growing area of Grande Champagne occurred to me: the Blackwater corresponding to the Charente and limestone determining the drainage and soil quality of both regions.

Contrary to all my expectations, Killavullen turns out to be a dry place to visit at this time of day with the doors of its two licensed premises firmly shut to exclude thirsty walkers in need of a drink to soothe a parched mouth and throat. A similar fate befell AOL in 1959 when he enquired if a cup of tea was available in any shop in the village, the response was negative. Apparently, the early generations of the Hennessy family to settle in France consigned a case of brandy every Christmas to the parish priest of

Killavullen. His generosity was greatly appreciated until a stern advocate of temperance and a devout follower of Fr Matthew became parish priest. Instead of responding graciously to their generosity this priestly ascetic rebuked the Hennessys for daring to send him 'their devil's broath.' He admonished them, in no uncertain terms, that such munificence would no longer be appreciated. Subsequently, after the death of the teetotaller Parish Priest, his successor wrote a warm letter that only drew the abated response of a single bottle.

I greet a group of workmen, laying tarmacadm, which bubbles and smells like the witches' cauldron in Shakespeare's *Macbeth*, I tell them (idle banter) that the two the pubs are shut. Their reply, delivered in a strong Cork city accent by the more outspoken one, settles the matter for me, 'They're probably too mean to buy a drink around here.' City slickers have to have their laughs and fun at the expense of honest, hard-working, frugal country people.

There is, however, one question, which I hope to settle here in Killavullen village today:- to see and inspect the confessional box in the nearby parish church, a short walk away from where the men from Farranree toil with the bubbling tar.

During the summer holidays of 1972, I met a fomer classmate in the Ocean Lounge Bar in Youghal, who had become a woodwork teacher in west Cork. In answer to my query what he was doing for the summer, he casually replied, 'I am making a confessional for Killavullen Church.' Thirty–eight years have flown since that meeting, but amazingly, the story has remained with me, and here I am now about to inspect the penitential masterpiece that Ger made in the summer of 1972. How well has all his sawing and planing stood up to the tribulations of the four decades that have passed since we met? What anguished tales of venial misgivings the smoothed and wax polished timber might tell if it too could speak like the oak tree that spilled the beans on Lowry Loingseach 's horse's ears.

St Nicholas's Church, with a tasteful façade of red sandstone on its eastern gable and entrance, was built in 1868. One hundred and forty-two years later, it stands gleaming in the mellow September sunlight, reflecting the care that the community has lavished on their place of worship. Entering through the lobby, I dip my index finger into the holy water font, and, opening the door, I enter into a space of light and peace. Immediately, my eyes dart from the left-hand wall to the right wall but, to my astonishment, there is no confessional to be seen affixed to either wall. Walking towards the altar, I hope that a confessional will manifest itself in some quiet corner but once again my search for the handiwork of my

St Nicholas's Church, Killavullen

former schoolmate draws a blank. Then, one final hope, – a secluded area that contains the baptismal font at the back. But not even there can I find the decorated carved wooden box where the penitents of Killavullen could purge themselves of 'the sins of a lifetime.'

Later in the local supermarket, I broach the subject of the confessional, asking the shopkeeper what has happened to the confessionals in the local church. A customer, who is busy packing the last of her messages (goods) into her shopping bags, tells me that she is not from the Parish but that they go to Saturday evening mass in Annakissa or Sunday morning mass in Ballyhooly. And so the mystery of the disappeared confessional has remained unsolved. Having purchased a sandwich and can of Fanta, I have more than a slight inkling that the lady behind the counter is not interested in any further queries from *Walking Man* who is about to withdraw to a parking space outside. The sandwich, boxed in a plastic triangle, is fresh and satisfying. Tired limbs gain some ease from the travails of the morning.

As I glance around me, my eyes fix on the national school, directly across the road. In keeping with the church, the school looks neat and well organised. Judging from the silence, the pupils would appear to have settled in quickly to a spate of serious study. It just reflects the wisdom of the adage that all work and no play makes Jacqueline and Jack less than enthusiastic about their studies.

From my own experience, as both a national teacher (5 years) and as a secondary teacher (35 years), pupils are more interested and eager to learn in September than they are prior to the long vacation. From October on, interest wanes and the task of teaching becomes progressively more challenging. Scanning the entrance, I read a sign informing parents that interviews with teachers must be arranged by prior appointments.

Retracing my footsteps back to the bridge, I follow the angler's path to Monanimy Castle (*Móin an Ime*, 'The Bog of the Butter'), built on a low hill north-east of the village. Having negotiated my way through the dense vegetation of briars and bushes, I step over the fence into the lower reaches of a pleasant terraced garden. I am intensely aware that I am intruding into private property and I have a sincere apology composed if confronted. I soon notice an busy gardener, tending to shrubs and other flowering plants, on a higher terrace. I call out 'Hello,' but the lady, absorbed in her task and with her back to the river, fails to hear my greeting from the lower reaches. Perhaps, I should have approached her and explained to her that I am walking the Blackwater from 'source to sea,' but, instead, I decide to speed up and exit her garden before she has observed me. In my haste, I fail to notice two strands of barb wire, suspended near the ground but easily missed by an interloper. I am brought to a sudden halt as I feel the sharp end of a barb piercing my right shin. Looking down, I see the first drops of blood forming and the foreboding fear of tetanus flashes through my mind. I am, of course, the author of my own bloody mishap which can only be resolved by fleeing from the garden. As the Irish proverb goes, *Is fearr rith maith ná drochsheasamh/A good run is better than a bad stand.* Within a short time, I emerge from the woodland that forms the outer reaches of the Castle grounds, and, pausing for a moment, I wipe clean the stream of blood that has by now coursed beneath my walking sock.

Some time later, I visited Renate Richter, and narrated the story of my brief incursion into her garden. Smiling in amusement, she responded, 'I spend a lot of time in my garden.' Klaus and Renate purchased the ruined castle of Monanimy in 1981. Natives of Bavaria, they had made up their minds to purchase a holiday home somewhere in the south of Ireland. 'We saw the old castle. It was burnt in 1940s, so we had a huge job on our hands. We completed the sale within three days. My husband had to stay in Germany where he worked very hard to finance the restoration of the place.' Pausing for a moment while recalling that time in their lives, 'It was very hard, we had to import a lot of the material from Germany that we couldn't source in Ireland.' The Richters succeeded in their task of preserving the architectural character of their aged building. Sadly, her husband Klaus died in 2003, leaving Renate and her son to continue to manage the castle and grounds in a manner that suggests care and attachment.

The issue of access to farming land and private ground for walkers,

Monanimy Castle

Monanimy nameplate

ramblers, anglers and others, has become a controversial subject in recent years with landowners denying access to people who may wish to walk along old pathways that have been traditionally regarded as 'rights of way.' The fear of an insurance claim for any injuries that could occur in the event of a walker having an accident while on private ground, has alarmed many landowners and caused them to erect signs warning people not to trespass on their lands. To my own utter astonishment, a farmer in this area told me two years later that I had broken gaps in the fences and that he had to go out fencing a few days after my visit to prevent livestock from breaking into his land. 'Put a bush in that gap before it gets any worse,' was a familiar phrase employed by farmers before electric fences became so widespread. After that shot across my bows, he quickly forgets my trespass, and, instead, begins to talk about the restrictions that the Rural Environment Protection Scheme (REPS) has imposed on them,

'You can only cut hedges at certain times of the year; you have to wait until you're told.' And then, pausing to put his thoughts in order, he adds,

'You have to watch everything nowadays. You can't put out all the fertiliser you'd like. And you have to write down everything you do.'

A glance around his fields reminds him of the beet-growing era that came to a close just five years previously,

Beet was a great crop: you'd put out ten hundredweight of fertilizer to the acre, and you'd get a fine crop of barley out of the same land for two to three years after the beet. I used to grow seed barley for Powers' Seeds, just up there. You have to be very careful, and spray it to keep the wild oat from growing in it.

Wood, water and land, Bridgetown Lower

Bruised and bloodied though not broken, the river calls me and urges me to walk on again. A broad meadow stretches invitingly before me. Here the banks have all been stripped of alders, ash and the other trees that must have bedecked them previously. On the opposite bank, a dense wall of trees obscures the lower part of Carigacunna Castle leaving only its castellated battlements projecting skywards. Sir Richard Nagle, attorney general for King James II and speaker of the House of Commons in Dublin along with being an MP for County Cork, lived in this residence. Another and even more famous politician, Edmund Burke, though born in Dublin, 1727, spent his formative years in this area, Ballyduff, where his mother, Mary Nagle, had grown up. While domiciled with his Catholic relations, Burke attended a hedge school managed by Master O'Halloran in the grounds of Monanimy Castle, 1735-41. Reared as a Protestant but inheriting a sensitive awareness of the delicate status of his Catholic cousins, Burke used his abilities as a statesman to allay the harsh demands of more extreme parliamentarians who sought to rid the country of any surviving pockets of papists.

While walking along this stretch, the thought or rather the question occurs to me why none of the local residents seem to keep or use boats for leisure purposes. Does the explanation lie in the fact that nothing is permitted to obstruct the angler in pursuit of his catch on a river that has been regarded by many anglers as one of the great salmon rivers of Europe if not of the world? Surely, the resources and potential of the Blackwater could be utilised to greater effect for the welfare and emotional well-being of people of north Cork. I acknowledge that the water level is low at this time of year though this would not be an obstacle to canoeists or kayakers who can skim along on a mere inch or two of water. I fear that we have strayed away from nature with its variety of flora and fauna.

Soon the river takes a decisive turn north, forcing me to reassess my options – whether I should wade across here where a natural ford affords me such an opportunity or, instead, to follow the curve of the river. Deciding to adhere to the course of the river, I find myself back on the public road but, within a short distance, I manage to double back to my riparian companion who has been my faithful guide for the last four days.

Approaching Clifford House, I pass a number of places on the banks from which local and visiting anglers cast their lines. Similar to Carrig, Adams included Clifford among the best known fisheries on the Blackwater. Prior to this walk, I had never heard of Clifford House nor was I aware of its reputation as being one of the premier 'seats of gentlemen' along the Backwater. In my enthusiastic ignorance, I blunder unawares into the uncultivated wild parts of its grounds. The drone of an electric pump destroys the peace and harmony of this stretch. Someone has been busy here with the strimmer, saw and slashook as heaps of cut branches, briars and other vegetation have been cleared away, probably for the convenience of anglers who have permission to fish the Clifford stretch of the river. A few steps further on, I come across a smouldering pile of vegetation with a few dying embers still glowing vividly.

The author, J.R. Flanagan, tells his readers that Clifford was the 'seat of Bart Lloyd, Esq. at the time of the publication of his book, *The River Blackwater in Munster*. Flanagan admired the house for its appearance from the river, describing it as a 'comfortable dwelling.' Designed and built by Richard Martin c. 1790, Clifford House is now a protected building which according to the National Inventory of Architectural Heritage is noted 'for the quantity and quality of the historic fabric retained such as the varied small-paned sash windows and slate roof that help to maintain the integrity of the composition.' But, today, the House remains completely obscured from my view. Martin, the original owner, had an inscription in Latin 'inscribed on a tablet in the hall,'

> Parvus domus! Nemorosa quies,
> Sis tu quoque nostris hospitium laribus
> Subsidium diu: postes tuas Flora ornet
> Pomonaque mensas.

A sense of bygone days still lingers in these haunts – a time when refined ladies and their consorts strolled by the river, enjoying the woodlands and the sparkling river with the dark Nagle mountains brooding gloomily some distance to the south. Today we spend most of our lives struggling to keep apace of an ever-shifting and ever-changing world. We are driven by superimposed forces of greed and grandeur, nonchalantly defined as progress and development.

Formerly, a large concrete urn, resting on a pedestal with an inscription, was a very admirable feature of the garden,

> Monumentum hocce
> Diis manibus R.M. posuit
> A.D. 1790.

The initials, of course, are those of Richard Martin, who continued the inscription with a delightful message admonishing the perambulating ladies and gentlemen to beware of the insidious encroachment of the enemy – 'Time.'

Nor does Time wait for *Walking Man* whose mobile phone begins to burble in his pocket. My brother Joe has arrived in Ballyhooly and is wondering where we will rendezvous. I give him directions to drive towards Castletownroche but to turn left for Bridgetown Priory before reaching the village. Approaching the ruins of what was once a substantial monastery that accommodated a community of Augustinian Priors, I experience what Olivia Laing expressed so graphically in her account of walking the River Ouse,

> Sometimes the lone walker feels that he is moving backwards through time, and sometimes that he stands at the threshold of a different world... The landscape hasn't changed, not in any way that can be articulated, but a sense of strangeness seeps up from all around.[9]

---

9   Laing, Olivia, *To the River: A Journey Beneath the Surface,* p. 73

Bridgetown Priory

The grey limestone walls of Bridgetown Priory loom large before me as I approach the junction of the Blackwater and its tributary, the Awbeg (*Abha Bheag*, 'The Small River*)*. Bridgtetown Priory was established by Alexander fitzHugh Roche, the Norman lord of nearby Castletownroche, for a community of Augustinian Regulars, 1202-16. Fitzhugh granted them thirteen carucates of arable land, one third of his mills and fisheries and all tolls from the bridge which once stood there. Bridgetown and Ballybeg (close to Buttevant) were the only two Norman monasteries established in North Cork prior to 1250. The imposition of political control by the Normans occurred slower here than in the neighbouring counties, and for this reason, 'The absence of medieval monastic architecture in North Cork is quite striking.'[10]

I am so absorbed in the history of this place that just for a brief moment I think I hear the psalms being intoned by the tonsured monks at vespers in their chapel. But at that very moment, twenty-first century life and reality intrudes when Joe calls to me from somewhere within the walls.

'Where are you?'

Overlooking the monastery from the elevation of the ground immediately to the north, I catch sight of him before he sights me, and I respond, 'I am up here.'

10 Department of Environment, Heritage and Local Government, *An Introduction to the Architectural Heritage of North Cork,* Dubin, 2009, p. 10

Uncertain from what angle the answer came, he glances around, wondering if I am concealed among the tombs of the Roches, or perhaps, under the arches of the cloister. A moment later, when we come face-to-face, he is aghast at the sight of my shins and knees: stained, scratched and splotched with blackened congealed blood, and, in brotherly concern, he inquires, 'Good God, what happened to you?'

BRIDGETOWN PRIORY

Bridgetown Priory was built to what is known as a *claustral* plan, in which all the essential buildings—the church, dormitories, business rooms, and dining hall—are arranged conveniently around a central *cloister* (*claustrum*) or courtyard, rather than scattered haphazardly.

Water supply was an important consideration—perhaps the most important—governing the site chosen for a monastic house. The availability of water affected not just the daily activity within the monastery such as washing, but it contributed to its economic health as well, since communities were involved in milling and fishing—sometimes creating ponds or pools to trap fish.

A mill, supplied with water diverted from the river Blackwater, was built in the middle ages here on the south side of the priory, and members of the community returning from the mill would have entered the monastery through the narrow passage between the Refectory and the Kitchen.

This plan was used in monasteries across Europe from the 9th century onwards, but only appeared in Ireland in the 12th century. The first Augustinian monasteries to have been built to the claustral plan were probably those founded by the Normans, such as at Bridgetown.

Acquiescing to the fact that his older brother has no need for sympathy, Joe comments on how fascinating the extensive ruins are and admits that he had no prior knowledge of this glorious monastic ruin. We pause before a notice erected close to the parking space by Cork County Council which informs us that Bridgetown Piory has been under the care and maintenance of the Council since 1976. In fact, it's the only such monument under their care in the entire county. On the occasion of Ó Liatháin's visit in May 1959, he bemoaned the neglected state of the Priory and he feared that, unless some heritage organisation intervened, that the monastery would crumble and disappear as its monks and founders had.

> 'Tá an-chuid dena ballaí ar tí titim agus scrobarnach thiubh de sceacha, driseacha agus neantóga á múchadh agus a gcreimeadh' (Many of the walls are in danger of collapsing with a thick undergrowth of bushes, briars and nettles undermining their stability.)

Fortunately, the intervention of the Council has saved these ancient ruins for future generations. Reading the detailed information board at the entrance, I learn that up to three hundred monks, dressed in black from head-to-toe, lived in this community. I pause before the tomb of the Roches in the chapel, which, supposedly, dates from the early years of the fifteenth century. It features a fish on an upside shield: the roach being an obvious pun on the family name while the inverted shield symbolises death. The extensive cloister and two-storey refectory clearly indicate the large number of monks who prayed and worked here.

Early 15th century tomb of the Roches, Bridgetown Priory

Detail of fish on upturned shield on tomb

Expressing a strong wish to return sooner rather than later for a more relaxed and informative tour of this medieval monastery, we reluctantly depart.

A short distance from Bridgetown Priory, the Awbeg River joins the Blackwater from its source in the Ballyhoura range. Its course of thirty-two miles extends from close to Ardpatrick (Co. Limerick) to Buttevant, and from there to Ballybeg Abbey. After Ballybeg it flows past Kilcolman Castle where the poet , Edward Spenser lived and wrote parts of his great work, *The Faerie Queen.* From Kilcolman, it continues its course to Doneraile, Shanballymore and Castletownroche. Beyond Castletownroche it enters a limestone gorge and passes beneath the Kilcummer viaduct to join the Blackwater between the townlands of Bridgetown and Kilcummer.[11] Fording the shallow Awbeg, I recall Spenser's verse in which he immortalised the Awbeg, renaming it as 'Mulla.'

> There was the Liffey, rolling down the lea;
> The sandy Slane, the stony Au-brian;
> The spacious Shenan, spreading like a sea;
> The pleasant Boyne – the fishy, fruitful Ban.
> Swift Auniduff, which of the Englishman

---

11 Milner, Liam, *From the Kingdom to the Sea,* Cork, 1976, p. 66-79

> Is called Blackwater, and the Liffar deep,
> Sad Trowis, that once his people overran;
> Strong Allo tumbling from Slew-logher steep,
> And Mulla mine, whose waves I whilom taught to weep.

Most likely, he derived the name 'Mulla' from the old Gaelic name for Buttevant, *Cill na mBallach*. Spenser's most recent biographer, Andrew Hadfield, writes that the Awbeg was navigable at that time and claims that the poet could have navigated from Kilcolman to Youghal to visit his friend, Sir Walter Raleigh.[12] Appending the possessive adjective 'mine,' would seem to signify ownership and attachment on the part of the poet towards the river that meanders slowly through the land that Spenser occupied albeit for a brief period of time. Despite the charm that the Irish landscape exercised on the poet, the native Irish 'never made their own' of him.[13] He remained a *conquistador* in their midst whose presence has been almost completely erased from the land he sought to subjugate.

The scholar and author, P.W. Joyce, wrote that the Munster Blackwater was never named 'Auniduff' by the people of Ireland who referred to the river as 'Avonmore,' derived from the Gaelic *Abhainn Mhór*. Joyce offers the opinion that 'Auniduff,' more likely, referred to the Ulster Blackwater. In Spenser's era, English speakers referred to the Munster Blackwater as 'Broadwater,' on account of its broad expanse as it enters its final phase from Cappoquin to Youghal. Gerard Boate in his *Natural History of Ireland* wrote, 'The two rivers of Munster are Sure [Suir] and Broadwater, the city of Waterford being situated on the first...the other [Broadwater] passeth by Lismore and falleth into the sea at Youghal.'[14]

The reference to 'Strong Allo tumbling from Slew-Lougher steep' requires further clarification. Joyce, citing the eighteenth-century historian, Charles Smith, believes that Spenser was referring to the Blackwater rather than to its minor tributary the 'Allo' (Allow) which flows from the direction of Kanturk and joins the Blackwater close to Ballymaquirke. (See Day 3).[15] The grounds for assuming that the Blackwater, rather than the Allo, was intended is based on the fact that the Blackwater has its source in the upland

12 Hadfield, Andrew, *Edmund Spenser: A Life,* Oxford University Press, 2012, p. 198, 'Spenser would also have made use of the waterways, in particular the Awbeg, which was navigable in this period, and the Blackwater, and would have taken him down to Youghal..'
13 Ó Faoláin, Seán...cited by Mary Leland in *The Lie of the Land: Journeys through Literary Munster,* Cork University Press, 199, p. 167
14 Joyce, P.W., *The Wonders of Ireland*
15 Smith Charles, *The Antient and Present State of the County and City of Cork,* 1750

area of *Sliabh Luachra* [Slew-Logher] rather than the Allo that originates close to the village of Boherbue, a distance of twelve miles from the nearest part of the elevated area of *Sliabh Luachra*. Furthermore, describing the Allo as 'strong' would seem to be misapplied, considering its brevity and minor status.

> It would be strange indeed if Spenser who knew so well and designated with such precision the features of the other chief streams of Ireland, should confound two rivers in the immediate neighbourhood of his own residence; one of them, moreover, being a mere rivulet, and the other a stream of the first magnitude – for Ireland.[16]

Joyce believes that the name 'Allo' must have been accepted as the name of the section of the Blackwater between Ballymaquirke and Mallow. In support of this view, he quotes the topographer John O'Donovan (1806-1861) who made a detailed study of Irish placenames as well as the names of rivers, mountains and other physical features: 'From this name (Moy-Allo, Mallow), it is evident that the name Allo was anciently applied to that part of the Blackwater lying between Kanturk where the modern Allo ends and the town of Mallow.'

Born in East Smithfield, London, 1552, Spenser first arrived in Ireland as secretary to Lord Grey de Wilton who had been appointed Lord Deputy in July 1580 with the specific task of quelling the Desmond rebellion in Munster. Spenser's early hopes of advancement had not been fulfilled; consequently, a career in Ireland could give him the chance to acquire property that he could never acquire in England. He witnessed Grey's initial defeat at the hands of Fiach McHugh in Glenmalure, August 1580. In November he travelled south to Kerry with Grey's army where he witnessed the massacre at Smerwick when 600 Spanish and Italian papal troops were butchered after their commander had surrendered at Dún an Óir. Spenser in his communiqués to Queen Elizabeth staunchily defended Grey's decision not to show mercy to the defenders of the fort. In their eyes, war was war and those who had blindly committed themselves to rebellion against their legitimate sovereign, had to suffer the consequences of their own actions. By the standards of the present day, Grey and his commanders would be arraigned for war crimes before the International Court of Justice in the Hague.

Most likely Spenser observed the dreadful destruction and the dire state of Munster, formerly 'a moste riche and plentifull Countrye ful of Corne

---

16 Joyce, *Wonders of Ireland*

and Cattell,' during his travels with Grey.. His graphic description of human degradation, written fifteen years later in 'A View of Ireland...' still has the power to shock a present-day reader,

> Out of every corner of the woods and glens they came, creeping forth upon their hands for their legs could not bear them, they looked like anatomies of death, they spake like ghosts crying out of their graves, they did eat the dead carrions, happy where they could find them, yea, and one another soon after, in so much as the very carcasses they spared not to scrape out of their graves; and if they found a plot of water-cresses or shamrocks they flocked as to feast for the time... yet not able long to continue therewithal, yet in short space there were none almost left and a most populous and plentiful country suddenly left void of man or beast, yea sure in all that war there perished not many by the sword but by the extremity of famine which they themselves had wrought.

It seems that Spenser was subtly suggesting that the Irish, being a barbaric race, should be left to perish from natural consequences rather than having to waste precious resources to subdue them. Having being granted a generous 3,000 acres of land at Kilcolman after the confiscation of the Desmond lands, Spenser began to devote more time to his poetic composition, *The Faerie Queen*. He brought tenant farmers from England to cultivate his estate. He modified the old tower house, turning it into more of an English manor with the comforts that befitted the status of an eminent man of letters. His second wife, Elizabeth Boyle, the daughter of the fabulously wealthy, Lord Boyle, bore him three children: Sylvanus, Peregrine and Katherine. Ironically, his eldest son, Sylvaus married Ellen Nagle, a member of the illustrious Anglo-Norman family and forebears of Nano Nagle. Sir Walter Raleigh most likely visited Kilcolman where the two settlers would have discussed poetry, especially Spenser's progress on *The Faerie Queen*.

Having crossed the Awbeg, I pause to admire the great Kilcummer viaduct that spans that river. From 1860 to 1963, the train from Mallow to Fermoy and from there to Dungarvan ran along this line. This magnificent structure looks almost as imposing today as it originally did. Eight tapering limestone piers rise tall from the ground to support the wrought-iron lattice girders across which passengers, excursions and wagons of sugar beet were consigned until 1963 when the line was closed down.

One illustrious visitor, who passed over the great viaduct, was the English poet laureate, John Betjeman (1906-1984) on his way to visit and stay with the family of the Duke of Devonshire in Lismore Castle. Probably

Kilcummer Viaduct straddling the River Awbeg

to pass the time as well as amusing himself, Betjeman composed a rather maudlin piece of versification entitled 'A Lament for Moira McCavendish.' In these verses, he extolled the rustic beauty of a 'colleen' with 'wiry black hair' who lived in 'her brother's wee cabin...where the Blackwater flows.' Besides depicting the charms of a delectable native, Betjeman painted a picture of an attractive though forgotten world that time seemed almost to have abandoned.

> Twas smoothly we raced through the open expansion
> Of rush-covered levels and gate-lodge and gate
> And the ruined demesne and the windowless mansion
> Where once the oppresser had revelled in state.
>
> At Castletownroche, as the prospect grew hillier,
> I saw the far mountains to Moira long known
> Till I came to the valley and townland familiar
> With the Protestant church standing locked and alone.[17]

I struggle up through a deciduous wood before emerging into a large and recently-harvested corn field through which the railway line formerly ran. The only evidence of the line is the isolated limestone bridge, marooned in the centre of the field. Having gained higher ground, I can now glimpse the Blackwater at the base of a great limestone outcrop. A large modern house,

17   Michael J. Walsh, 'Sir John Betjeman and the Mallow-Waterford Rail Line' in *Mallow Field Journal*, 2007

close to completion, occupies a very desirable site at this point. Pressing on, I find a vehicle track that leads downhill to the river.

Christy Roche, author of the history of Ballyhooly, has told me about Spencer's Oak somewhere along this stretch of the Blackwater. According to Christy's directions, I should be close to the renowned tree where Spenser came for solitude and to enjoy the solace of the river. A winding angler's path suggests that I am on the right track until a great barrier of brambles brings me to an abrupt halt. After a trojan effort of slashing with my hazel stick, I succeeded in breaching this formidable obstruction. And, within a short distance, I reach the longed-for-sight.

A sessile oak (*Quercus petrea*), coated with moss and polypody fern, leans over the river. The local story is that Spenser used sit on a favourite branch with the muse of poetry feeding him elevated thoughts, images and language for a higher mental state. The story is plausible as Spenser celebrated the Irish rivers, mountains and woods in his work and would have been clearly aware of their strategic importance as waterways. A contemporary map of Munster (1586) shows the principal rivers as great masses of water, probably emphasising their crucial importance as routes of travel and commerce. [18]

Legend or fact? We will never know. Considering that the townland of Renny was granted to the poet, he may have visited the riverside and spent time there. However, a more likely explanation is that his grandson, Hugolin Spenser, who had been granted land in the Cromwellian confiscation, lived here. Possibly, people may have confused the poet and his grandson.[19]

Meanwhile, Joe has driven on to Ballyhooly where we plan to enjoy a pint and meet some of the local men. Glancing at my watch, I realise that I will have to hurry though my preference would be to saunter and to absorb the autumn glow and colour of the woods and trees. From Spencers's Oak, the river deviates to the Nagle Mountains that overlook the sheltered valley through which the mature Blackwater serenely flows. Along this stretch, I am on the lookout for the ancient fence known as the 'Cliadh Dubh' which runs for 22km from the Ballyhoura Hills to the Nagle Mountains. Having assumed that it would be a large earthen embankment, I have to confess that I experienced a measure of disappointment on sighting this linear

---

18 Hadfield, *Edmund Spenser*, p. 198-199
19 Roche, Christy, *The Ford of the Apples: A History of Ballyhooly, Earliest Times to 2008*, Éigse Books, Fermoy, 2008, p. 20-21

earthwork about which relatively little was known until a few years ago.

Reading an interesting essay later in the Mallow Field Club Journal (MFCJ), my sense of disappointment was duly abated on reading the comment, 'It [The Cliadh Dubh] does not have a uniform morphology and is generally not outstanding. Sometimes it is a higher and broader-than-usual fence...topped by a dense growth of native trees and bushes.'[20] Though indistinguishable from the ordinary field fence, Canon Patrick Power claimed that it served as a boundary fence between the two cantreds that constituted the ancient territory of 'An Chaoille' which is described in the fifteenth-century Book of Lismore though the 'Cliadh Dubh is not actually mentioned by name in *Críochad an Chaoille*. As a result of Power's research, the ancient fence is included in the contemporary Discovery series of OS maps (1:50,000). Resulting from field work, Eithne Verling claimed that the 'Cliadh Dubh may have been little more than a pre-historic cattle fence.'

Whatever the true nature of the old fence, I am quite pleased to know of its location and to connect with such ancient features of our landscape. Allow me to digress here for a moment: the early Irish divided and organised the territory of Ireland into a series of divisions, known as 'Tuath(s)'that were subsumed into the Norman structure of baronies and later into the present day counties. *An Caoilli* was the general name for the area that now includes Fermoy, Mallow, Buttevant, Mitchelstown, Castletownroche, Doneraile and other places. An awareness of placenames, of legends and the history of one's own area gives one a 'connect,' an anchor that roots the members of a community in their own territory. Having crossed the Cliadh Dubh from Renny into Convamore, I have entered the former estate of the Earl of Listowel who lived in the great house until it was burnt to the ground in April, 1921. The placename 'Conva' is from the original Irish, *Con Mhaigh* or *Conbhá* ('The Hound-Plain' or 'Hound-Drowning')) as legend has it that Bran, the favourite hound of Fionn Mac Cumhaill, was drowned in the Blackwater along this stretch of the river.

The margin is 'willow-veiled' though there are bare stands, at intervals, where the angler comes for his leisure. The tell-tale signs of the great estate are all present here: the walled garden; the groves of yew; the rows of lime trees; the limestone pillars and boat jetty with stone seats. Echoes of the past, sad and happy, resound here, but the residents and their servants have

---

20 Gerard Condon, 'The Cliadh Dubh: A Linear Earthwork in North Cork' in *Mallow Field Club Journal*, No. 28, 2010, p 15.

Galloping horses close to river bank

departed since the night of the great conflagration when a tall halo of light illuminated the surrounding countryside. The most prestigious visitor to Convamore had been the Prince of Wales in 1887. On that historic occasion, a great beacon was lit on the roof of the house to welcome the future Edward VII who spent three days as a guest there and partook in fishing and woodcock shooting on this extensive estate.[21]

The forebears of the Earl, the Hare family, came from Norfolk to Cork City in the seventeenth century where they engaged in business. They accumulated considerable wealth that enabled them to purchase 25,000 acres from the Earl of Kerry in 1783.[22] Around 1800 they purchased Convamore from the O'Callaghans. Both son and father were elected members of parliament, and having voted for the Act of Union in 1800, they were duly rewarded with titles though resented by true-blue blood aristocrats. Captain Roberts, owner of the nearby Cregg House, used to address Lord Listowel as 'Lord Candlegrease' on account of his background in the commercial world. After Roberts' death, Listowel purchased his land and had the army blow up the house of his detractor.[23]

He then commissioned the architect brothers, George and James Pain, to design and rebuild his own mansion along classical lines to mark his elevation to a peerage in the House of Lords. Convamore House was beautifully situated, facing south to the Nagle Mountains and the Blackwater, reflecting the sky, clouds, hills and trees of a benign

21 Roche, *The Ford of the Apples,* p. 37; Kevin Myers, 'The Hares of Convamore, Ballyhooly,' in *Mallow Field Club Journal*, 2006, p. 30, 35-36.
22 Myers, 'The Hares of Convamore, p. 30
23 Roche, p. P. 35

countryside. Its proud owner must have thought that his splendid new home would last for centuries; despite their hopes, it failed to reach its first centenary in 1925.[24]

The IRA attributed their burning of Convamore to the 'anti-Irish' attitude of the Earl. His predecessor, the first Earl, had voted against measures to bring about Catholic emancipation during the campaign led by Daniel O'Connell. On the other hand, the Listowels imported blight-resistant varieties of potatoes during the Great Famine to enable their small holders to survive.[25]

According to Ernie O'Malley, the IRA commandant, Liam Lynch had been greatly agitated by news of the burning of six homes, belonging to well-known Republicans. O'Malley narrates that 'Liam's eyes blackened with rage.' His response, 'I'll bloody well settle that; six big houses and castles of their friends, the imperialists, will go up for this,' was duly carried out within a short time.[26]

On the night of 30th April, 1921, while the Earl was away, his niece, Miss Barbara Beecher, heard a loud knocking on the entrance door. Having opened the great oak door, she came face-to-face with a group of grim-faced men. One of them handed her a typewritten document from the IRA headquarters in Cork,

> On Wed, the 13th inst, the enemy [British military] bombed and destroyed 6 houses of Republicans as reprisals for IRA activities on the 10th inst. You [the Earl] being an aggressively anti-Irish person and your residence being in the Battalion area of enemy reprisals, I have hereby ordered that the same be destroyed as part of our counter-reprisals.

The IRA activists ordered her to save her own personal belongings but not to include any of the Earl's personal effects. They then sprinkled petrol on the stairs and set the house ablaze. Miss Beecher and some servants fought the forest of flame with a hose and managed to save the servants' quarters.[27]

Two more of the great houses of north Cork, Ballywalter in Shanballymore and Rockmills, near Killdorrery, were also burnt on the same night.

Elizabeth Bowen, the novelist who lived about 15k from Ballyhooly, transposed the events of that Stygian night to her novel, *Another September*. Naming three fictional houses: Danielstown; Castle Trent and Mount

24 Ibid., p. 35; Myers, p. 32-34
25 Myers, p 29
26 O'Malley, Ernie, *Another Man's Wound,* cited by Myers, p. 29
27 Myers, p. 39

Elizabeth, she described their 'execution' on that fateful night in language that painted the burning as a horror that inverted the natural order of day and night.

> A fearful scarlet ate up the hard spring darkness: indeed, it seemed that an extra day, unreckoned, had come into abortive birth that these things might happen. It seemed, looking from east to west at the sky tall with scarlet, that the country itself was burning. [28]

Bowen knew, loved and portrayed the great houses and landscape of North Cork most vividly. Despite her evocation of a utopian life in her autobiographical writings, there was a deeper, more enduring sense of insecurity, even hostility, between the Anglo-Irish and the native Irish. Her fictional *personae* sensed that the Great Houses were imposed, un-embraced presences in the landscape that would inevitably have to reckon with a poignant destiny in the years ahead.[29]

The burning of Convamore and other great houses could be regarded as an act of wanton destruction. The attritional nature of warfare has always involved the burning of towns, settlements and houses. Both sides resorted to the use of fire in the Irish War of Independence. Contemporary nationalists tend to take a pragmatic view – that the great house could have become a cultural centre, a select guesthouse for anglers fishing the Blackwater or a residence for a rich industrialist who might bring employment to the area. A deeper, more atavistic instinct was unchained where the oppressed seeks to erase the cultural landmarks of the oppressor.

The Earl claimed £150,000 compensation at a hearing in Fermoy in October. He denied, through his solicitor, the accusation of the IRA of being 'anti-Irish,' and claimed that he had lived on good terms with local people for over sixty years. He added that he had given 'very great employment' to local people. He was awarded £85,200 for the loss of his home and property. In reality, the Hares were absentee landowners for six months of the year, preferring to winter in London rather than endure the travail of winters in Ireland.

The farmyard complex, situated a short distance from the ruinous mansion, has remained intact to the present day. Featuring ashlar limestone and two pairs of symmetrical-arched entrances, the complex stands as a reminder of past glories when coachmen and footmen guided elegant barouches through the north-west entrance. A cupola with a clock on the east

---

28 Bowen, Elizabeth, *The Last September,* London, 1928
29 Eibhear Walsh, 'Several Landscapes: Bowen and the Terrain of North Cork' in *Estudios Irlandeses, No 0,* 2005, p. 141-147.

range regulated the hours of work for gardeners, grooms and farmhands.

At the edge of the former estate, all exits are securely locked, forcing me to climb over an eight-foot high wall into the grounds of Christ Church where the members of the local Anglican community assemble to worship. Memorial plaques, recalling the military careers of members of the Hare family, decorate the interior walls. The limestone edifice, opened here in 1881, was originally erected in Bridgetown close to the Augustinian Priory, 1860. However, it was closed after a few years due to the very limited numbers attending services there. The church authorities had it de-constructed stone by stone, and transported to Ballyhooly to be reconstructed in this elevated site over the Blackwater.

Here too stands the daunting mausoleum of the Earls of Listowel and their families. The passer-by can read the inscription in French and Latin over the doorway which also features their family crest – a coronet.

Guilelemus
Cones de Listowel
Sibi et Suis
1846

The name 'Ballyhooly,' according to legend, originates from the story of St Carthage (also known as Mochuda) who, while crossing the Blackwater, offered an apple to the daughter of a local chieftain. The young woman had a withered arm. The saint, however, refused to release the apple from his

Christ Church, Ballyhooly

Earls of Listowel mausoleum

grasp until she reached her disabled hand to receive his gift. On grasping the apple, her arm was miraculously cured, and since that time the area has been known as Baile Átha hÚlla ('the Town of the Ford of the Apples'). The story of the miraculous cure is beautifully depicted in a Harry Clarke stained-glass window in the Honan Chapel, UCC.[30]

My brother Joe has already parked and is waiting for me outside the Church of the Nativity. Glancing around us we notice a large sign, advertising newly built houses in an appropriately named estate, Gleann Úll. Unfortunately, only some of the houses have been completed: half of the houses 'remain uninhabited; electricity to provide lighting has not been connected and manholes protrude from the access roadway.'[31] The lure of country living, free from the pressures of city estates has not been fulfilled for families who made the break from Cork City. Adding to this planning problem, two more estates, close to the village, 'are similarly uncompleted and ... remain a long term difficulty' for the community especially for the local tidy town [village] committee that, in the view of the adjudicators of the Tidy Towns competition, has done commendable work.

With the railway station closed since 1963 and small grocery stores going out of business in recent years, the main street is dominated by the Catholic Church on the left side and Ballyhooly House on the right. Ballyhooly House was once the home of the steward of the Convamore estate. Three licensed premises and a supermarket cum filling-station help to meet some of the everyday needs of local consumers and visitors.

Our visit to Grindel's Bar helps to make up for the disappointment of the closed pubs in Lombardstown and Killavullen. With the exterior painted in green and white and the name H.M. Grindel embossed in large red lettering, two panels inform about-to-be customers that 'Guinness, Stout, Best Whiskies, Brandies, Wines and Minerals' are all available within.

The barman ignores our entrance, which is par for the course in most of our rural licensed premises. ' If you think I am going to bend over backways to get your custom, let me tell you, you are in for a big shock.' Two male customers at the bar eye us up and down but as this cat-scan reveals nothing contagious or threatening in our demeanour they resume their quiet conversation. *Walking Man*, having called for two pints of stout, is in one of his daring moods and boldly releases the pin in one of his hallmark rhetorical grenades. 'Is there a good pint of porter in these premises? He

30 Roche, *The Ford of the Apples: A History of Ballyhooly,*, p. 14
31 Louise Roseingrave in Irish Times, 'Cork, The Kids' Playground is just Waste Ground,' Oct. 22, 2010, p. 13

outrageously inquires. Neither proprietor nor customers take the bait. They are old hands at fielding rhetorical questions and know from long experience that such questions do not demand an answer either in a chapel, kirk or licensed premises.

The barman, who already has the first glass angled towards the tap, pauses ever so briefly, and then recommences his task, determined to silence the effrontery of a brazen customer who dares to ask the one question that should never be asked in a rural pub.

While waiting for our two glasses to fill, Joe asks the local men if all the corn in the area has been harvested.

'Yes, 'it's all over for another year.'

One of the men replies, and after another draught of stout, he adds, 'We're tidying up the straw at the moment. There's great demand for straw in parts of Kerry and west Cork.'

After what seems a longer than usual 'filling,' two pints are placed before us with a silent challenge. Another subtle pause ensues as the local men and the proprietor monitor our reaction to the first sip, 'That's good,' I respond, and Joe adds his affirmative view. The tension dissolves and we sip and chat about local events and about the village. Yes, the world famous dancer, Michael Flatley, calls in occasionally from his residence in Castlehyde. We drain our glasses, thank the barman and say goodbye to the local men.

It is time to return to the Blackwater to resume my journey and to

complete today's trek to Fermoy. I have chosen to walk the south bank as a sizeable number of large walled residences occupy the northern bank while the south bank, which is liable to flooding, has not been built on. I can only glance at Ballyhooly Castle and the old church as we drive downhill past tasteful houses built of cut limestone.

Then across the limestone bridge, built as recently as 1955 when a flood swept away the old wooden bridge that had ferried coaches and cars across the Blackwater from 1844-1955. At Ballyhooly crossroads, I glance back to Ballyhooly Castle. Built in 1314 by the Roches to guard a prominent ford, the main tower (keep) survives as a sentinel guarding all approaches to the river. In recent years a modern fishing lodge has been erected in the foreground of the castle courtyard where anglers sleep after a day on the beats. The silent Blackwater has witnessed the building of the castle and knights in armour riding through the shallow waters; it has watched travellers: peasants wading and lords riding in their carriages in the same quiet way that it now observes my arrival and my departure.

Glancing at my watch and entrusting my knapsack to Joe, I set out again to continue my walk through the fields of Gurteen, Ballylawrence and Ballymacallen. I am on my own once more, but not alone, for I have the Blackwater *'scamhóg anála na Mumhan'* (the breathing lung) of Munster as my travelling companion.

Back once more to the challenge of the fields – their fences and streams and patches of briars, I am on my own again and free to return to the river that the writer and journalist, Liam Ó Muirthille, referred to as the 'scamhóg anála na Mumhan or the 'breathing lung of Munster.' Such a perceptive metaphor, redolent of the historic events along the Great River and of its physical character though expressed silently in summer manifests another mood in its winter rage.[32]

Buoyed up by the 'good pint' from Grindel's, I head off across the fields hoping that the unforeseen fences won't force me into time-wasting diversions. I manage the first, second and third field without undue difficulty, skirting around the wetter areas and managing to sidle through the boundary fences. The quiet and companionable presence of the river, on my left hand side, reassures me that I am making progress on this fulfilling journey. The northern bank features a densely wooded slope while the southern side with its line of ash, alder, sycamore and other trees appears to be an ideal place for anglers in their quest to land salmon or trout. But

---

32 Liam Ó Muirthille in 'An Peann Coitianta,' *Irish Times*

where are the anglers? Why are they not availing of this quiet evening with the declining sun casting a soft lambent glow on the water?

Here in Ballylawrence, I pass through the land owned by the Grahams (known locally as Grimes) in the time of the penal laws (1797-1884) when Catholic schools were banned and priests were outlawed. The enforcement of these tyrannical laws against Catholic priests tended to be sporadic, depending on the attitude of local officials and how zealous they were in enforcing the penal code. The Grahams, the owners of the land through which I am now passing, took it upon themselves to report priests to the authorities for the reward of £5, offered on their heads. Accordingly, Major Graham and his three sons, residents of Ballylawrence House, decided to capture a local priest, Fr John Walsh, who lived in Killathy (*Cíll Átha*, 'The Church of the Ford'), and to claim their reward for his capture. The lack of a bridge in Ballyhooly, however, forced them to ride to Fermoy and from there along the northern bank of the Blackwater to the priest's hiding place. Fortunately for the priest, their plans were overheard by one of their workmen, 'a simple lad named Peter,' who, using a horse's collar to support himself, waded across the Blackwater to warn the priest of the deadly danger that was about to envelop him. The grateful priest thanked him and prayed that Peter would not drown on his return across the Blackwater, 'Go easy Blackwater and do not drown Peter the fool.'[33] The priest hid in the ruined church of Killathy and escaped the clutches of the Grahams who, according to the local folklore, died shortly after that incident and are buried in Killathy in a stone crypt though their names have not been carved on their grave.[34]

Recently, Christy Roche, took me to see Ballylawrence House. At this stage the house, smothered in overgrown trees and vegetation, is scarcely visible. Dense boles of ivy have ripped the plaster of the walls and pierced the crevices between the stones through and through.

After the poignant reverie of the penal age, I mentally readjust my sights again to the river and to the land, wondering if I will meet a farmer or angler along the way. In the next townland of Ballymacallen, I can see a large farm a short distance away with a cluster of sheds, silo pits, a tractor with a loader and a slurry spreader attached. A thin wisp of smoke rises from the chimney. In the river field a large herd of Friesian heifers graze on higher ground, and lucky for me, access for them to where I am is cut off by an electric fence.

Next, I come to a deep drain where, fortunately, a resourceful angler has

33 Roche, *The Ford of the Apples, p. 25*
34 Roche, p. 25

Angler Johnny Guerin fishing on a 'wonderful stretch of river'.

put two short metal ladders in place: the first to the bottom of the drain and the second to help one surmount a formidable fence. As I climbed up from the bottom of the trench I had an eerie feeling of what it must have been like for soldiers in the trenches in the Great War. Up and over, I notice an angler fishing in midstream.

For a minute or two, I observe him as he casts his line into dark, still pools under the overhanging branches of the northern bank. He seems utterly

absorbed – a consummate angler, trying to outwit the wily salmon who has escaped the barb hooks of the scheming anglers from early spring 'til now – late summer. The scarcely visible line scythes through the swarms of midges in the soft light of this September evening. And then casting an eagle-eye glance over his shoulder, 'my consummate angler' spots the uninvited spectator who thought that he had been observing the fisherman unawares. I call out a quick 'Hello,' followed by the usual predictable query, 'Any luck?'

Reeling in his line and wading towards me, he responds, 'They're quiet at the moment; they were jumping more early on but those fellows could be up at Ballyhooly Bridge by now.'

Having informed me that he lives in the Blarney-Blackpool suburb of Cork, he adds that he grew up in Listowel where his father had a fishing tackle shop until the 1960s and that he fished and poached in the River Feale from an early age. Nowadays, he pays an annual fee to Simon Hirsch, the owner of Ballyhooly Castle, for the pleasure of fishing what he regards as a 'wonderful stretch of river.' He quickly adds, I'll be disappointed if I don't catch a salmon this evening.'

In response to my question of whether the low level of the river affects the fishing, he declares that it can be an advantage, 'When the water is low, the salmon tend to stay in the pools, and you can concentrate on those parts.'

Distracted for a moment, he stoops and picks something from the grassy vegetation at our feet, 'You wouldn't want to leave the evidence lying around.'

Asking him what he means, he explains that he was cleaning up scales that had fallen from a five-pound salmon that he had caught the previous week.

His favourite lure is the 'Flying C' or 'Condom' as it is known to the French who invented and popularised it, 'The French brought it around here first. I use nothing else now, a yellow one when the water is dirty but a black one is better.'

And clearly, Johnny Guerin could continue to talk and to discuss lures and fishing for the rest of the evening.

Glancing at his wrist watch and wishing Johnny 'good luck,' *Walking Man* says goodbye and recommences his tramp along the river. Reaching

Johnny with his catch of the day

Colourful store of fishing tackle

[127]

Creggolympry (*Creig O Loimpre*, meaning not known), what plainly appears to be an opulent and tastefully designed mansion has been built on higher ground to escape the floods, that ensue here, and to enjoy the visual amenity of the beautiful Blackwater. I keep close to the river and well away from the building while casting envious glances in its direction, imagining what a pleasurable place it would be to live, where one could observe the river in all seasons. Nearing the boundary of this extensive site, I try one path and then another but, frustratingly', I fail to find any exit-point to the next section of the river. So, nothing to do except head for the official entrance where, to my utter dismay, I find a heavy-duty steel gate barred and locked, allowing no one to leave or enter. Peering to the right or left of the gate, I similarly fail to find the slightest chink that would enable me to slip through to continue my trek unimpeded. Climbing over the gate is not an option as the manufacturers have left no place to plant one's foot. In semi-desperation, the Irish proverb occurs to me, *Is cuma nó muc duine gan seift*, (literally and bluntly, 'A person without a stratagem is no better than a pig.'). Having peered around both sides and looked over the gate, I look downwards, espying an opening of approximately 10-12 inches between the gate and ground – just about enough to allow me wriggle underneath. Stripping off my tee-shirt and laying a pullover on the ground, I shuffle and writhe uncomfortably though effectively to shift my head, trunk and legs underneath the great barrier. My main concern, of course, is that someone may appear out of nowhere or a motorist who may stop wondering what exactly is happening. In a jiffy, I am back on my feet, fully clothed and bounding away along the public road. Luck is on my side and I soon find a path that leads directly back to the river.

Within a few minutes, I find myself standing and staring across the Blackwater at Castle Hyde – the preferred home of the 'Lord of the Dance' – Michael Flatley. My discretion in avoiding the northern bank, has now been rewarded with a grandstand view of this 'storied mansion' that has been comprehensively refurbished since the Dancer purchased a building that had been progressively stripped of its furniture and ornaments and allowed to deteriorate. Having purchased the property for £2 million, Flatley, it is claimed locally, has spent €18 million in restoring the great house to its former splendour and glory.

Built in the last quarter of the eighteenth century for Arthur Hyde, the building was further enhanced with the addition of two-fronted pavilions. The Hyde family retained ownership until 1851 when family fortunes declined, forcing them to move to Cregg House about half a mile upriver from Castlehyde. The Hydes, originally from Berkshire, were granted a huge tract

Castle Hyde, residence of MIchael Flatley

of land (11,762 acres) in this area by Queen Elizabeth I as a reward for their raising a battalion to defend the realm against the threat of the Spanish Armada in 1588.[35] Taking up residence in the four-storey thatched castle of the banished Maloneys, the family remained in Castlehyde for 250 years.

How absurdly ironic to think that a descendant of Elizabethan planters gave independent Ireland its first president – the scholarly Douglas Hyde (1860-1949) who learnt the Irish language from the peasants of his native Roscommon, collected the folk songs of Connaught and committed himself passionately to the preservation of a language that Elizabeth had sought to eradicate.

The new owner had to replace all the two-hundred year old windows at a cost of approximately half a million pounds. So the great house has been rescued along with its extensive gardens, tree-lined avenue, farmyards buildings and riverside walk, and should survive for another two hundred years. However, I persist in asking myself whether I find the edifice a pleasing spectacle in an aesthetic sense. While Castlehyde occupies a magnificent scenic location and has an impressive harmony of proportions, framed against a background of mature beach, oak and other trees, I feel

---

35   Hajba, Anna Maria, *Houses of Cork, Vol 1 – North Cork,* Ballinkilla Press, 2002

that it is too obviously self-important. Wrestling with such thoughts, I set off again ever watching and observing the river that has by now assumed a visible magnificence.

Curving like a great but pliant serpent, the Blackwater flows onward in all its watery grandeur with a teeming population of trout, salmon and flies dancing in the lambent glow of a September evening. Around the curve, I catch my first glimpse of [mute]swans on the river – two adults and two juveniles – who seem content in their river home. Only then does it strike me that I had not seen swans anywhere else along the Blackwater and, in mock humour, I begin to parody Bob Dylan's lyric, 'Where have all the *swans* gone? Nor have I seen water hens though mallards, herons and even the little egret can be seen and heard along most stretches of the river. The commonly held explanation for the disappearance of water hens and swans from our rivers is that the predatory mink are destroying their eggs and preying on their fledglings. Anglers, especially, have noticed the reduced numbers of these birds on many rivers. The accidental introduction of mink to the Irish fauna since the 1960s when they escaped from mink farms has had drastic repercussions for wildlife on the coast as well as on streams, lakes and rivers.

Continuing my journey, I hear a hollow rumbling sound accompanied by the whine of an outboard motor engine. Within a second or two, the senior ladies' team 8+ of the Fermoy Rowing Club glide past in a gracefully synchronised movement of bodies, arms and oars with their blades dipping lightly into the dark waters. But, out of synch, their coach in his grey rib, begins to remonstrate with them about technique, stroke, posture and all the rest that will help them win regattas in late summer. Anyway, I am transfixed, listening into a very serious coaching session over a megaphone – eight young ladies, a coxswain and their coach about a mile upriver from Fermoy town. Here at last, I witness and marvel at the spectacle of 'comely maidens' engaged in the intensely competitive sport that rowing is.

We under-utilise the resources of our rivers, and in the case of the Blackwater, it appears to me that angling has been prioritised to the detriment of other water activities. In fact the relationship between kayakers and the angling community has often been fraught with tension and misunderstanding that, on some occasions, boils over into confrontation. Sensing my presence, the coach glances in my direction, and sends me a discreet, unspoken message to move on. Time is of the essence for *Walking Man*, and the traction of the ever-moving river cajoles and beckons me to follow.

At this juncture, Joe, having driven to Fermoy with my knapsack, should

Short restpite · Training session of the senior ladies from the Fermoy Rowing Club

be walking from the quayside to meet me as I approach the end of Day 4. But another obstacle lies in wait for me: this time an almost insurmountable barb wire fence: five strands high, securely fastened and, obviously, designed to exclude the casual walker, the angler or mitcher, following where the fancy leads, who might take it into his head to ramble along the Blackwater.

I stand still for a moment to focus my mind on my current predicament to determine what I consider to be the best solution to the quandary that now faces me. With no way through and no way under, I conclude that my only option is the risky one of climbing over the rusty wire with barbs as sharp as pirhana teeth. Then, gripping the branch of an ash tree with my left hand, I place a foot on the lower strand, then the other foot on the second strand, and in that fashion, I climb upwards to the third and fourth strand, but as I precariously begin to rest my weight on the fifth and final strand, its hold on the tree gives way, causing me to drop downward carrying the fourth strand with me but, luckily, the third strand arrests my fall. Drawing a breath of relief, I jump clear to land safely on softer ground underneath. *Walking Man* picks himself up, brushes himself down and heads back to the riverside. In the distance I see Joe approaching. Before I can inform him of my close brush with calamity, he tells me that he has just visited Grange Stud and that he has seen Oscar and Vinnie Roe. He adds that there's plenty to see around Fermoy

Jim and Christy Roche near Woodville House on Glanabo bridge

and that he will definitely return at a later date.

Happy in each other's company as we would have often been at home many years before, Joe and I stroll off together. Like two pupils playing truant we joke and chat and admire the fleet equine pedigrees that kick up their hind legs in the air and gallop away over the folds of the extensive meadow that we are not traversing.

In the next field, we find to our amazement a small suckler herd of Highland Cattle who eye us suspiciously, fearing that we may be intent on kidnapping their calves from them.

We walk jauntily past Gleannabo bridge and join the Barnane riverside walk where couples, young and old, are strolling in the evening sunshine. After the trials of the day, this final phase is a luxury that we both relish. The river bristles with activity: canoeists; scullers and kayakers about to conclude their training and haul their craft ashore to the premises of the Fermoy Rowing Club where Christy Roche, local historian, is awaiting our arrival. Earlier in the year, I had approached the caretaker in the clubhouse and informed him of my plan to walk the Blackwater. His immediate response was, 'You should talk to Christy Roche. He's just driven up there (referring to the riverside walk), and he should be back down shortly.'

Sensing that I might not have had time to spare, he remarked,

> Come on, we'll walk up after him. Christy has a great interest in walking and has designed walks around Fermoy and Ballyhooly. Christy is your man; he'll tell you everything you need to know about the Blackwater.

A few moments later, I am introducing myself to Christy and explaining to him that I am planning to walk the Blackwater from source to sea. I immediately sense his interest and I quickly realise why the caretaker told me that Christy would be the right person to talk to. Within a minute, we begin pouring over an OS map of the Blackwater valley as he points out various landmarks along the way, giving me useful advice concerning accessible routes particularly whether I should take the north or south side of the river from Ballyhooly to Fermoy.

Herd of Highland cattle

Meeting him again after four months, Christy points out various landmarks – the house where James Joyce's father lived as well as the residence of James Roderick O'Flanagan (J.R. O'Flanagan), the Fermoy barrister-at-law who wrote the first book on the Blackwater. He refers to John Anderson, the Scottish entrepreneur who bought the lands to develop the town of Fermoy. Pausing a moment, he adds,

> Of course, Anderson made the mistake of building on the flood plain of the Blackwater, and we're living since with the consequences of his error.

Pausing again and glancing at the river flowing past us – calm, peaceful and strong – but Christy knows the hidden menace that lurks in the depth and volume of those black waters hurtling eastwards from the mountain fastness of Duhallow to their ultimate destination, the Atlantic Ocean off the south coast of Ireland. 'The Blackwater in flood is an awesome sight,' he comments while looking towards the monumental limestone bridge that spans this ancient ford.

In medieval times the Cistercian monks operated a ferry to transport travellers across the great river. Their monastery was dissolved in 1539-41.[36] The first bridge in Fermoy over the Blackwater, most likely a wooden structure, was built by the Earl of Cork, Richard Boyle, in 1625 at a cost of £500. Boyle saw the bridge as vital link that would facilitate his many business interests in the area.[37] Unfortunately, the bridge was swept away by a flood within three years. The urgent need for a strong bridge troubled him even on his death bed.

---

36 Brunicardi, Niall, cited by O'Keeffe & Simington, p. 169
37 O'Keeffe & Simington, p. 169; Dickson, David, *Old World Colony: Cork and South Munster 1630-1830*, p. 22

I desire the ease and safety of the neighbours and travellers, and to have a strong and substantial bridge of lime and stone built in the place [Fermoy as it is at Moyalla [Mallow]. I do here signify that it is my will and desire that my brother-in-law William Fenton, Knight, Richard Fishers Esq., His Majesty's Attorney in Munster, and Joshua Boyle Esq., with the assistance of my tenant George Hartwell should cause a very graceful and substantial bridge to be built of lime and stone over the river of Fermoy.[38]

His wish was duly carried out in the 1670s. This bridge lasted almost two hundred years until it was demolished *circa* 1860 and it was replaced by the present magnificent structure in 1865.[39]

Yes, 'the brown god – sullen, untamed and intractable' that flows so placidly beneath the great bridge this peaceful September evening, remains 'untamed and unpropitiated…but waiting, watching and waiting'.[40] As Eliot implies, the threat from a great river is never entirely solved. Nevertheless, an extensive programme of flood prevention has been carried out here in Fermoy in a determined effort to eliminate or to significantly alleviate the devasting floods from the Blackwater that have caused so much damage to commercial and residential buildings in the centre square of the town and other low-lying areas.

The modern town of Fermoy became a great garrison town from the late eighteenth century and with a large barrack, housing hundreds of soldiers, it remained a stronghold of security for colonial rule until the dawn of Irish Independence in 1921-22. Thirteen years after independence, the parade square of the barracks became the new home of Fermoy GAA club and was subsequently called Fitzgerald Memorial Park in honour of the local patriot Mick Fitzgerald who died after sixty-five days on hunger strike. I recollect a Sunday in late September, 1955, when I attended my first big game of hurling. I was a big man then, all seven years of me raised up and perched on my father's shoulders so I might see afar. My older brothers were there as well. I remember it graphically. Youghal versus Mallow in the final of the Intermediate Championship.

The ruined walls of the deserted military barracks stood sentinel in the background with supporters from both clubs, taking up advantaged viewing positions in the gaping windows. Fifty-five years have passed since that memorable day when Youghal, my own club, triumphed over their rivals.

Of all the towns and villages on the Blackwater, it seems that Fermoy

38 Ibid., p. 169-170
39 O'Keeffe & Simigton, p. 170
40 Eliot, T.S., *Four Quartets: Dry Salvages,* Faber & Faber, paperback ed., (1959), p. 35

more than any other settlement has embraced the great river, considering that not only has it a rowing club but a sub-aqua club along with trout, salmon and coarse fishing associations. Consequently, the young, middle-age, elderly, women and men can enjoy the facilities that the flowing water of the Blackwater offers to them. Sadly, the waters bring heartbreak to other families who have lost loved ones through accident or misadventure.

Tonight, I am staying with my cousins, the Mulcahy family, who live on a farm about seven miles from Fermoy in the picturesque parish of Conna. We are late but Neilus, after a busy day minding his suckler herd of Aubrac and Romanola cattle, has the fire lit and wants to hear a detailed account of my walk. But before relating the adventures of the day, and while we tuck into two generous and tender steaks, Nelius, Joe and myself reminisce and talk about farming, horse racing and hunting. Nelius and all belonging to him love the hunt.

The practice jumps in the paddock area, outside their kitchen window, clearly demonstrate that their children, Cormac and Áine, are serious about hunting across the countryside during the winter months. Tonight they have their homework completed, their school bags packed while Cormac checks some project work on the computer and Áine browses through show jumping books. Rosettes and other awards, won at equestrian events, are arranged at various display points around the house.

Today's trails and travails have taken their toll on me. I feel exhausted but very satisfied. Joe heads back to Glanmire and I take up the kind offer of a cosy bed. My body longs to rest and sleep but not before I have read a few more pages from Willy Vlautin's best-seller, *Lean on Pete*.

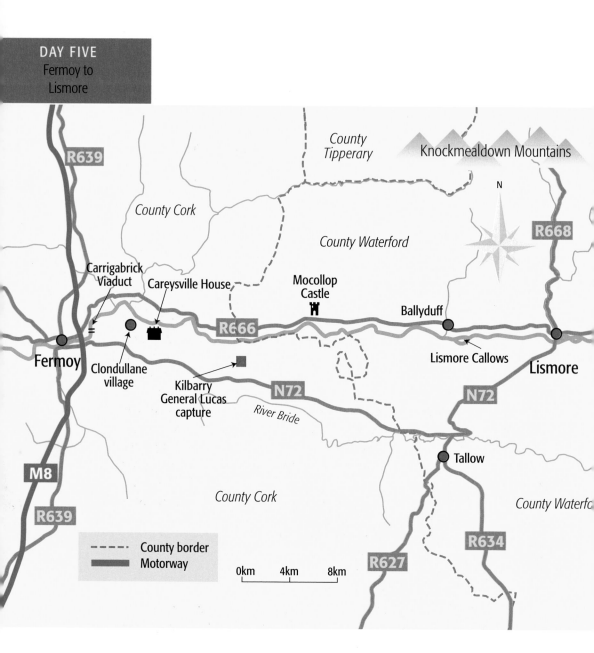

Fermoy to Lismore

Fermoy to Ballyduff to Lismore, 26 km (approx. 16 mls)

'Rivers run through our civilisations like string through beads.'[1]

A T 5.00 am the Mulcahys' rooster announces daybreak as the first rays of light steal through the bedroom window. My head, suspended somewhere between sleep and wakefulness, struggles with thoughts and plans for Day 5 but weary legs and shoulders rebel and demand more sleep which, thankfully, descends again after the cockrel's rude announcement of morning. Two hours later, I can hear footsteps around the corridors as Áine and Cormac get ready for the school bus which will bring them to their schools: Loreto Secondary School and St Coleman's College. Aine has just enrolled and is enjoying the excitement of new subjects, new teachers and new friends while older brother Cormac has completed two years of post-primary education and is busy studying for the Junior Certificate examination next June. Their mother, Mary, a primary school principal, wishes me 'good luck' before heading off to Ballynoe N.S. Nelius has already visited his livestock and is busy tending to a variety of jobs around the farmyard.

As Nelius drives me back to Fermoy, he draws my attention to significant landmarks along the way. We pass through Clondulane that was nothing more than a hamlet with a church, school, public house and a shop until the Celtic Tiger came to maraud the landscape.

Though the builder's hammer and chisel are now silent, a crescent-shaped estate of houses remains unoccupied. In fairness, the development

---

1   Laing, Olivia, *To the River: A Journey beneath the Surface,* Cannongate, London, 2011.

seems to have been completed satisfactorily along with approach roads, footpaths and green areas. Consequently, the impact is not such an eyesore here as in other locations; however, building development that would disproportionately increase the population in a relatively short time can scarcely be considered desirable.

Pulling into the lay-bye near Fermoy Hospital, Nelius directs me to the well-worn track that anglers and strollers take to reach the bank of the river. Tallow horse fair is on today, an important occasion in the calendar for all horse lovers in the region who, whether buying or selling, will enjoy their yearly reunion and exchange yarns and racing lore along with the more serious subject of breeding good hunters or racers. Before he can rush off to the fair, I entrust him with the task of transporting my knapsack to Lismore. Relieved of my bag, I feel that the walk ahead will be more manageable and enjoyable. In fact, I am eagerly looking forward to this stretch where the Blackwater develops into a strong-flowing and mature river.

Having bid goodbye to Nelius, I ramble down the angler's path to the river that flows serenely past. There is scarcely a puff of wind to ruffle the calm, glassy surface of the deep water where I stand in awe before striding through the fields. Glancing to the west, I observe the new concrete viaduct, bestriding the Blackwater like a Colossus, bearing cars, lorries and other vehicles freed from the traffic congestion in the town of Fermoy. Opened in 2006, the new viaduct has significantly reduced the volume of traffic through the town as well as greatly conveniencing commuters, travelling south to Cork or north east to Dublin. Turning my back on the concrete super-structure, I walk downriver to the older Carrigabrick viaduct, constructed in 1872, over which trains passed connecting Fermoy to Lismore, Cappoquin, Dungarvan and ultimately to Waterford city. Supported by five rock-faced limestone piers, it fits snugly into the landscape unlike its modern, concrete and gigantic counterpart straddling the N8. The sight of the viaduct brings back memories of the epic first World War film, *The Blue Max*, in which an ace German pilot flew his aeroplane under the central span of the bridge to escape from his allied pursuers. Starring George Peppard, James Mason and the Bond star-to-be, Ursula Andress, the opening sequence was filmed here in October 1965. A year later, along with a few companions, all destined to be national school teachers, I saw the film in the Ambassador cinema in the Rotunda, Dublin. No harm to admit now, that the generously endowed starlet raised testosterone levels in us celibate students. But, of course, it was innocent

Carrigabrick viaduct

fun in comparison to modern cinematic fare with its undiluted portrayal of sexuality.

Prior to the construction of the rail line, the Duke of Devonshire, Lord Mountcashel and Sir Richard Musgrove of Toureen had proposed that the river Blackwater would be made navigable as far as Fermoy to allow for a steam riverboat as a means of public transport. Instead of acceding to their proposal, the authorities of the time favoured the construction of a railroad. Musgrove, in his enthusiasm for the project, had even purchased a barge, called the *John Anderson* and succeeded in doing trial runs to Fermoy.

It's time to walk, to follow the river eastwards to Ballyduff and from there to Lismore. But just as I am about to begin, a large fish leaps out of the water, causing a loud splash behind my back. A pity I missed that wonderful sight – must keep my eyes peeled – nor have I seen a kingfisher on my walk – that flash of steel-blue coursing arrow-like through the air. September tends to be a quiet time for anglers though, judging by the well-trodden track along the bank of the river, the local rod men are more than familiar with this stretch of river. The Fermoy District and Anglers' Association was founded in 1935, and since that time, judging by the history of their group, they have enjoyed the challenges posed by the great river with its plentiful stock of trout and salmon.[2] Being an outsider, who knows little about the rods, reels, lines and baits used by the piscatorial confraternity (anglers), I

---

2   *Fermoy & District Anglers' Association: 60 Years a Growing 1935-1995,* Fermoy, 1995

Careysville Estate with angler midriver

am fascinated by their enthusiasm, their knowledge of the water's secrets and especially by their skill in naming their favourite flies: Red Spinner, March Brown, Orange Grouse, Light Olive Quill, Badger Quill, Silver Partridge, March Brown Spider and many more designed by gifted rod-men who, with their dexterous fingers, can tie the miniscule components to make their own special baits. Their knowledge of the river, its flora and fauna is beautifully illustrated by this excerpt:

> Fly dressers may question the use of Heron Herl as this noble bird is protected...but they do drop wing quills by the river bank...and the observant angler will keep an eye out for them. Believe me this herl is an excellent material for the fly dresser.[3]

Sadly, the anglers witness the deterioration of the water quality; the floating refuse, the discarded plastic, the oily film on the surface and, surely the most distressing sight of all must be the appalling spectacle of a large

---

3   *Fermoy & District Anglers' Association*, p. 85

fish-kill. The morning of 13th August 1987 was a black day for the Fermoy anglers as reports came in of a massive fish-kill along three miles of the Blackwater below Fermoy Bridge. The scale of the damage with 'salmon, trout and coarse fish...killed in their thousands'[4] gave rise to more stringent measures to prevent run-off from agricultural sources and faulty septic tanks that leads to a build-up of nitrates that affects the spawning beds of salmonoid species. We cannot afford to be blasé about a range of indicators that will ultimately, if not prevented, dramatically affect a great salmon river such as the Blackwater.

Despite the failure of the kingfisher to display its unmistakeable bright plumage, nature has reserved a different treat for me: after ten minutes, I disturb a fox, nosing around for a rabbit, thinking, perhaps, that the nocturnal Reynard was tucked-up deep underground. On my approach, the wary predator bounds away through the nearest gap, out of my sight. Two fields further on, I again espy the foraging fox, now stationary, before a brake of brambles. Pausing in my tracks, I observe him for some time and notice, to my astonishment, that he's plucking blackberries for his morning snack. I see the briars springing back into place when released from his teeth. Though foxes are carnivores, they will eat fruit such as blackberries, mushrooms and strawberries in season when more meaty fare is not readily available.

Picking up my scent, he hurriedly departs from his blackberry fare. Yes, I am thrilled that nature in its discretion has revealed one of its precious secrets to me. If you're patient, keep your eyes open, listen to the sounds, be still and allow yourself to be absorbed into the scene then you begin to observe animal and bird movements that are usually overlooked. *Éist le fuaim na habhann agus gheobhair breac.* For that reason, I never use an iPod to listen to downloaded music whether it be Leonard Cohen, sonorously telling us that 'Suzanne takes you down to her place besides the river,' or Johnny Cash, telling us that the tears that 'he cried' are gonna flood 'Big River.' Anyway, the Blackwater today flows almost silently, just a barely audible swoosh as it spills over grit and gravel and washes nonchalantly against the lower part of the banks.

Moving on, I reach the first limestone outcrop and am forced to detour around a series of paddocks where skewbald ponies and their foals graze contentedly. Nearby, stands an old unoccupied farmhouse with sheds and stables.

---

4   Ibid, p. 35

One of the most pleasant aspects of this walk is that I am never sure what awaits me in the next field or around the bend. I know, however, that the premier fishing location on the Blackwater lies on this stretch of the river. Careysville Fishery has attracted keen and amateur anglers down through the generations – politicians such as Harold Macmillian, film stars such as Fred Astaire and mega-sports personalities such as Tiger Woods. Admission to Careysville is not a casual matter yet *Walking Man* is prepared to breach security in the belief that his mission to walk the Blackwater will guarantee him safe passage through this exclusive haven where the great and mighty cast their lines in the hope that they will hook and land the king of fish now returned from its ocean sojourn.

Careysville House was built in 1810 on the site of Ballymacpatrick Castle. Formerly the residence of Edward Carey, this fine Georgian mansion overlooks the Blackwater from a limestone escarpment that towers above the flowing waters. With an estate of 175 acres and 1.75 miles of bank with numerous pools, beats and glides, Careysville is regarded by many fishing enthusiasts as one of the finest stretches of salmon fishing in the country.

The first obstacle I encounter is a rusty barb wire fence which I easily surmount, then through an arbour of great beeches and along winding paths to return to the river again. I can glimpse the lawns and mansion through the shrubs and foliage that adorn the setting of the house. My intrusion remains unnoticed and the thrill of invading Careysville has turned into an anti-climax. Approaching the great weir, erected to halt the salmon in their journey upriver and to corral them in a pool of water where those who relish piscatorial pursuits can lure them on to their baits, I pause and observe the cascading waters for a moment. I text my daughters in Dublin to inform them that I have reached Careysville where Dukes and their parties flock. But before I can finish texting, I hear approaching footsteps. A ghillie, attired in all the fabric of his trade and with waist-high waders, is approaching in a manner that suggests authority. A man of few words,

'This is private,' he informs me.

I know exactly what he means. Deciding for the moment to pocket my belief that the 'Great River of Munster'/*Abhainn Mhór na Mumhan* belongs to all the people of Ireland, I respond calmly,

'I know,' and speedily add the explanation and apology, 'I am walking the Blackwater from source to sea. And this is Day 5 of my journey.'

Having heard my explanation, he noticeably relaxes. And then, pressing home the advantage, I add that Annraoi Ó Liatháin walked the Blackwater in 1959 and wrote a colourful, lyrical account of his experience in *Cois Móire*. The ghillie, swarthy and approximately forty years of age, is not at all interested, but his next comment, delivered in a strong Cork accent, offers me a piece of very helpful advice,

> When you get to the end of this place [Estate], you'll find a large drain blocking your path but, if you walk back along the drain, you'll find a fallen beech tree that you can use as a bridge.

Walking together, we saunter towards the anglers' shelter (a cricket pavilion brought from Sussex), he informs me, in answer to my query, that the level of water is too low for good fishing. To illustrate his point, he indicates the marker that shows the level of the water, and adds that it should be two to three feet higher at this time of the year. We bid one another goodbye, and thus my visit to Careysville is brought to an amiable conclusion.

Careysville House, land and fishing rights were acquired by the Duke of Devonshire in the 1930s and are now managed under the business title of the Lismore Estate. The fishing fee for a day or a week is exorbitant, probably a €1,000 a day. At this very moment Lismore Estate is embroiled in a dispute with the OPW concerning the removal of the weir to enable the returning salmon to travel unhindered up the Blackwater. Their *rationale* for this request is that the weir is hindering the free movement of salmon, trout, the freshwater lamprey and the allis shad to their spawning beds further up the river. A spokesperson for Lismore Estate has defended the existence of the weir, claiming that the migrating salmon use the pass in the barrier and that the pool offers the fish a convenient resting habitat on their journey to the spawning beds. The Duke of Devonshire, the owner of Lismore Castle and Careysville, has threatened to initiate legal action against the Irish government to prevent the loss of his lucrative fishing business. Luckily in 2011, wiser council prevailed in advance of a court case, according to which the parties involved 'will bear their own costs and Lismore Reality Ltd and Lismore Trust Ltd will pay all reasonable costs of the removal of Clondulane Weir to allow for the free and uninterrupted passage of migratory fish, as required by national and European legislation.' Negotiations have been on-going and in the interim the weir remains in place.

The presence of weirs on the Blackwater posed problems for people navigating the river even during the reign of Henry VIII (1491-1547) when a 'statute was enacted aimed at the removal of obstructive weirs.'[5] The problem

---

5   O'Keeffe & Simington, p. 51
6   Ibid

persisted to the early seventeenth century and caused tension 'between those who wanted to remove and those who wanted to retain them.[6] Obviously, the weirs caused problems for woodmen who floated 'sawn timber...down the Blackwater to Cappoquin, where it was loaded on lighters for transport to Youghal.'[7]

Four centuries prior to the Elizabethan plantation, this stretch of the Blackwater valley was covered in dense woodland. Led by Sir Walter Raleigh and later by Richard Boyle, the commercial felling of the great Irish oak woods began in earnest in the last decade of the sixteenth century. Raleigh brought in 200 English timber workers to fell the mature oaks that adorned the banks of the Blackwater. Such was the intensity of their enterprise that within a century the character of the landscape had been altered dramatically.[8]

I stride off across an extensive field that leads to another field round which the river bends in a parabola-like curve. Across the river stands a belt of mature Scotch pine trees that offer shade for the patient anglers who return day after day in the hope that good fortune will favour their perseverance. Beyond the trees, the farm land rises steeply to an altitude of 300-400.' Having reached the boundary of the Careysville Estate, I find the fallen beech that offers me a safe bridge into the next farm and into the next townland of Kilbarry where momentous events occurred on Sunday, 26th June 1920.

Here in Kilbarry my thoughts turn to three English gentlemen who found, to their great personal discomfort, that Irish hospitality did not extend to them on their fishing trip. I am, of course, referring to three of the leading commanders in the Fermoy military barracks during the Irish War of Independence (1918-21): Brigadier General Cutbert Henry Tindall Lucas and his companions, Colonels Danford and Tyrell. Lucas, a veteran of the Boer War, had fought at Gallipoli during World War 1. The prospect of a relaxed days fishing on the Blackwater must have made him and his companions discount any danger to their personal safety. Liam Lynch, the IRA commander had hatched a daredevil plan to abduct General Lucas along with his companions – an escapade intended to embarrass the British military command and to further undermine the stability of colonial rule in Ireland.

IRA volunteers had observed the movements of the military personnel from Fermoy to Kilbarry and quickly conveyed the information to Lynch and his fellow-conspirators, Sean Moylan, George Power and Paddy Clancy. Moylan had provided the car for the operation and had picked up Lynch

---

7   Ibid
8   Smyth, William, J. *Map-Making, Landscapes and Memory: A Geograpy of Colonial and Early Modern Ireland c. 1530-1750,* Cork University Press, 2006, p. 93-95

Area where General Lucas was captured

along with his assistant, Power. Meeting Larry Condon at the site of the operation, he directed their attention to a small fishing lodge which he believed was occupied by a number of British soldiers, detailed to escort the officers. At a given signal, the four IRA men charged the house but only found an old lady and a young girl. A search for weapons in the house yielded nothing. The band of volunteers remained hidden in the shrubbery for an hour until they saw three men approaching from the direction of the river. The two officers and their batman put up no resistance and were brought inside the fishing lodge. The third officer who had remained on the riverbank was taken into custody and brought to the Lodge where the batman prepared a meal for the prisoners.

The decision by the IRA to use the officers' car, in addition to the car that Moylan had borrowed earlier, to transport the prisoners led to unforeseen consequences. Moylan and Power drove ahead with one of the prisoners while Clancy and Lynch travelled in the second car with Clancy sitting between General Lucas and Col. Danford. After some time, Power, noticing that the second car was no longer following behind them, ordered the driver to turn around to retrace their journey. After a short distance they found the second car ditched and a dog fight in progress between Clancy and Danford and between Lucas and Lynch. A shot rang out that resulted in one of the British officers being wounded. His companion, realising that further resistance would be fruitless, immediately surrendered.

General Lucas and Col. Danford had held a conversation in Arabic during which they had decided to overpower their captors. The driver lost control of the vehicle and crashed into the margin. Lynch and Moylan decided to release Col. Tyrell to attend to their wounded colleague. Subsequently, the IRA held Lucas captive at a number of secret locations in Counties Limerick and Clare and succeeded in frustrating the enormous dragnet that the military launched all over Munster.

In reprisal, the Fermoy military subjected the town to a night of unrestrained lawlessness during which private property and shops were burned and looted. Lucas cut through a bar in the window of the room where he was imprisoned and succeeded in making his way to Pallas, RIC barracks. The incident represented a major propaganda victory for the IRA who, according to Lucas, treated him with due chivalry during his captivity. For weeks afterwards, young local men whistled and taunted the military with a ribald version of the popular ballad, *Where the Blarney Roses Grow*,

Twas on a Sunday morning out a-fishing he did go,
And when he had his fishing done he was caught by Who You Know!
They said, 'You'll have to come with us, or else down you will go
For that's the way we'll treat you where the Blarney Roses grow.

Visitors from the UK continue to visit, fish and live along the Blackwater. A

Kilbarry riverbank

more recent arrival, Doug Lock, having grown up in rural Devon, developed a passionate love of fishing and rock music. His love of rock led to his involvement with well-known groups such as Motorhead and the Moody Blues.

In 1998 Doug Lock put aside his guitars, drums and music sheets. He settled down with his partner, Joy Arnold, here in Kilbarry where he ran salmon fly-fishing courses and bred skewbald ponies. Such was his enthusiasm for this equine species that Lock established the Irish Piebald and Skewbald Association and succeeded in having these horses recognised by the Department of Agriculture. A brass plaque on the entrance to his residence, Ghillie Cottage, features the inscription, 'Tresspassers will be Prosecuted, Poachers will be flogged and sent to the Colonies.' That could have been me, but, I imagine if Doug found me crawling under his electric fences, his sense of humour would probably have come to my rescue and sent me back to the Blackwater.

Today tranquillity hangs over Kilbarry and the Blackwater. The dramatic events of that Sunday in 1920 have almost been forgotten except in the memory of the older generation. Later, during the course of writing this account, I asked a number of local people who told me that they had never heard of the episode.

I hope to meet and to walk with my colleague, Hannah Joyce, from UCC. Hannah grew up on a nearby farm in Waterpark. Hence, she is familiar with the river and its environs from her childhood.

Emerging through a narrow opening in a hawthorn hedge, Hannah walks towards me. She tells me that she hasn't walked the banks of the Blackwater for thirty years. Her most vivid memory of that time seems to be the stern warning of her parents to keep away from the dangers. She recalls that the drowning of two water bailiffs some time in the 1950s frightened all the parents of the place. Now living about a one-hour drive from the Blackwater, she hasn't forgotten how to cope with electric fences.

We ramble along and time passes almost unnoticed, passing Capel Island where we sight the sole occupants of this two acre island – a gennet and a goat. No one knows for certain how these close companions found such an unlikely sanctuary. I have been informed by a local resident that the animals manage to survive the floods by retreating to a raised tree stump which has just about sufficient standing room for them. A vet has examined both animals and found them to be in good condition with adequate herbiage and grass to graze that ensure their welfare. The winter months provide a tougher test but, nevertheless, they pull through though leaner than the sleek animals that we now observe. We pass a young man at work with a strimmer, clearing away the weeds, willow and alder saplings that could impede the casting of a dedicated angler who has paid a tidy sum to enjoy a few days on this great salmon river. One such angler, mid-stream in the low waters, ignores our arrival, such is the intensity of his task. Hoping to draw a comment, I call out, 'The patience of the angler!' To which he instantly responds, 'You need lots of it.' A repartee that tells the whole story of his day's fishing. Perhaps, he may not catch a single fish on the Blackwater but he will savour the gentle breeze, the fresh air, the flowing water and the sight and sounds of the animals that graze peacefully in the fields that slope gently to the water edge.

We pass through Ballydorgan, Rossnabrone, Ballynerroon West and East and Cloonbeg. Across the river are the townlands of Inchaleama, Carrigane and Mocollop. I am anxious to sight Mocollop Castle, the ruins of which stand sentinel over the Blackwater. Written references to Mocollop (Máigh Cholpa, 'The Plain of the Steers?') appear in documents as early as the thirteenth century. Cromwell's guns reduced what must have been a formidable stronghold, built by the Desmonds, to protect their extensive territories along the river. Originally built in 1220 but rebuilt substantially in 1432, it contained a circular keep with square towers at the base, a type of fortification which, according to J.R. O'Flanagan was 'similar in

Mocollop Castle keep

Remnant of Mocollop Bridge

character to many of the old border-fortresses between England and Scotland.'[9] O'Flanagan also tells us that the 'winding staircase is still perfectly tolerable, and is worth ascending for the sake of the rich prospect from the summit of the castle.'

A short distance upriver from the old castle, a wooden bridge spanned the Blackwater, until it was swept away by a flood in 1838. The embanked approach on the Waterford side is still evident though largely obscured by trees and other vegetation, while on the Cork side one can still make out the remnants of the stone abutments that supported the timber structure. The approach to the vanished bridge is faintly evident in the townland, the palimpsest of another time almost forgotten except for a few keen historians who scan the pages of the landscape.

Niall O'Brien, a farmer and historian, who lives a short distance away from where we now stand, writes that the early Mocollop ferry and later bridge linked Kilworth to the *entreport* of Tallow through which goods were imported and exported but the development of the modern Tallow-Fermoy road led to the decline of the Mocollop route. Niall has been fascinated by the topic of trade and navigation on the Blackwater for many years. With such a passionate interest, he has uncovered an enviable amount of archival material that professional historians had assumed to be lost. The outcome of this labour of love was the publication of his book, *Blackwater and Bride: Navigation and Trade, 7000BC to 2007*, in 2008.

---

9   O'Flanagan, p. 61

Before leaving Mocollop, Hannah and I gaze across the river at a lush field of grass from which silage has been harvested earlier. Stretching from Carrickabrick to Cappoquin, the marginal or contiguous fields along the Blackwater have been designated as a Special Area of Conservation (SAC) under EU legislation. This river-side land is subject to winter inundation and, consequently, attracts waders such as curlews, godwits and especially whooper swans. The whoopers migrate from Iceland to winter here where the mild temperature and a ready supply of grass, winter cereals and formerly sugar beet enable them to survive in relative comfort until March-April when they return to Iceland where they rear their young.

Driving from Fermoy to Lismore, one tends to assume that the whoopers are sheep rather than swans. A few years prior to my walk, my brother Joe, assuming that they were farmyard geese, tried to take a close-up photograph but only succeeded in scaring them away like the young William Butler Yeats at Coole Park,

> The nineteenth Autumn has come upon me
> Since I first made my count;
> I saw before I had well finished
> All suddenly mount
> And scatter wheeling in great broken rings
> Upon their clamorous wings.

The riverside farmers show a great deal of tolerance to these wonderful snow-white creatures with their beaks of yellow and black that winter in their fields and help themselves to the farmers' grass and other crops. Flocks average around three hundred birds most winters but their numbers can vary, depending on the severity of the weather. By late March or early April, they depart for their breeding grounds in the far north.

Leaving Mocollop behind, the Blackwater has expanded into a great mass of flowing water with its tributaries, the Funcheon and the Araglin, having joined it from the hills to the north. We skirt around minor lagoons and thickets of sally trees (*Salix cinerea*), but eventually the ground becomes too wet, and we're forced to retreat to the nearby road close to the river. From there we set our sights on Ballyduff, a quiet village slumbering in its natural afternoon siesta, on the Waterford side of the boundary that separates Cork and Waterford. We will reward ourselves for all our trundling troubles with a cup of tea or a glass of ale.

Crossing the old iron bridge over the Blackwater, we pass the small Carnegie Library, the local parish church, community hall and a few quiet shops. To our dismay, all of the five public houses are closed so a large paper cup of coffee from the machine in the Centra supermarket suffices. Within a short time, we strike it lucky when the doors of the 'Sibín' open for business.

Formerly owned by the Feeney family, the bar has been renovated and expanded to suit the needs of the present day clientele. Hannah reminisces about attending school and going to Sunday Mass in the local church though her home place lies in the nearby parish of Castlelyons which is in the diocese of Cloyne. A young local man informs us that the entertainment at the Booley House has concluded for the summer. This form of entertainment – music, sketches, cabaret as well as storytelling is quite unique to Ballyduff, and, as such, it attracts both local people and tourists. The word 'Booley' is derived from the old Gaelic practice of 'booleying' which involved moving livestock to the higher pastures in summer where the family, or a younger member, would live with the herd while sheltering at night in a temporary building.

Glancing at my watch, I realise that it is almost five o'clock, and that I must leave the company to complete the remaining five miles to Lismore.

The quiet village of Ballyduff

The young local man has kindly agreed to drive Hannah back to her car which is parked four miles away in Waterpark. I wave goodbye to Hannah, now invisible behind the blacked-out windscreen of a boy racer type car. I am on my own again and feeling sluggish after the good fare of Ballyduff.

I slip through a gateway on the northern side of the river, walk past a herd of bored cows, climb over an electric fence and pass through two fields from which silage has recently been cut. I hug the river bank, bedecked with angling huts and stands at varying intervals. All is quiet with only a few sleek herds of sucklers grazing contentedly and swatting the troublesome flies with their tails. After one mile, I sight Fort William, the former residence and fishing lodge of the Duke of Westminster. I have since learned that the house and 400 acres have changed hands again for the princely sum of €8 million – an apt illustration of how marketable an estate with fishing rights on the Blackwater remains for those who have the means to acquire possessions on such a scale. Nearby lies the Glencairn Convent in which a community of Trappist nuns reside who keep the rule of silence and support themselves by producing their own vegetables, bake their own bread and design and print memorial cards.

The sluggish feeling has abated and I stride out along a cowpath. I make headway and savour the solitude that envelops the water and the land. Then back to the retaining bank, built to contain and channel the seasonal floods of winter-time and those that occur during periods of heavy rainfall when the river invades this low-lying land, making it a haven not only for the whoopers but for other waders who chose to winter here. Gradually the effort of walking begins to take its toll and I find my energy levels steadily dropping but there is no other option only to trudge on through these undisturbed fields that seem to recall a sense of bygone times. Nearing Lismore, I know that I have entered the Lismore Castle estate when I sight an enormous, prize-winning Hereford bull, quietly chewing the cud, and supervising a herd of Friesian weanlings that keep him company now that the great beast has concluded his task of impregnating their mothers to produce the next generation of calves.

Keeping a peeled eye on the bovine behemoth, I stick closely to the river course in the presumptuous strategy that the water offers an escape route if the chewing giant should head in my direction. But only the distracted calves come nosing at my heels and, to my annoyance, persist to the very fence.

I had a strange sensation on this particular evening. For no particular reason a cloud of despondency descended me. It suddenly dawned on me that my initial excitement at the prospect of walking *Abhainn Mhór na Mumhan*

Lismore callows where whooper swans winter

was now beginning to wane. I actually asked myself what was I doing here. Was I playing a childish game of lost adventure? I felt like an intruder and a fake in a world where I didn't really belong. I am reliably informed that this a normal enough reaction about the halfway stage in a physically challenging undertaking. You begin to doubt yourself and to suspect your motives for undertaking the challenge. To be honest with you, I felt like packing it all in and returning to my wife, my family, my cat and my garden where I belonged. On the other hand Dervla Murphy does not seem to have encountered this low trough in her travels along the Blackwater:

> Here in west Waterford the river has come a long way from its source near the Cork/Kerry border...It flows between steep wooded ridges – sombre in winter, lacy green in spring, heavily green in summer and in autumn a glowing conflagration...one winter morning I met an otter on the path, sitting on its haunches, sucking a swan's egg. (Irish Times)

The magic and the mystery of the great river has dimmed for me, in fact, I feel as if I am an uninvited intruder in comparison to Dervla Murphy who has described her own intimate relationship with the Blackwater in such resonant prose.

Thankfully the clouds of this fleeting despondency vanished as quickly as they had come. I was an empty vessel once again ready to be filled by the wonders of the river. The swallows skim the glassy surface – a sure sign that rain is on the way. A greyness masks the surrounding fields, the trees and the sky overhead. Anticipation of arriving at Lismore Bridge with its towering Castle has receded, leaving me to anticipate the comforts of warm accommodation instead. Anyway, Ballyin House and gardens halt my walk along the river and force me to detour though the margin of Lismore golf course on to the road from Ballyduff. I had planned a stroll across the bridge and, perhaps, a short sojourn in the Red House pub to savour the local atmosphere. Lismore has attracted and continues to attract writers, anglers, dukes, dancers, princes and other visitors who have left numerous accounts of their impressions. Hardly necessary for me, therefore, to add another ream of prose to what has already been recorded. Instead, I will let Mr and Mrs Hall tell their readers of the grand sight that unfolds on Lismore bridge,

> And the castle, high above the level of the water, is kept in view nearly all the way, and crowns a landscape that is at once magnificent and graceful. The castle is situated on a steep rock which rises perpendicularly from the river. To look down from one of its chamber windows would make the clearest head dizzy, and there is a tradition that James II darted back in terror when he was conducted to a lattice to take a view of the surrounding scene; the window still bears his name.[10]

J.R. O'Flanagan similarly extols its beauty,

> Lismore now appears above the trees on the south side of the river – the majestic castle, seated proudly on its throne of rocks, and the slender spire of the cathedral shooting into the liquid sky.

And even the nationalistic Annraoi Ó Liatháin, with all his love of Gaelic antiquity, allows his account to take flight,

> *Eiríonn sé go maorga aníos as mothar crann agus crochann a chuid túiríní agus túr go hard os cionn na habhann. Is cosúil é le Lios na Sí nó dún i scamall taibhrimh.*[11]

According to the Halls, there were no fewer than forty-two salmon weirs on the Blackwater between Youghal and Lismore,' and they add that the one [weir] immediately under the castle was the most productive where up to 600 fish could be taken at a time. Mr & Mrs S.C. Hall first toured the country six years before the desperation of the Great Famine afflicted the labouring classes and cottiers.

With such thoughts and feelings coursing through my brain, I turn my back on the town and head for Ballyrafter House Hotel (*Baile an Reachtaire,*

---

10 Mr & Mrs S.C. Hall, *Hall's Ireland: Mr & Mrs Hall's Tour of 1840,* condensed edition, Sphere Books, London, 1984.
11 *Cois Móire,* lch, 116, 'It [castle] rises majestically upwards to exhibit its towers and castellations high over the river. It resembles the fairy stronghold or castle of our dreams.'

Lismore Bridge

'The Homestead of the Steward') where Joe and Noreen Willoughby extend a warm welcome to *Walking Man*. Later on that night, I confide the purpose of my mission to them.

After a delicious dinner, I join the chat in the lounge bar where anglers exchange stories, debate the virtues of various baits and the best pools along the river. Joe supplies the rods and all the necessary tackle along with taking an active part in the management of their charming and commodious hotel which was in times past a hunting lodge belonging to the Duke of Devonshire. Joe confides that the Duke calls round and enjoys a pint in the company of the locals. The fleeting thought crosses my mind what would I have said to him if I had met him on the banks: would I have been so bold as to question his ownership of the fishing rights along the Blackwater or would I have opted to discuss less contentious matters.

Sir Walter Raleigh

In 2008, however, one persistent RTÉ journalist, Liam O'Brien, managed to arrange a meeting with the Duke as part of a radio documentary, 'Fishing the Blackwater.' Descending from a line of aristocrats, Peregrine Andrew Mornay Cavendish (known to his friends as 'Stoker'), 12th Duke of Devonshire is a close friend of the Prince of Wales and acts as Her Majesty's representative at Ascot. His principal residence is Chatsworth in the Peak District, Derbyshire where he lives with the Duchess. Their house has 365 rooms and a vast estate that amounts to 200,000 acres. In contrast, his Lismore estate of 1,000 acres plus tracts of mountain land is modest. An aristocrat manages to pick up a range of verbal thrusts, argumentative sallies and, of course, anticipation of your opponent's queries. Liam Ó Brien lost round one when he conceded the right to the Duke to pick the venue.

The background of this documentary involved a controversy between people with fishing interests in Youghal Harbour, the Youghal Urban District Council (UDC) and the Duke who informed the individuals concerned that he owned the bed of Youghal Harbour, and that, consequently, his permission would be required to place fixtures in the harbour for the purpose of mussel harvesting.

In fact, the Duke owns 2/3 of the fishing rights of the Blackwater from Youghal to Cappoquin, approximately 18 miles of river, and the full stretch of river from Cappoquin to Lismore. Accordingly, fishermen were/are obliged to pay for an annual permit to allow them fish in the harbour and on the river. Relations between the boat fishermen and the Lismore Estate seem to have been generally conducted in a spirit of cordial co-operation. Nevertheless, the Duke does not hesitate to safeguard his ownership which, he claims, dates back to the Earl of Desmond, to Sir Walter Raleigh, as the Duke conceded in the interview due 'to a series of convoluted and complicated happenstances, we do own quite a large part of the Blackwater.'[12] Even in the context of the current suspension of salmon fishing, the Duke has been careful to point out that his rights are only 'suspended' but not 'abandoned.'

---

12   Duke of Devonshire in 'Fishing the Blackwater,' April 2008

Two legal cases, featuring the right to fish, in 1826 and 1827, were decided in favour of the Duke. Subsequently in 1882, the House of Lords delivered a judgement confirming the ownership and the rights of the Duke of Devonshire.

O'Brien interviewed a number of the stakeholders on the subject of the ownership of the fishing rights on the Blackwater and repeatedly posed the question, 'Have you ever met the Duke?' Finally, this intrepid young journalist succeeded in arranging an interview with the Duke in Pratt's Gentlemen's Club, St James's Place, London. Clubs are, of course, quintessential English institutions into which Irishmen seldom stray. Even in contemporary society, women are not accepted as members of this world of privilege and power. In conceding the venue, the journalist

The 12th Duke of Devonshire

conceded the advantage as the Duke opened play with a strong forearm, welcoming and relaxing his interviewer, with deft silky replies. Even when O'Brien managed a volley, his opponent smoothly discouraged any further daring questions. Within ten minutes it was game, set and match to the elder Cavendish over the youthful O'Brien.

Nevertheless, Ollie Casey, a former member of Youghal UDC, is adamant that Folio 1645 in the Land Registry shows that the Youghal Harbour Authority (now the UDC) owns the riverbed from the Sloblands, heading out into the river for hundreds of metres and all the way out on 'our' side of the river as far as Dysert on the front strand.[13] Two diametrically opposed views. The Duke maintained in the radio documentary that his ownership of the river is 'firmly and securely based in law.' Ollie was later interviewed by Radio Yorkshire on a programme where the interviewer hoped that the Duke would participate and reply to his claim that Youghal UDC owns the river bed. Having spoken for half an hour, the interviewer failed to make contact with the Duke. The Duke did, however, met the UDC sometime after the radio programme and had hinted that some concession or arrangement might result from their meeting. This meeting duly took place without any tangible outcome being negotiated by the two parties.

To conclude Day 5, and on this occasion, I totally agree with the Duke in his comment that the 'Blackwater was the Valley of Slumber...a place where you sleep better than anywhere else.'

---

13   The reference to 'our side of the river denotes the town of Youghal, built on the west boundary of the harbour in Co. Cork where the speaker, Ollie Casey lives.

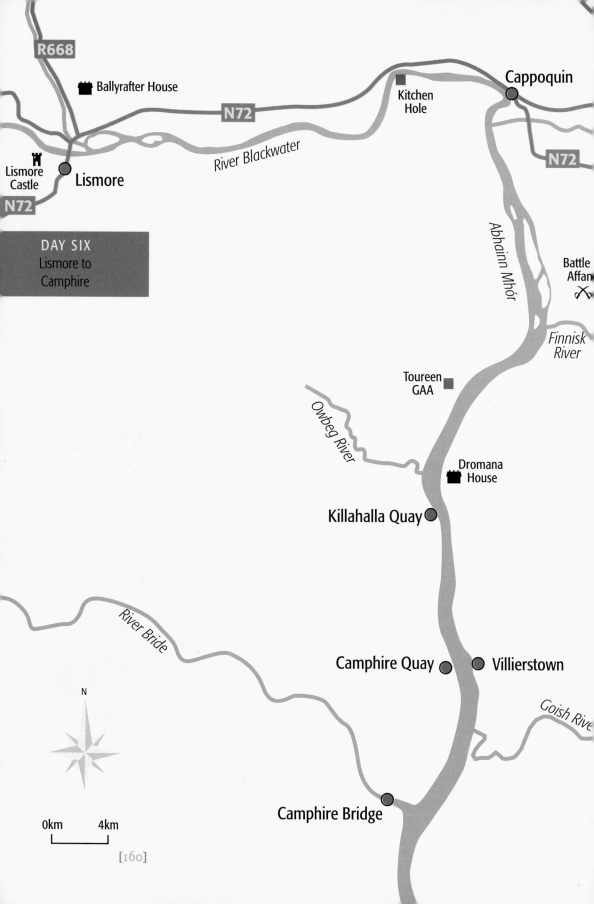

R668

Ballyrafter House

N72

Kitchen
Hole

Cappoquin

N72

Lismore
Castle

Lismore

River Blackwater

N72

DAY SIX
Lismore to
Camphire

Abhainn Mhór

Battle
Affan

Finnisk
River

Toureen
GAA

Owbeg River

Dromana
House

Killahalla Quay

River Bride

Camphire Quay

Villierstown

Goish Rive

N

Camphire Bridge

0km   4km

Lismore to Camphire

'Spring fishing opens in February, and some very large fish are caught; a forty-pounder is by no means unusual. The grilse begin to run in June, but the Spring fishing is by far and away the best.'[1]

MY NIGHT OF SLEEP has been punctuated by loud gusts of wind, blasting the tall coniferous trees around Ballyrafter House, and the incessant pounding of rain that persisted through the night. Mick Sheehan, YCR, blasts away the last prospect of some late slumber when he phones me live on his early morning chat-show at 7.30 a.m. Mick is well primed: how far have I progressed on my walk? What obstacles I've encountered? What sights I've seen and what are my impressions? Why I am walking the Blackwater and my plans to write a book on my experiences? For about fifteen minutes, Mick poses a pleasant flow of questions while I am propped up in bed. And to round off, he questions me about my plans for the day ahead which involves a walk from Lismore to Cappoquin and from there to Camphire Bridge where the Bride, the main tributary of the Blackwater meets the *Abhainn Mhór*.

Breakfast proves to be a delightful gourmet experience that includes cereal, fresh fruit and cooked trout. I may as well savour the culinary delights, harvested, or more appropriately angled from the river that has been my faithful companion for the last five days. The grey mood of the previous evening has lingered, causing me to drag my heels before setting off. The overnight rain, though persisting, has lightened off appreciably. Joe and Noreen bid me farewell as I face a short descent downhill to the junction where I can follow the Flats walk along by the river or take the

---

1   Adams, Joseph, *The Angler's Guide to the Irish Fisheries,* Hutchinson and Company, London, 1924.

footpath along the main road to Cappoquin. I opt for the direct road, fearing the fences and the pools of water that have built up overnight. AOL found this stretch with its numerous barb wire fences, drains and other obstacles most forbidding even though he was a formidable walker who claimed that he had once walked seventy-two miles in twenty-four hours. Besides, I have previously walked from Round Hill, a motte and bailey developed by King John, to the carpark below the cathedral of St Carthage. Some historians believe that it was from this dramatic landmark that Lismore got its name, *Lios Mór* ('the great ring fort').

Having arrived too late and too tired the previous evening to view the castle and the Blackwater, I decide to stroll to the great bridge before beginning my trek to Cappoquin. Standing at the mid-point of the giant arch, I glance left at the soaring spire of St Carthage's Cathedral, and to my right at the castle, built by the fifth Duke of Devonshire in 1775. The cathedral and castle represent two contrasting ages in the story of Ireland.

Little trace of the great monastery of Lismore, founded by St Carthage in the seventh century, has been located in the vicinity. For close to five centuries scholars from all over Ireland and also from continental Europe flocked to this very place. According to medieval sources, the mud and wattle huts of the scholars occupied an extensive stretch of the south bank of the Blackwater. Here they prayed and studied theology until the Vikings made their way upriver to plunder their manuscripts and other precious belongings.

The original castle, built by King John in 1185 on the great limestone outcrop over the Blackwater, was besieged and ravaged by fire over the centuries. In the Elizabethan era, Sir Walter Raleigh gained ownership of the castle and a huge estate of land stretching from Lismore to Youghal. Raleigh, however, soon sold the castle and his entire estate to William Boyle, the Earl of Cork. Boyle's descendents, allied through marriage to the Duke of Devonshire, have retained their title to the present day.

The magnificent bridge was built at 'the sole expense' of the fifth Duke of Devonshire in 1775. Thomas Ivory, a noted eighteenth century Irish architect, constructed the 100' arch to channel the broad river, and a series of six lesser arches under the rising causeway to take the flood waters when the river overflows. His engineering feat ensured that the main arch withstood the violent storm and flood of the 3rd November, 1853 though some of the dry arches were destroyed. [2]

---

2   O'Keeffe & Simington, p. 253-256

Lowering my hooded head against the wind and rain, I set off along a wide path. By my own reckoning, I should complete the four-mile walk to Cappoquin in an hour-and- a-half. The Blackwater, swollen after the rain and sporting a grey clayey hue, hurtles onward in its eagerness to immerse itself in the Atlantic. The fields that separate me from the 'Brown God' offer me a safety margin from the perils of walking its banks. I am no Huckleberry Finn who can relish the pleasure and abandon of hurtling downriver to the moorings in the towns or hiding in the islets to escape his pursuers. The wooded slope on the northern side of the road climbs steeply, first, to the heights of Glentan West and then to Monaman Lower. The district of Cappoquin has boasted a centuries-old reputation for growing fruit, especially apples. Cappoquin cider was a favoured drink for those seeking to quench their thirst in the summer time. The high well-drained ground with its exposure to the mellow sun of autumn aided the ripening process. Charles Smith (1715-62), the Waterford historian, described the production of cider in the Cappoquin area as follows,

> In the west of this county…our cyder has of late years been brought to great perfection; and besides enough for our own consumption some hundred hogsheads are yearly exported, in good fruit seasons, sent   by sea to Dublin and other places.[3]

Railway historians also testify to the fruitfulness of the area as large quantities of strawberries and other fruits were loaded on to the trains that ran from Mallow to Waterford at Cappoquin railway station. But the crowning testimony to the fruitfulness of this area is the river head sculpture that symbolises the river Blackwater on one of the Custom House windows in Dublin. When James Gandon was designing this building in 1785, he soon realised that the beauty and harmony of his design would be greatly enhanced by the addition of tasteful sculpture. Gandon, a young Englishman and unacquainted with building in Ireland, consulted his stone-cutting contractor, Henry Darley, who promptly recommended Edward Smyth, the son of a stone-cutter from Meath.[4] His recommendation

---

3   Smith, Charles, *The Antient and Present State of the County and City of Waterford,* 1746; 2008 limited edition published by Waterford Co. Council, cited by Elizabeth Healy, p. 20

4   Healy, Elizabeth, *The Wolfhound Guide to the River Gods,* Wolfhound Press, Dublin, 1998, p.7

proved to be an inspired choice. Smyth suggested to Gandon that the keystones in some of the arch windows should include carvings of the thirteen great Irish rivers with the Atlantic Ocean included as a fourteenth.

The head representing the Munster Blackwater is crowned with a pattern that clearly suggests a fruit basket laden with apples while underneath the basket, the salmon and trout, for which the Blackwater has always been recognised, are represented. Strands of river weeds hang over the cheekbones of the saturnine head.[5]

With such thoughts and recollections churning through my head, I saunter along until I come to a point where the Blackwater, curving to the north, flows alongside the road. Pausing to peruse an information board in the carpark, my eye falls on the line, 'The Blackwater's banks bear visible imprints of the progression from one age to another.' And if that is not enough to keep me reading, the next line stirs my romantic imagination, '...in the middle ages the area became adorned with castles and churches, including Kilbree Castle...' that stood directly across from where I now stand.

At the lower end of the carpark, a young man stands on the low wall directly over the river and throws out coils of line, laden with bait, over the river. Clad in torn denim jeans and a faded brown leather jacket with a baseball cap on his head, his energetic arm movements suggest an unusual

---

5   Healy, *The Wolfhound Guide to the River Gods*, p. 20

degree of eagerness. Pausing a short distance from him, I observe his casting for a while before casually querying,

'Are there any salmon down there?'

Possibly, sensing an unspoken implication in my question that his chances of catching anything are about as remote as winning the national lottery, the exuberance of his answer startles me,

'Hundreds...there's hundreds of them down there. The problem is to hook one of them before they move off up the river.'

And before I can ask a further question, he recommences the reeling in and casting off, no doubt envisioning with the right combination of skill and luck that the prize of a glittering salmon, snatched from the river bed, will be his. He means business and is not prepared to entertain further idle questions from passing walkers. Nevertheless, I am determined to fish some more information from him,

'What name is this stretch of the river called?'

The answer is given with the same energy and eagerness that characterises his fishing,

'It's the Kitchen Hole pool...they hole up here...dozens and dozens of them.'

Wishing him better luck, I saunter a few yards further on and then pause where an elder and gentlemanly-type of angler is engaged in the same frustrating quest of landing the elusive silvery fish. A relaxed smile from him encourages me to exchange a few remarks. Shifting his attention from reel and line,

> No luck this morning but it's nice to be out here... It's just a lovely soft drop of rain that should clear up within a short time...a lovely stretch of the Blackwater called the Kitchen Hole...It's called that name because this was the source of water for Salterbridge House up there on the hill.

A notice, erected by the Cappoquin Salmon Anglers' Association, refers to the long tradition of angling in the area and explains that the attraction of fishing here can be attributed to the spate rivers and streams that provide the Blackwater valley with 'excellent spawning and nursery grounds for salmon and trout.' The notice also warns anglers 'to give way to fly fishermen at all times.'

It is interesting to note here that Charles Smith, the eighteenth-century historian, recorded that country people gathered up horse-mussels from the Blackwater between Lismore and Cappoquin. He writes that 'seed-pearls' were occasionally found in them but adds that it was not 'for the sake of the mussel, or the thought of the pearl that these people gather up these fish, but for the shells, which they use for spoons.'[6] Clearly, Smith was referring to the freshwater pearl mussel (*Margaritifera margaritifera*) that is nowadays listed as an endangered species. He adds that the 'country people' gathered a type of manure from the river, known as 'triskar' which was 'a collection of weeds, grass, straw, mud...'[7] He further refers to the custom of bringing 'sea-sand' from Youghal up the Blackwater.

Smith's history of the county was first published in 1746 and a second edition was brought out in 1774. Realising the importance of his work, Waterford County Council published a modern edition in 2008 under the editorship of the county librarian, Donald Brady. It is from this edition that I am now taking relevant details.

Smith described the land lying along the Blackwater as 'well-cultivated' especially as limestone was available at Lismore, Cappoquin, Toureen and Affane. [8] In contrast he described the land to the north and in many other parts of the county as being 'rude...little removed from the state in which nature originally formed it...'

Resuming my walk, I pass the lodge at the entrance to Salterbridge House which remains discreetly out of view from the lower level of the Lismore-Cappoquin Road. Built by Richard Musgrave in 1750, this large Victorian residence was reconstructed in 1949 and occupied by the Chearnley family until 1947.

Amazingly, the upheaval of the Irish War of Independence did not affect the ownership of landed estates and great houses here in west Waterford. Whether such preservation of the social and economic status quo can be attributed to a benign relationship between the landed class and their tenant farmers or, perhaps, a lucky anomaly that enabled the Keanes, Musgraves, Duke of Devonshire, Chearnleys, Villier-Stuarts and other families to retain their ownership, cannot now be easily explained. Today in the twenty-first century, one senses an air of quiet contentment and harmony over the area.

Step by step, I near the peaceful and almost forgotten town of Cappoquin, languishing at the bend on the river. Rows of tall poplars line the margins of the river through which the anglers tread their paths from January to October. I recall my early memories of Cappoquin as the source from which the salted bacon came, the staple diet for farming families before refrigerators came into common use. I can still recall listening to a

---

6   Smith, Charles, p. 194
7   Smith, p. 40
8   p.40

conversation between my parents one Sunday evening when they discussed the subject of feeding a growing family of six children. Their proposed solution was to send a fatted pig to the bacon factory in Cappoquin, have it salted there and then returned in a barrel from which all of us could enjoy a good meat diet with home-grown potatoes, cabbage and milk. Initially, the novelty of having our own supply of bacon acted as an inducement to eat up; however, as the quantity of meat dropped in the barrel, so too did the flavour which, within a few months, became almost inedible. Nevertheless, we weren't going to disappoint our mother and father, and so we persisted eating up though not quite finishing off our portions until the work-men on the farm, my father and eldest brother could no longer cope with such pickled saline fare. The remaining portions were consigned to an abandoned quarry in the Glen.

Approaching the town, the old disused railway bridge stands over the river while a few slow-moving vehicles cross the Avonmore Bridge that carries traffic south to Youghal. Before heading for a coffee break, I walk to the middle of the bridge to observe the dramatic bend that alters the course of the Blackwater from flowing in a west-east direction to a north-south direction. How can such a dramatic alteration be explained? What geological events determined that the Blackwater, instead of following a predictable course towards Dungarvan, should make a full right-angle turn and flow, instead, southwards to Youghal harbour? Having followed the North Cork/Dungarvan syncline for 60km, the Blackwater at Cappoquin is only 18km from the sea at Dungarvan and at a height of only six metres O.D.' Instead of following the easier route to Dungarvan, the river opts for a significantly more challenging course. Its path, due south to Youghal Harbour, was barred by four sandstone synclines/ridges with crest lines of more than 100 metres. Similarly, the Rivers Lee and Bandon follow a due east course before turning dramatically south into Cork and Kinsale harbours respectively.

According to the local oral tradition, the Blackwater formerly entered the sea at Whiting Bay, about four miles east of Youghal. And in support of this belief, the storytellers cite the Gaelic name for Whiting Bay –*Béal na hAbhann* ('The mouth of the river').The first scientific theory posited by geologists was that of 'river capture.' In ancient times South Munster consisted of a system of ridges and valleys that ran east-west. These ridges and valleys were buried under a layer of soft chalk that sloped towards the south, consequently, the rivers flowed south according to the slope of the chalk. [9] The Blackwater was then a large south-flowing river that included much of today's Suir. The soft chalk was slowly worn away, so that the underlying east-west ridges and valleys were gradually exposed. The great rivers continued to flow southwards, but they now flowed across the grain of the countryside. In some places, these rivers managed to cut right through the gradually exposed east-west ridges such as the deep gorge that the Backwater has cut through in the Villierstown area. Geographers refer to the cutting of such gorges as 'Superimposed Drainage.'[10] The Dromana gorge, five miles south of Cappoquin, is an excellent example.

Following the erosion of the chalk, new rivers began to form in the east-west valleys, such as the Blackwater. Rivers, depending on their volume of water and the gradient of their flow, can be powerful agents of erosion. Not only do they deepen and alter their own courses but they can cut back into their valley heads to capture neighbouring streams. These streams/rivers then abandon their old course and join the more powerful river. This phenomenon is known as 'river capture' and is responsible for the complex pattern of drainage that has evolved in the upper catchment territory of our rivers.

Seventy million years ago the River Suir flowed south from Ardfinnan to Youghal harbour until an adjacent river flowing east eroded back into its valley. The old river bed through Ballinamult to Cappoquin dried up. Possibly, the Glenshelane and Finnisk rivers that join the Blackwater south of Cappoquin may be remnants of the ancient river system.

The unspeaking waters of the Blackwater will not easily yield up their secrets but the stones of the bridge on which I am now standing bear evidence of more recent events. This solid limestone bridge, originally named Victoria Bridge, is now called the Avonmore or simply Cappoquin Bridge. Built by Sir Richard Keane of Cappoquin House as a relief project during the Famine years, 1845-47, it was opened in 1851. The title 'Victoria' was later chiselled from the name plaque by local nationalists who resented the bridge being called after an English monarch. Stooping down, I can barely decipher the erased word from this palimpsest of stone as a faint outline of V.I.C.T.O.R.I.A. still lingers on the stone. The local IRA attempted to blow up the structure in 1921 and though they succeeded in breaching a

---

9 Herries Davies, G.L and Stephens, Nicholas, *The Geomorphology of the British Isles: Ireland,* Methuen & Co. Ltd., 1978, p. 103

10 The latter part of this paragraph is based on a note prepared by Charley Hayes, M.Ed, writer of geography secondary school texts.

span on the southern side, the bridge was repaired and continues to serve the community since those troubled times. I am reluctant to leave my viewpoint. To my left stands the red-roofed boathouse of Cappoquin Rowing Club. And below in the water two crews are limbering up for a training session. It seems that they are slow to get going but the 'f' word flies through the air and jolts the oarsmen into action. Cappoquin people are proud of the long tradition of rowing in the area. Their club premises served for many years as a concert venue and theatre where illustrious actors, such as Hilton Edwards and Micheál Mac Liammóir, brought Shakespeare to the community.

It is time to interrupt this riverine reverie. Up main street, past Uniacke's, Lehane's, Seargent's Garage, the Toby Jug and other business premises,to Barron's Bakery where I have arranged to meet brother Joe as well as Denis Burns. While I am waiting I enjoy a chat with a lorry driver from the Mount Melleray area, seven miles from Cappoquin on the lower slopes of the Knockmealdown mountains. Half expecting sympathy on his part for the neighbouring county of Tipperary in tomorrow's all Ireland hurling final, I pose the question,

'Who do you think will win?'

Allowing his fork and knife to rest for a moment, he tells me,

'The Cats, of course, by eight or nine points. I can't see Tipp matching them. They're not up to it.'

No, he won't entertain any possibility that Tipp may exact revenge for their defeat against the same opposition the previous year. Mention of the

Barron's Bakery

Cappoquin

Cats, of course, reminds me of the well known pub, 'The Cats,' where hearsay has it that young men, entering the Cistercian community in Melleray, have their last drink before forsaking the more conventional lifestyle for a life of prayer and meditation. Yes, he agrees that the drink-driving restrictions have hit the trade of rural pubs such as 'The Cats' but he can leave the car at home and stroll down the road three or four nights a week.

Joe is the first to arrive, having driven from Glanmire and picked up my heavy knapsack at Ballyrafter House. Then Denis appears, smiling broadly, and querying how my walk has progressed since he said goodbye to me in Millstreet on Day 1. We signal to the young lady behind the counter and order tea for three: a custard flap; a slice of Chester cake and apple pie. She informs us that she is studying Social Care in the Cork Institute of Technology (CIT), and that she has been working in Barron's for the summer. Denis jokingly wonders why she didn't opt for UCC where he and his colleague Dan O'Sullivan organise the course, 'Diploma for Learning Difficulty for primary and secondary teachers'.

The three of us settle down to a most enjoyable and relaxing chat about hurling; we are three hurling men though Denis has the main claim to fame, having won All-Ireland medals as a member of the Cork hurling panel three-in-a-row, 1976-78. The stories and the yarns about games and hurlers fly thick and fast among us. Time passes pleasantly though an insistent voice whispers to me, 'What about your walk? Time to resume your trek, *Walking Man!*' So after a restful hour in Barron's we depart. Denis intends to walk a few miles with me.

Just outside the door, I greet a tall man, wearing a trade-type coat with a few touches of flour who is engaged in removing cake and bread trays from his delivery van into a store next to the cafe. We exchange greetings and a few comments about the day and the weather prospects. Then it occurs to me that rather than pass anonymously through Cappoquin, I should let him know that I am walking the Blackwater, from source to sea and that I have two days left before reaching the end of my trail – the mouth of the river. His warm and spontaneous response startles and delights me.

'That's wonderful. I wish you luck.'

Later I realise that I have spoken to Joe Prendergast who manages the bakery with his wife, Esther Barron. Commenting that we have just enjoyed a pleasant visit to their cafe and sampled their produce, he explains that he has just returned from his Saturday morning delivery run to Dungarvan farmers' market.

Two years later, the story of Barron's Bakery was described in a book that has won considerable acclaim from newspaper reviewers and food experts. The survival of the Bakery since its foundation in 1887 to the present day is a tribute to three generations of the Barron family and their loyal workforce that continues to bake and market a variety of bread and confectionery despite the aggressive practices of the large retail outlets. Their bread – pans, cobs, grinders, basket pans, blaas and barmbrack, is still baked in the original Scotch brick ovens that give it 'a unique taste, flavour and crust.'

Bidding farewell to Joe [Prendergast] though adding that I will call again, I face up street to where Denis is searching in the boot of his car for some item. Instead of retrieving footwear or rain cover, he produces a seasoned, banded hurley with 'Cumann Barra' branded across it.

'You haven't really hung it up, Denis?'

Denis chuckles and explains,

'I bring it [the hurley] with me when I go walking; it's my walking stick. The old hip is giving me a bit of bother and I need it for a bit of support.'

In response my brother Joe produces a hurley and sliotar out of his boot and challenges Denis to an impromptu session on the streets of Cappoquin. Moving uphill, across Main Street into Castle Street, Joe fires a high looping ball to Denis who grabs it in his left hand and promptly returns a low well-directed ball to him. They continue with great glee for about three minutes, watched by an anxious house owner who fears that one of her windows may be shattered into smithereens at any moment. *Walking Man* is the only other spectator and he's focusing on the tight wrist-control that Denis is exhibiting in directing each ball low and straight to the target, typical of the Barrs, whereas the east Cork man [Joe] has an entirely different style of broad strokes with the hurley moving in an arc-type trajectory. The 'puck-around' draws to a close without any damage to windows, street lights or car windscreens, and the hurleys are returned to their respective car boots.

Standing at the junction of Main Street, Castle St and Cook St., we notice a large boulder resting against the wall of the Blackwater Bar and partly obtruding on to the footpath. Named the 'Cornerstone,' it is connected to the Faustian legend of a local nobleman, Tomás Bán Fitzgerald, who made a deal with the Devil in the guise of 'Maistíní' or Hell Hounds that in return for fleeting riches, he would surrender his first born son to them. Tomás, a bachelor, remained blithely unconcerned until his marriage twenty years later to a French noblewoman, who bore him a son, changed matters immensely. The 'Maistíní' soon returned to claim their payment but Tomás

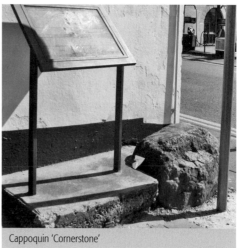

Cappoquin 'Cornerstone'

refused to surrender his beloved infant. Sometime later the child died of a mysterious illness to be followed by his mother who died of a broken heart. The grief-stricken Tomás forsook Ireland, swearing never to return, and lived out his days in a French monastery. Before leaving he took the cornerstone of the fireplace in his castle upon which the malign bargain had been written and rolled it away from his castle until it came to rest at the spot where it now rests.

Accompanied by Denis, I retrace my steps down main street, noticing the discreet paving stones that commemorate local events and personages. Outside the Toby Jug, my gaze rests on one such paving tile that preserves the memory of Pádraig Denn (1756-1828) who taught school here and composed Gaelic poetry devoted to the contemplation of the sufferings of our Saviour and the need for repentance from mankind. Denn was the first poet, writing in the Irish language, who had his poetry published during his own lifetime. *Aighneas an Pheacaigh leis an mBás* ('The Contention of the Sinner with Death') was published in 1814. A man of Calvinistic ardour, his poetry was recited at wakes in Munster into the twentieth century while today we can still listen to recordings of the Ring *sean-nós* singer Nioclás Tóibín singing poems and songs composed by Denn.

We press ahead: Denis with a hurley and *Walking Man* with his hazel stick. Pausing briefly, we observe the river negotiating the great bend or elbow before setting forth on its final surge to the sea. Hard to believe that steamboats once moored blow the bend and took passengers on pleasure outings to Youghal from 1878 to sometime in the 1920s. Steam propulsion seemed to offer a ready solution for coping with the problem of the daily tides. Vessels such as the *Star, Countess, Daisy* and *Fairy* enabled visitors and locals to enjoy the magnificent scenery along the course of the Blackwater from Cappoquin to Youghal. The *Star* offered 'three classes of passenger space: first class paid 1s 4d, second class paid 8d and the third class paid 4d for standing on deck.'[11] Daniel O'Connell's [The Liberator] jibe about the danger of such travel, 'How can the wives of Cappoquin...let their husbands trust their lives to an old tea kettle of boiling water,' could be attributed to political rivalry with the candidate of the Duke of Devonshire during an election campaign when the Duke had supporters transported to Waterford on such a craft.[12]

Even more dramatic than its change of direction, the Blackwater becomes a tidal river from Cappoquin south to Youghal. The daily rise and fall of the tides transforms the whole character of the river. From here it expands into a force of nature with a greatly broadened channel through which an enormous mass of water surges south only to slow and pause before the alignment of the moon and sun reverses its flow and sends an immeasurable volume of water back to where it has commenced its course. The muddy banks, over which a few waders pick their steps and probe for invertebrates, are banished from view; stranded boats rise and shift with the inflowing tide that laps around the piers where formerly sea-going vessels moored to unload their cargos of coal and other products, and, perhaps, equally significant, the communities of the east side and west side are divided to an extent that makes them almost strangers to one another.

We pause again at the lay-by in Drumroe (*Droim Rua*, 'the Red Ridge') to read the information board on the surroundings. Looking directly across the now broadened river, I take particular notice of the willow carr-type woodland intersected by numerous channels. The area is known as Lefanta (*Na Liatha Bána*), and, archaeological finds here offer evidence that this part of the Blackwater was possibly occupied by an early hunting-fishing community similar to that found in Mount Sandel on the River Bann. The plentiful availability of salmon, eel and trout in the river would have ensured a ready source of food for such early settlers. Closing my eyes, I envisage canoes hewn from large trees, paddled by skin-coated hunter-fishermen,

---

11 O'Brien, Niall, *Blackwater and Bride: Navigation and Trade, 7000 B.C.to 2007*, p. 245-249
12 O'Brien, p. 244.

gliding in and out of the series of channels that run through the grove of willows. But all we see in broad daylight are the single skullers of Cappoquin Rowing Club straining every muscle in their bodies to achieve that extra degree of strength and agility that will carry them to victory in the next regatta.

Forced away from the river, we follow the road to Toureen where we hope we can rejoin the Blackwater. *Giorraíonn beirt bóthar* ('Two shorten a road'), as the old Irish proverb tells us. Soon we reach Toureen Cemetery, and rather than walk past, we enter through the side gate and walk between the rows of graves and headstones, silently reading the names of families: McGraths; Powers; Fives; Dooceys; Kielys and other distinctive Waterford names, found here in the Déise. We traipse steadily along, discussing the pleasure of walking, the attractions of the area and previous visits until we come to the Toureen-Ballinwillin GAA field. Having read the information about 'the smallest club to win the Waterford [senior] championship on the lectern in the Market Square, Cappoquin, we're both interested in learning how this small club is managing to survive, considering that its potential for recruitment is entirely rural. Lacking even a small village, it draws its players from a limited number of local families who tend to be intensely committed to their teams: supporting the players; attending games; organising fund-raising events that will ensure the survival of their club. The club colours are red and white vertical stripes while the football side [Ballinwillin] wear royal blue and white. Their triumph over the famed Mount Sion team in the Waterford senior hurling championship in 1950 has been their greatest achievement – a true example of a David slaying a Goliath. However, a recent disclosure in the biography of John Keane, the *Unconquerable Keane: and the Rise of Waterford Hurling*, takes some of the gloss off their triumph. The author, David Smith, attributes the victory of the underdogs to a sporting gesture by Keane who pleaded with the referee not to send off a Toureen player early in the game as a depleted Toureen side would most likely be overwhelmed by the city team that contained all the stars. Keane, the captain of Waterford in their All-Ireland triumph, 1948, was hugely respected; consequently, the referee acceded to his plea, and due to his intervention, the offending player was allowed to stay on the pitch. The Toureen men proceeded to pull off the greatest surprise ever in the history of Waterford hurling.

Leaving the playing pitch behind us, the two of us turn left down a cul-de-sac that leads back to the Blackwater. Within five minutes, we reach the water edge where we fall into a silent reverie at the sight of the great body of water flowing past. Denis has to walk back to his car in Cooke Street but before parting we take a short break seated on a nearby stone. The invasive Himalayan balsam (*Impatiens glandulifera*), stands erect along the bank. A passing brush from an animal or a light tap from my walking stick causes the ripe pods to burst and scatter seeds all around.

Before saying goodbye, Denis catches me completely off guard when he comments,

'This is about you, Jim. Isn't it.?'

For a second, I remain silent before responding with some uncertainty, 'Yes, I suppose you could say that.'

He elaborates further,

> I said to Phil [Denis's wife], "Men need to undertake challenges" such as something like you're doing now.' And she replied to me, 'What are you going to do?'You see, women are different but we need some kind of benchmark to check where we are at certain stages of our lives.

Relaxing after the surprise of Denis's comment, I begin to recount how I described my motives for the walk to Noel Cronin, YCR, in an interview with him prior to undertaking this river journey.

> In a sense, I am connecting my past, my younger life in the Youghal area, to my present life in Kerry where the Blackwater rises. You could say, completing the circle...connecting my past and present lives.

Warming to the topic, I add some more thoughts,

> All journeys are a search for meaning. It's more than a straightforward walk; something else is going on at a deeper level.

Denis bids me good luck and turns to walk back to Cappoquin. I climb over a tubular gate into Tourin demesne, owned and managed by the Jameson family who live in Tourin House. Now I am on the land side of a huge embankment that keeps the Blackwater from inundating the land ahead. Knowing that the river flows close to me, I follow a browned track that the sheep graze on between the river and the wetter ground – the type of walking ground that I can exult in. The three Jameson sisters, members of the whiskey dynasty, manage the extensive gardens around the house and have commendably planted 70 acres of oak and ash that seem to be thriving in this lower wet ground. After half a mile, I encounter more briars, furze bushes and prolific stands of tall reeds (*Phragmites australis*). The situation rapidly deteriorates to such an extent that I have to beat my way through a dense mass of foliage which takes almost half an hour before I reach a solidly constructed barb wire fence that I just manage to surmount.

The most pernicious are the great growths of tussock sedge (*Carex paniculata*) that can grow up to 150cms with razor-sharp margins on its long tapering leaves.

Turning aside from my battle with the sedge and reeds, I pause at a small slip-way from which a local farmer and rowing enthusiast, Denis Murray, carries on a business venture that involves bringing individuals and groups for outings on the river. Denis, a seasoned member of the Cappoquin Rowing Club, made the decision in 2008 to diversify from his suckler cow farming by setting up his company, Blackwater Boating. Enjoying the goodwill of his neighbours, the Jamesons, he houses canoes, kayaks and other craft in their nearby farm buildings and launches them from the slip-way where I now stand. The presence of his parked jeep suggests that Denis is on the river with customers, guiding them safely along the river as well as informing them of the built and natural heritage of the Blackwater,

> It's not just canoeing. If you go out canoeing, you're looking not just at the river but at the history and environment of the area.[13]

How wonderful to know that members of the local community have begun to use the resources of the Blackwater in such an environmentally sensitive way.

The expanded Blackwater from Cappoquin to Youghal almost precludes me from describing the eastern side of the river. Despite being at a physical distance, I am determined to incorporate places and events in the barony of

'Hindu-gothic' gate lodge Dromana

'Decies without Drum.' Almost directly opposite Tourin Quay, the Fi(n)nisk (*Fionn uisce*, 'Fair water.') joins the Blackwater. The bridge over the river features the quaint but elegant Hindu-gothic gate lodge which is regarded by architectural authorities as the only example in Ireland of 'the Brighton Pavilion style of architecture.' The original structure was built in 1826 from wood and papier-mâché to greet Henry Villiers-Stuart and his wife Theresia Ott on their return from their honeymoon. The couple were so utterly charmed by the novel structure that they had it permanently built in stone some years later. [14]

The unique gate lodge remains obscured from my sight but an event that took place in the same locale three centuries earlier had profound repercussions for all of Munster. I am, of course, referring to the Battle of Affane (1565), between the forces of Gerald Fitzgerald, the Earl of Desmond and the Earl of Ormond, Thomas Butler in January 1565. The Fitzgeralds (Desmonds) controlled huge tracts of land in Cork, Limerick and Kerry while the Ormonds (Butlers) held sway in Tipperary, Waterford and

---

13 *Irish Examiner Farming* [supplement], interview with Conor Power, 'River of Opportunity,' May 27, 2010.
14 WWW. Archiseek

Kilkenny. Relations between these two great land-owning families had been characterised by rivalry and tension over disputed claims. The marriage of Gerald Fitzgerald to the widow of the Earl of Ormond in 1561 had eased the tension between the two families but the death of Lady Jane in 1564 saw old quarrels being resurrected again.

Desmond remarried and during his honeymoon he decided to sort out the failure of a kinsman, Sir Maurice Fitzgerald of Dromana, to pay due tribute to his overlord. Sir Maurice sought the protection of Thomas Butler to protect himself from whatever penalty Desmond would seek to exact. The forces of Desmond and those of Ormond came face to face in Affane in January 1565. By the end of the day three hundred men had been killed, including soldiers who in seeking to escape across the Blackwater were shot from armed boats and drowned. Ormond emerged victorious but Queen Elizabeth 1 was exceedingly annoyed by the spectacle of two of her loyal subjects resolving their conflict on the field of battle. Both men were summoned to London where Ormond succeeded in winning the Queen's favour but Gerald, the fifteenth Earl of Desmond was detained in the Tower of London for an extended period of seven years.[15]

Ironically, the sequence of historic events has unfolded in reverse for me. My walk began on Knockanfune Mountain where I saw the outline of the Earl's refuge, *Réidhtheach an Iarla* (see page 4).

Having emerged from the jungle of Tourin and gained higher pastures in Pallis, the expanding Blackwater lies beneath the woodland while across the river I sight Dromana house, probably the most dramatically situated of all Irish houses, perched high over the water on a rocky ledge that descends perpendicularly to where the river laps and lashes against its base; a Geraldine house and the home of the Villiers-Stuart family since the thirteenth century. Turning my back on Dromana and surveying the system

---

15 To mark the 450 anniversary of the Affane Battle, the Cappoquin Heritage Group have produced a concise and informative booklet that describes the background, the location, the course and the outcome of this conflict between the Fitzgeralds and the Butlers.

of grazing paddocks ahead, I immediately spot the Aberdeen Angus bull with this year's weanlings. The shortest diagonal route to the nearby road to Camphire would compel me to mix with the bull and his progeny. Instead, I follow the line of the electric fence while the livestock, on the other side of the fence, follow me in parallel motion. Fortunately, the roadside hedge allows for a quick exit back on to the Cappoquin-Youghal road. Following a gentle decline, I soon cross the Owebeg river (*Abha Bheag*, 'the little river'), which is something of a misnomer as its lower reaches are tidal and debar me from any attempt at wading across.

It is a pleasant Saturday evening; the easy atmosphere of the weekend has enveloped this wooded area on the western bank of the Blackwater. The western part of Co. Waterford, a hidden triangle of scenic and fertile land, stretches from Youghal Bridge to Cappoquin and Lismore and from there to Tallow and Ballyduff. It remains undiscovered by tourists, excepting the anglers, and has languished economically since the opening of the new Youghal bridge in 1963. The erection of a modern concrete bridge from Rhincrew to Ardsallagh placed an unmoveable obstacle in the way of ships travelling up the Blackwater to Cappoquin. The previous metal bridge (built 1883) had a swing-span that allowed sea-going vessels through in the convenient time of two and a half minutes.[16] However, the fact that river traffic had declined significantly by the late 1950s points to other factors such as the growth of road transport which offered a quicker service than vessels that were subjected to the delays caused by rising and falling tides.

Pondering on the beauty of land, trees and rivers of the *hidden triangle*, the song *Cois Abhainn Mhór na nDéise* comes to mind. Sung most fittingly by Nioclás Tóibín, it celebrates the natural beauty of a countryside rich in beauty, bird song and wild life,

> Is ró-bhreá an dúiche a mbéarfainn liom tú
> Ar chois Abha Mhór na nDéise
> Mar a mbíonn an smólach is an lon go ceolmhar
> Is fia na mbeann á thraochadh ann.
> Bíonn torthaí cumhra ar chrannaibh á lúbadh
> Is mil na gciar á thaoscadh ann;
> An chuach gan amhras i dtús an tsamhraidh
> Is an traonach ag labhairt sa bhféar glas.[17]

An idyllic picture that celebrates some of the most visually attractive and haunting landscapes that can be found anywhere in Ireland. Notice too how

---

16 O'Brien, p.327
17 CD, 'Nioclás Tóibín: Rinn na nGael,' Cló Iar-Chonnachta, 1999

the songwriter has added a claim, on behalf of the Waterford people that the Blackwater is their river, that it belongs especially to the ancient sept of the *Déise, Abha Mhór na nDéise.*

Having crossed over the Owebeg river and walked from Pallis to Killahalla (Coill na hAille, the Wood of the Ferry Ford),[18] the road veers back towards the Blackwater. Here an enclosed area of four to five acres has been colonised by Himalayan balsam or Bumbee as it has been nicknamed in the UK on account of the manner in which bees, in search of the copious quantity of honey within, immerse themselves so completely that only their rear ends can be seen. While the flower is attractive, the establishment of the species on such a successful scale here must surely mean that native species, such as purple loosestrife (*Lythrum salicaria*) is losing its habitat to this exotic plant. Similarly, extensive wet meadows on the east bank of the Blackwater, have been extensively colonised by this flamboyant invader. Reaching Killahalla Quay, I enjoy a grandstand view of the Blackwater, of Dromana House and of the woodlands on either side of the river. Here the river enters a gorge, flanked by steeply-sloped ground on both sides with coniferous trees on the west and deciduous on the east. A picture of harmony with the land channelling the water but unable to contain the mass of water on its seaward journey.

Vessels, such as *De Wadden*, moored here at Killahalla to unload coal for the merchants of Lismore and Cappoquin. Having discharged theirs cargo, the loading of pitt props for the coal mines of Wales and elsewhere, commenced. From here too, a light boat ferried local people across to Dromana. The age of shipping has passed and the channel has silted up with material shifted and transported by the Blackwater from its upper reaches. Today, people such as Barbara Grubb, Dromana House, wonder how the river with all its attraction could be made more accessible to visitors. The silted channels, the daily fall and rise of the tide plus the need for infrastructural development present daunting difficulties to be overcome. Great rivers are relentless in eroding their banks and in depositing material.

Niall O'Brien describes how a dance platform was often erected here when the pitt props were removed, and local people and others from across the river would came to socialise and dance to the quayside after their day's work. Even more fascinating are the details that the same author recounts

---

18   Power, Patrick, *The Place-names of Decies,* Cork University Press, 1952, p. 46; cited by O'Brien, p. 131

Dromana House

Dromana gorge

of the Dromana Ferry which he discovered on a 1767 map of the Blackwater. He narrates that when Earl Grandison, or any member of the Villiers-Stuart family, wished to travel to Youghal, their coach would be driven to Cappoquin and from there along the west bank to Killahalla. After a two-hour journey, 'a horn would sound to inform his lordship that the coach was ready. The family then crossed the river in a simple rowing boat and proceeded upon their journey.'[19] O' Brien adds that the meaning of the placename offers evidence that the ferry probably operated before the Norman invasion (1192).

Thankfully, the recent water-skiing venture, on this stretch of river, seems to have been wound up. A speed-boat with a fully throttled motor, toeing an attached skier, greatly diminished the tranquillity of the river. Today, a harmony of all the elements of nature pervades the scene apart from the quiet lapping of the water below the road. A drowsy heron, disturbed by my arrival, flaps his cumbersome wings and flies away to the sanctuary of the wooded slopes on the eastern bank. Following the quiet road with a slow contented pace, I marvel inwardly at the splendour of the great river, *Abhainn Mhór na Mumhan*, wishing that this glorious stretch would continue to the unreachable horizon of the ocean's curve. But soon, too soon, river and road divulge from one another. Yet, the steady rhythm

19 O'Brien, p. 131

of my walking allows me to absorb, to marvel and to reflect on the canvas unfolding before me. Car travel telescopes our experience of distance and time. While we spare precious time in our cars, we lose the physical experience of traversing distance, a task that the vertical human frame has been evolved to achieve. In opting to walk rather than drive, we are returning our physical being to a mode of translocation for which our feet, our frame, eyes and mind were originally designed.

After a distance of one mile, I reach the new concrete bridge over the River Bride (Camphire Bridge), the largest of all the tributary rivers flowing into the Blackwater. The Bride, though tied forever to its riparian overlord, deserves due recognition of its own. Flowing eastward for a distance of 54km (25 miles) from its source close to Glenville and following a parallel course to the Blackwater, it passes villages such as Rathcormack, Conna and Tallow. Below this latter town, the tidal waters surge almost as far as Tallow Bridge, a feature that allowed access to sailing vessels and other craft to Janeville Quay and to even to smaller craft close to Tallow Bridge Quay. Lacking the width and water mass of the Blackwater, vessels could not turn and were, therefore, forced to travel in reverse until rejoining the larger

Bridge keeper's cottage, Camphire Bridge

Harvested stack of Bride reeds, Camphire Bridge

river. The tide has begun to ebb and what stands out most notably are the muddy banks and stands of reed. A harvested stack of reeds has been placed by the bridge to remind passers-by of the former importance of Bride reeds for thatching in the area. The culture of harvesting the reeds has ceased in this area. People here in Coshmore and Coshbride refer to reeds as 'Spire,' clearly an Anglo-Saxon derivative. Reeds or 'spire' need regular cutting to guarantee that they reach thatching quality. Nowadays reeds are imported from Hungary and other eastern European countries.

Luckily, the records of vessels that passed under Camphire bridge from 1902 have been preserved. These log books show, for instance, that the bridge was opened 32 times in 1902, 30 times in 1903 and on 54 occasions in 1904. These vessels were mostly schooners, brigantines, ketches and motor boats. A smaller type of craft, lighters, used the river frequently without the bridge having to be opened. Coal was the main import with cargoes of 140 tons and 134 tons being imported in 1903 while potatoes, oats and timber were loaded for the return journey to Liverpool, Bristol and other ports.

I am due to be picked up here by my brothers Frank and Joe at 5.00 p.m. While waiting for their arrival, I look down below at the bridge keeper's thatched house and notice the wheel that was used to unlock the old bridge up to 1956 when shipping ceased on the Bride. The risen tide has transformed this tributary into a formidable waterway though upriver, it reverts to the status of a small and quiet-flowing waterway. In her teenage years, Dervla Murphy entered the Bride about a mile from where I stand without calculating the risk that the retreating tide entailed. Swept downriver and unable to return to her starting point or even to wade ashore, a greatly shaken young lady managed to haul herself to safety here at Camphire Bridge. Needless to say, Dervla went on to travel extensively in Europe, Asia, Africa and South America.

Sadly the Bride did claim the lives of three young men rowing across the river in a small cot. The purpose of their crossing was to bring a football for a local game between Lismore and Kilwatermoy. Their boat, unable to withstand the high water and the current of the tide overturned and the three men were drowned.[20]

After Frank and Joe arrive, we decide to do some exploration before heading to our old homestead in Clasheel, four miles north-east of Youghal. We follow the unsurfaced road to Camphire Quay which lies directly across

---

20   O'Brien, p. 130, as told to him by Frank Mills, 24 June, 2007.

the Blackwater from the Villierstown Quay. Frank is particularly interested in the land and the type of farming carried on the area. He tells us that international horse trials were held here a week previously on the estate of the late Susan Dobbs who began the trials in 2000 to provide experience for young riders. Now established as an annual event, riders, horse owners and other equine enthusiasts flock here from all over the country as well as from the UK. Featuring dressage, show jumping and cross country, the venture has been a major success for the organisers and provides a welcome boost for rural tourism and for local farm produce.[21] Today, all we see is the trampled grass and a few jumps waiting to be dismantled.

We gaze across the Blackwater at Villierstown Quay which served as a ferry landing point in the eighteenth century and afterwards as a 'stopping point' for passengers on the leisure steamers that opened up the Blackwater for tourists. A rowing boat was used to ferry passengers from Camphire to Villierstown at the cost of one penny per person. A large flat-bottom raft

---

21   Ray Ryan, 'Best Foot Forward for Horse Trials' in Irish Examiner, 22 July, 2013

Villierstown Quay with Knockmeldowns Mountains in background

was used to transport animals, carts and gentlemen's carriages. An ingenious method of powering the raft involved the use of a chain secured at both ends to firm steel posts. Two men worked a winch on either side which manipulated the chain, tied around a drum on the bottom of the raft, and, in this manner, local people could do business and socialise with their cross-river neighbours. Pupils, attending Lismore (CBS) used the ferry up to 1958 when Waterford Co. Council discontinued the service. Niall O'Brien offers the opinion that the river ferry created closer ties among the river communities than is the case at the present time.

Villierstown or *An Baile Nua* was founded by John Villiers-Stuart in the late eighteenth century to which linen workers from the north of Ireland were attracted with the offer of work in the area. Though the new industry faltered after twenty years, many of the families remained in the area, resulting in such unusual northern Irish surnames as Arrigan, Bullan, Doublet, Goodbody, Manktelow, Stears, Horson, Poyner, Sage, Boorn, Head, Gee and Iddon persisting there to the present day. The erection of a millennium stone at the crossroads in 2000 records a total of eighty-four surnames in the parish.

River Bride

Camphire Quay

Villierstown

Goish River

Camphire Bridge

N

Strancally Castle

Tower

R671

Knockanore
village

Poul na Béast

County Waterford

County Waterford

Old Strancally Castle

Clashmore Broads

Newport

Clashmore

Glendine

Licky River

Ballinatray
House

R634

Dairinis Island

†
Templemichael
Cemetery

Ardsallagh

County Cork

Youghal
Bridge

E30

Tourig River

Metal
Bridge

Cork/Waterford
county border

R634

Ferrypoint

0km   4km

E30

Youghal

Youghal
Harbour

Strancally to Youghal

'There are few localities in the British Isles so rich in picturesque scenery, historical associations and monumental remains as the Valley of the Blackwater.'[1]

Today is the final day of my Blackwater journey. For the last six days I have been cocooned in a world of my own making, casting the odd cursory glance at the billboard affairs of the outside world. So much so that it had almost slipped my mind that today is the Sunday of the All-Ireland Hurling Final between Tipperary and Kilkenny.

Frank drops me off at 6.45 a.m. close to the entrance of Strancally Castle. All is still and the stubble in the harvested field is laden with droplets of dew. Putting on my walking boots, I sight three fallow deer slinking silently into the Coillte plantation across the road. The sky is overcast and at this stage not even a vestige of the dawn light is filtering through the leaden pall overhead.

The nineteenth-century castle slumbers peacefully close to the banks of the Blackwater. Walking near the iron railings of the avenue, leading to the castle, I note the helipad from which the occupants of the castle can fly clean away to their destination either in Ireland or abroad or else they can take the cabin cruiser, berthed at a modern wharf, for a more leisurely outing either up or down the river. Lines from my teaching life flash across my mind,

This castle hath a pleasant seat; the air
Nimbly and sweetly recommends itself unto
Our gentle senses.

---

1   O'Flanagan, J.R., *Historical and Picturesque Guide to the River Blackwater in Munster*, 1944

Strancally Castle

...Duncan's reaction on entering Dunsinane Castle in Shakespeare's *Macbeth*. The modern castle here in Strancally (*Srón Caillí*, 'The Hag's Nose') was built c. 1830 by the architect brothers James and George Pain for John Keily who later became Sherriff of Waterford. From that time to the present day, a succession of owners have lived in the castle. Keily was replaced by the Whitelocke-Llyods, then came the Parkes and after them Mrs Henaghan who was followed in 1963 by a German educationalist, Dr Walter Greite. In 1976 ownership was assumed by the Croft-Greene family from Athlone. The Billensteiners came from Austria in 1995 and remained there until 2008 when the present owners, Michael and Giancaria Allen-Buckley, purchased the property.[2] Needless to say, *Walking Man* and the owners of Strancally Castle have lived and live in different worlds; nevertheless, the story of Dr Greite resonates with me.

Recalling an October evening, having cycled on my old Raleigh bicycle

2 Billensteiner, Friedrich jun. & Heffernan, Kieran, *The History of Strancally Castle*, 1996

the rising road from Youghal to our home in Clasheel, my mother Margaret told me that a college had been opened up for German students in Strancally Castle. She pointed to the report in the *Cork Weekly Examiner*.[3] Somewhat intrigued by the report, I set off on the old Raleigh the following Sunday to see the new college and, maybe, to espy some of the students in the castle grounds. Fortified with a bar of chocolate and a bottle of orange and driven by innate curiosity, I reached the entrance to the castle and glanced all around, hoping to see and, perhaps, to hear the guttural sounds of the Bavarian dialect floating over the tree tops. As the poet Walter de la Mare (1873-1958) wrote in *The Listeners*, 'All was locked and barred...'I knew full well that there were real people inside, not a 'host of phantom listeners.' Time passed and the story of the school was discarded to the bin of memory; however, this Sunday morning, forty-seven years later, the memory recurs and I wonder how long the project lasted and what the outcomes of this educational experiment were.

Dr Walter Greite, who owned a private college near Munich, wished to use the castle and its facilities as an adjunct to his German institute. Accordingly, he named his Irish school, St Marinus College, after an Irish monk who sought to preach the Christian faith in southern Germany but was murdered and buried there. Dr Grete's plan was to allow his students a six-month stay in Ireland to enable them to study and to improve their English while at the same time having an opportunity to learn more about another country and its people. School numbers soon increased to forty and Irish teachers were employed to teach Irish history and other subjects. From the limited evidence available, the school was managed efficiently but foundered after some years when Dr Greite and his wife, Charlotte, separated.[4]

Even though I am an intruder here, I sense a oneness between my presence and the stillness of the brooding woods. We seem at ease in one another's company. Nearing the boundary of the stubble field, I emerge on to the lane that leads downhill to Strancally Quay where a picnic table allows me to pause and to absorb the river at this early hour. A light mist shimmers over the still water which reflects the sky and the wooded slopes of the west and east bank . A solitary heron observes me from the muddy banks that the ebb tide has exposed. Two little egrets, alarmed by my arrival, fly across to the opposite shore where they recommence their probing for invertebrates

---

3   *Cork Weekly Examiner*, Thur., October 3rd, 1963.
4   *Cork Weekly Examiner, Oct. 3, 1963*, and reproduced in *the History of Strancally Castle*.

Strancally Quay

and other fare. The raucous and shrill cry of black-headed gulls pierces the morning stillness.

Here too stands Strancally Tower, a fortified stone building, three storeys in height and mounting to an open space at the top which is crowned fittingly with a salmon weathervane. I believe that the Tower is currently unoccupied; the gate is locked solid and a disused Mercedes van suggests that the owner has moved elsewhere. A tower for a poet, a scholar or writer who could watch the daily rise and fall of the Blackwater and acquaint himself intimately with the character and life of this great river – *Abhainn Mhór na Mumhan*.

On a recent visit to this very place, I spoke to a man from Cappoquin who had fallen under the spell of the river, 'It's an awesome sight,' he commented, 'to watch the huge volume of water surging back upriver.' He immediately lapsed into silence as if the spell of the river had reasserted

Strancally Tower

itself. This morning there is absolutely no one around with whom I can share the wonder of the water, the incomparable grandeur of nature and the sense of a primeval power which follows its own rhythm outside and beyond our inconsequential daily lives of work, exercise and relaxation. Reluctantly, I turn my back on the water, and follow a track through the woods of a much reduced Strancally estate.

I am uncertain of the way ahead but, luckily, the track runs parallel to the river. Wood pigeons coo to one another from their scattered perches and a startled cock pheasant flies away in alarm. One discordant note in this quiet place is the vast quantity of glass and plastic bottles and other containers that have been washed up beyond the reach of the tide. I make good headway and after fifteen minutes I reach Poul na Beast Quay (Poll na bPiast, 'The Hole of the Serpents). [5] Today no visible sign of a quay is evident but records show

---

5   Power, Patrick, *Logainmneacha na nDéise, The Place-Names of Decies*, 2nd edition, Cork University Press, 1952, p.22. Power explains that the name had legendary connotations.

that vessels discharged cargo here during the 1800s.[6] A boat called 'Three Rock 1' lies anchored a short distance from the edge of the water. From here the track veers back to Knockanore. The name Knockanore is an anglicised version of either *Cnoc an Fhómhair* or *Cnoc an Óir* ('The Hill of the Harvest' or 'The Hill of the Gold.'). Sloping from the Blackwater to a height of 300' over sea level, the fertile and well-drained land in this area is particularly suitable for grain growing, especially barley. I would conjecture that 'the Hill of the Harvest/*Cnoc an Fhómhair*' is probably the more authentic name especially on account of the orientation of the fields that allows long exposure to the ripening sun in July and August. Apart from cereal crops, dairying and suckler herds form a prominent part of the local economy. Sometime later, I had the pleasure of meeting Eamonn and Patricia Lonergan who have successfully developed a cheese-making enterprise, using the milk from their Friesian dairy herd to produce Knockanore Irish Farmhouse Cheese which is now widely available throughout Munster. The small village of Knockanore, with its parish church, national school, public house and GAA pitch is well maintained – evidence of a rooted and vibrant community that seems determined to meet the challenges facing rural communities in the twenty-first century.

Resuming my trek, I walk through a few smaller corn fields without undue difficulty until confronted by a formidable wall of briars and hawthorns, strong enough to prevent livestock from trespassing into the adjoining farm or forestry plantation as it turns out to be in this instance. Rather than retreat, I find a large fallen branch that I manage to place as a bridge over the briars. Having successfully negotiated this obstacle, I advance between rows of Sitka spruce, larch, beech and some stunted blackthorns. And then the unexpected sight of a red squirrel descending a tall beech tree brings me to an abrupt full-stop. Watching in fascination, he pauses mid-way on the broad trunk before resuming his downward movement as casually and sure-footed as a pedestrian moving through a shopping mall. Small and scattered populations of this declining species persist here in the western part of Co. Waterford with the Blackwater and the Suir, farther to the east, impeding the spread of the grey squirrel. Introduced into an estate in Castleforbes, Co. Longford, the new arrival has spread throughout most of Leinster. The grey squirrel has a greater appetite and is prepared to eat nuts and fruit that have not fully ripened. His less fussy palate results in a significantly diminished larder for the native red

---

6   O'Brien,. p. 306

squirrel. Having reached the ground floor of this mixed woodland, he quickly flees into the undergrowth and disappears from my view. Gradually the undergrowth of briars, blackthorn and furze grows denser, forcing me to change direction uphill away from the river. I am even forced into a crouched position to pass between rows of prickly Sitka until escaping out of the plantation into open pasture where a suckler herd lies contentedly chewing the cud. From this point I can hear the pulse of a milking machine from a nearby farm.

The open fields and the expanding light of the day come as a welcome relief after the claustrophobic gloom of the wood. A series of fields lie ahead, divided by electric fences and mature hawthorn hedges. Three thoroughbreds sight me from the far end of a large field and canter towards me; luckily, an electric fence keeps them from encircling me. Livestock grow accustomed to the coming and going of their owners and tend to remain largely undisturbed on their arrival; however, they recognise a stranger almost instantly and exhibit a mixture of excitement and fright. I manage to reach the gate and to climb over it, leaving these handsome equine creatures to resume their quiet browsing.

The Department of Agriculture has encouraged horse breeding in recent years through offering generous grants for the building of stables along with other facilities such as exercise arenas and horse walkers. Many farmers have begun to keep a pedigree breeding mare to produce a foal that can be sold for a good return. While some farmers and landowners have profited from the scheme, many others have been forced to sell their offspring at a loss.

From this elevated position over the Blackwater, the land slopes away to the water, granting me a magnificent panorama of landscape, east and west of the river, rounded into gentle contours and punctuated with farmsteads, woods, streams and a patchwork of superimposed fences. A mixture of elation and energy courses through my veins, sending me striding freely through mown and grazed fields until I reach a farm path surfaced with shale chippings. I exult in the joy of walking, in the beauty of the land and in the gentle buffeting of air as I stride downhill towards Newport Quay. The sight of Ballinclash Quay and the Clashmore Broads on the far side of the Blackwater stops me in my tracks. The Broads consist of a large area of salt marsh, divided into numerous islets through which the River Licky reaches the Blackwater. Charles Smith, in his history of Co. Waterford, refers to this area,

A little lower, the river forms a considerable *bason* (author's italics), called

View from Strancally to Coolbagh

the broad of Clashmore; on either side whereof; low marshy grounds called Inches, jut out in some places, which being covered with grass, seem, at a distance, to be so many smooth verdant islands.[7]

At this very moment, the weakling sun breaks through the clouds and lights up the numerous rivulets that drain the Licky into the Great River. From its source in the Drum Hills, this tributary river, *Abhainn na Leice* ('The River of the Flagstone') flows westwards to Clashmore before entering the sea between the townlands of Ballinclash and D'Loughtane.[8] The location of the 'Broads'compelled me to walk the western side of the Blackwater; otherwise, I would have been forced to follow a time-consuming detour around this extensive marshy area into Clashmore and from there along side roads back to the river. Annraoi O Liatháin, similarly, opted for the west bank. The Broads offer a sanctuary for threatened birds, such as the hen harrier and ornithologists have observed rare visitors here such as whimbrels.

Despite the pulse of a milking machine and other sounds from local farms, I have not sighted a living soul, and I presume that neither has

7   Smith, Charles, *The Ancient and Present State of the County and City of Waterford* (3rd edition), 2008, p. 37
8   Milner, p. 126-127

Ruined coach house, Srancally area

Walking Man been observed. Soon, I come to what appears to have once been a substantial holding, consisting of a two-storey farmhouse and slated outhouses, one of which still has two striking examples of a large arched entrances where horse-drawn vehicles were sheltered from the rain. The roof has collapsed and the extended and interwined branches of laurel bushes and other trees bar entry to the ruin. Then, to my surprise, I notice an electric light switch, still attached to a dangling cable, just inside the door. The grass grows to the very door of the old dwelling house and large clumps of nettles stand here and there around farmyard. Nature seems to be reabsorbing all the materials back into the earth.

Emerging from the abandoned farmstead, I cast my eyes along the river bank, trying to pinpoint the ruins of old Strancally Castle, a Geraldine fortress, built in the thirteenth century but destroyed in 1580. Legend has it that the tyrannical owner had a ruthless method for dispatching those who met with his disapproval. Having entertained them as guests, he would then usher them into a cave from which they would be cast through a hole cut in the rock into the Blackwater below. To the present time, it is known and referred to by local people as the 'Murdering Hole.'⁹

Today the ruined castle is obscured by a dense growth of bushes and ivy

9   O'Flanagan, p. 36-37

though the east-facing wall is clearly visible from the river. Another episode in the ill-fated life of Gerald, the fifteenth and last Earl of Desmond unfolded here. Having ransacked the town of Youghal for four days in 1579, he then withdrew his forces upriver where he deposited the spoils of his depredations within the walls of Strancally Castle. Within a short time Sir William Morgan set out from Dungarvan to capture the castle. As his force approached, the garrison set the building on fire and fled downriver.[10]

Here too a gigantic pylon bears three heavy cables overhead through which high-voltage electricity is transmitted from the Aghada gas-powered generating station to Waterford and other areas. To prevent swans and other birds from crashing into these cables and being electrocuted, large orange-coloured cylinders (game guards) have been placed at intervals on the cables where they cross over the river.

From this high vantage and high voltage point, I enjoy an uninterrupted view of the townlands of Ballinaclash (*Baile na Claise*, 'The Homestead of the Trench) and Coolbagh (*Cúl Beathach*, 'The Luxuriant Plot/Nook').[11] Continuing my journey, I am forced to walk around the perimeter of another coniferous plantation. After the travails of the previous woodland, I am resolved not to attempt walking through anymore of these dark and claustrophobic woodlands but to hug the light of the broad and casing air. Taking the long way around the plantation leads to an unexpected bonus for

10 Twomey, Michael, *Irish Heart, English Blood,* The History Press, 2014, p. 45-46
11 Power, p. 88-89

me when four fallow deer, three does and a fawn, break cover at the top of a stubble field and speed in their high-bounding leaps to the cover of the Sitka trees. After that delightful spectacle, I pursue a diagonal course downhill to the corner of the field close to the site of the quay. Entering into the narrow angle of the corner, I am quite surprised to meet a woman with a greyhound on a leash. Her surprise on meeting a stranger along the walking route that she uses regularly, is clearly greater than my own – in fact, she startles. To reassure her, I explain that I have been walking the Blackwater from source to sea since Monday morning.

In reply to my question,

'Where did Paddy O'Keeffe live?

She glances backwards at her own house which lies mostly obscured by surrounding vegetation and an outhouse,

'The middle section of our house was Paddy O'Keeffe's cottage. We have extended it over the years.'

The lady is well-wrapped up in anticipation of the rain that is expected later in the afternoon. Her greyhound is anxious to proceed with his usual morning stroll around the field through which I have just walked. She adds that she never met Paddy but that she has heard stories about him. Neither have I met him though I have read the colourful stories that Mike Hackett, the Youghal writer, has included in his books about Paddy.

A fisherman by trade, a character and raconteur by nature, a sociable neighbour of fun and laughter but, perhaps, most extraordinary was his intuitive knowledge of the Blackwater with its currents, its tides, its salmon season, the best places to fish and when to launch his boat. It was said of Paddy that he knew who was fishing from the sound of their rowing and movements on the river,

'Shouldn't you be fishing today?'

Paddy calmly responded, 'They're wasting their time. The wind is from the wrong point. It's not a day for fishing.'[12]

On another occasion, noticing his farming neighbour, Tom Dick Moloney, sheltering from a heavy shower while engaged in ploughing the nearby field, Paddy called him in to share the contents of his dinner pot. According to Mike Hackett, the two neighbours spent the evening chatting and joking about all the various matters pertaining to rural life.

It would be easy to deride the finely-tuned sensitivities of people such as Paddy. In this context they develop a keen awareness that enables them to

---

12 Hackett, Mike, *Echoes over the Blackwater, 1997, p. 71*

recognise the humour of the weather, the rhythm of the seasons, the haunt and tracks of the wild animals and song birds that live all around.[13] It is pertinent to point out that Howard Gardner, the Harvard psychologist, having proposed seven separate forms of intelligence in his theory of *multiple intelligences*, added an eighth form which he termed *Naturalistic* – the ability to classify and distinguish different species of plants, animals and other species.

Just past the old cottage, I pause at the refurbished slipway from where Paddy and other fishermen set off on their fishing trips; nowadays, the refurbished slipway is used occasionally for leisure boating. Save for the gentle lapping of the water, a tranquillity has descended over land, wood and water that is only disturbed by the liquid call of the curlew. An inimitable warbling sound, born out of the water and the wetlands. A redshank emits its alarm call and scythes through the air to safer ground, mallards dabble off shore, black-headed gulls, the sentinel heron and the newcomer – the little egret – grace the water and the mudbanks.

While the entire course of the Blackwater from Muinganine to Youghal is a journey through an absorbing and frequently magnificent landscape, here in Newport the river expands into *a considerable bason* and combines the land and sky in a harmonious embrace. Modernity, in the form of bungalows, slatted cattle units and electricity supply poles stands aloof, a respectful distance from the river. Strands of the purple sea aster provide a dash of colour and piles of strewn reeds on the road remind us of the winter storms when the swollen Blackwater clears the bank by the roadside.

The salmon fishing season on the Blackwater extended from 1 January to 31 July. Fishermen were required to pay an annual fee to the Duke of Devonshire and in addition had to pay for a licence from the state. Before the advent of the monofilament nets, they were frequently forced to fish in the dark of night as the wily salmon could see their nets in the daylight and would then swim away to safety. Fishing for five hours with the rising tide and three hours with the falling tide, they managed to make a reasonable living for themselves and their families. From Coolbaha Quay to Youghal Harbour, a stretch of four miles, eighteen families generally managed to make a good living from this livelihood.

However, one resourceful fisherman, turned to boat-building during the off-season. Pat O'Keeffe, Ballinanclash, born in 1912, began fishing at an early age. He designed carvel-type boats, measuring 5'x17', that gave

---

13 Hackett, *Echoes...*, p. 70-71.

fishermen extra stability when hauling nets. His boats proved to be popular and he managed to build 4-5 craft while he waited for the fishing to recommence in the early spring. Despite such enterprise, salmon numbers rapidly dwindled from the 1970s due to the industrial-scale fishing on the high seas that prevented the bulk of the returning salmon from reaching their spawning grounds. Nowadays, a few old boats lie decaying on the undisturbed quayside as testimony to a way of life that has passed.

Glancing at my watch, I note the time – 12.30pm. Walkers cannot be dawdlers and since time and tides don't hang around for anyone, *Walking Man* must press ahead once more. After a short distance, the road bends west to Ballynatray and Glendine, taking me away from the river again. Immediately ahead on the fringe of the Ballynatray demesne another large salt marsh bars the route ahead. After one mile, I reach the Newport entrance to the Ballynatray demesene where I conceal my knapsack in the undergrowth. My plan is to leave the Blackwater for 1-2 hours for the purpose of visiting the former home of Annraoi Ó Liatháin who previously walked the Blackwater and recorded a colourful account in his book *Cois Móire*.

Here in the parish of Knockanore-Glendine local people struggle to identify Annraoi Ó Liatháin; however, on giving some details, the penny drops and brings a dramatic response from your interlocutor,

'Oh! You mean Harry Lyons. They lived down the road by the waterworks in Boola.'

Whether, you call him Lyons or Ó Liatháin, I am undertaking a short pilgrimage in memory of the walker and writer who was probably the primary influence that motivated me to undertake the Blackwater journey. A few biographical details will help to shed light on the background and work of a man who led a full and varied life as a civil servant, an actor, a writer, a radio presenter and, probably, most significantly, as an Irish language activist. Annraoi (Harry) was born in 1917 in Portumna, Co. Galway . His father Michael came from Glenfarne, Co. Leitrim and his mother Annie McKee from Tyrone. In 1922 Michael was appointed as gamekeeper on the Holroyd-Smyth estate here in east Co. Waterford. Annraoi was proud of his Waterford heritage and identified himself as a *Déiseach*. Having attended Glendine NS, he received his secondary education in the Patrician novitiate in Tullow, Co. Carlow, where he spent three years, and in Youghal CBS where he completed the leaving certificate in 1936. He then entered the civil service and worked in the Valuation Office and later in the Department of Education.

He became an active member of *Conradh na Gaeilge* and was appointed as the first editor of *An Glór*, the magazine of that organisation. In 1951 he was elected as president of the *Conradh*. During that time, he broadcast talks on various topics in *Aeriris* as well as participating in the series *Idir Shúgradh is Dáiríre* on Raidio Éireann while at the same time taking part in Irish language productions at Halla Damer in St Stephen's Green. As a writer he wrote five fictional works which would probably have been classified as 'light reading' for teenagers or adults, a book for salmon angling enthusiasts, a history book on the Irish in Scotland as well as his two books on the Blackwater and the Suir.

His strong feelings on matters relating to the Irish language led to his dismissal from the civil service in 1946 when he criticised the government over the death of Seán Mac Eachaigh, a political prisoner, while in custody. After two years he was reinstated to his position on the election of the first coalition government in 1948. The loss of his salary must have led to severe hardship for his wife and family of eight.

The road from Newport to Glendine is all uphill and follows the wooded margin of the Ballynatray estate where mature sessile oaks create an old world atmosphere. Passing the water works at Boola, I almost miss the roofless cottage which the Lyons family occupied until the late 1950s.

The Lyons' home was a card game house where neighbours assembled in the long winter nights. The older generations of Boola like to recall the homely image of Mrs Lyons seated at the upstairs window and knitting while she waited for her four children to return from Glendine NS along the woodland paths.

Later Annraoi was to set some of his stories in this locale and, no wonder, they contain numerous references to the tall beech trees, the wood pigeons and woodcocks. Annraoi liked to revisit the area and often enjoyed a pint in Lombard's pub where he chatted with his former school mate, Frances Casey.

A homestead that has fallen into ruins stands sad and poignant in the countryside but keeps alive the memory of the family for a few generations but that memory fades as the physical structure crumbles back into the earth. Turning away, I retrace my steps downhill to the Newport Lodge where I retrieve my belongings. Approaching the keypad, I type in the code for opening the automated stockade-type gate and stand back waiting for a reaction. Within a second or two, I hear the quiet hum of a low mechanical sound; the gates divide in the middle with one half diverging to the left and the other to the right. Having walked past several estates during the course

House in Boola where Harry Lyons (Annraoi Liatháin) grew up

of my walk, I now have the pleasure of walking unhindered through the demesne of the Holroyd-Smyth estate. The last of the Holroyd-Smyths died in 1969 and the control of the great house, along with most of the estate, has passed into different ownership: from the related Ponsonbys to Serge and Henriette Boissevain and more recently to a Welsh businessman, Henry Gwynn Jones.

Immediately inside the gates, a large field, from which a crop of barley has been harvested, stretches over and beyond the brow of a hill. But what engages my attention most is a corner section of the field in which farm weeds have been allowed to proliferate – the yellow flowering charlock, the pale red persicaria, the corn marigold, scattered sunflowers and smaller

Newport gate lodge

annuals such as scarlet pimpernel, field pansy and various species of speedwells. Puzzled at first, I soon realise that this crop of seed-laden weeds has been designedly cultivated here for the game pheasants as both a source of food and cover. Already, I have noticed a few cocks and hens foraging along the margins. Later, as I progress along the estate road, I see and encounter pheasants everywhere that, instead of taking to flight, just run away in front of me. Obviously, these farm-raised birds have become domesticated to such a degree that shooting them no longer presents a challenge to the sportsman armed with a modern repeating game rifle. As in the UK, game shooting now constitutes an important part of the business enterprise involved in running large estates profitably. David Bellamy has been convinced that the rearing and shooting of game birds helps to reduce the dependence of landowners on intensive fertilizer farming and promotes greater diversity in the countryside. Opposed to that view, the nature writer John Mabey describes how piles of shot pheasants are burnt in Norfolk after the departure of the city fowler.

Mature sessile oaks over-arch the road. I ramble calmly and unhurriedly, delighting in the wood with its under storey of holly bushes. Every bend reveals a new vista ahead and glimpses of the river away to my right. The sunlight comes dancing fitfully through the leaf canopy, casting rays of light here and there on the woodland floor. During his walk of the Blackwater in 1959, Annraoi found much of the estate neglected with bracken and furze colonising large tracts of land that had been formerly cultivated. He writes

Cornfield with wild flowers

Entrance gate, Ballynatray Estate

that the herd of Kerry cattle were left unattended and, consequently, they startled and stampeded through the vegetation if disturbed by walkers or the estate workmen. He lamented the ageing of the Ballynatray House, fearing that it was approaching its demise unless finance could be found to save it from the fate of so many of the great houses of Ireland that were allowed to decay or else fell victim to the fiery holocaust during the Irish War of Independence, 1918-1922.

The timely intervention of the French-German couple, the Boissevains, most likely saved Ballynatray from inevitable decay. Having acquired the house along with its 850 acres, they ambitiously set about restoring it to its former splendour. Around the estate, wrought-iron gates were erected, new bridges replaced the tottering iron girders, cottages and lodges were refurbished, large scale plantings were undertaken and the walled gardens were open to the public for a period of the year. Sadly, dreams are but dreams, or, perhaps, the couple found seclusion here but not contentment, and departed for Seville where they bred Andalusian horses. The house and lands remained on the market for an extended period with rumours circulating that rock stars or other celebrities were about to set up home here. Instead, a practical and quiet businessman stepped in with an offer of €12 million which was accepted.

Nowadays the house and its facilities are marketed for weddings, conferences, filming, holiday and week-end vacations with fowling and stag stalking added to the extensive list of offers available to many different target groups.

Emerging from the woodland to the residential part of the estate, *Walking Man* encounters a younger couple who request his assistance to help restart their Renault Megane. The young man explains his predicament in a very apologetic tone but his girlfriend remains silent during the exchange,

> I left the parking lights on overnight and the battery has been completely run down. We're here for a quiet weekend from Limerick. Could you help us to push it? And, maybe we could restart it.

His girlfriend takes the driver's seat and, assuming a scrum stance, we push and push but, disappointingly, the engine refuses to spark into life despite our best efforts. Regretfully, I could not be of any further assistance to them. They thanked me for my help and I continued on my quiet way.

Approaching the eighteenth century Georgian mansion, I marvel at the picturesque setting of the great house and the harmony that the architect and Grice Smyth achieved between the built structure and the encircling hills to its rear. Likewise, the view from the frontal area of the house opens to a panorama of water, land, trees and sky. On-line images of the interior convince the web browser that the furnishings and decor create an ambience for a cultivated lifestyle available to the privileged aristocracy and to the moneyed *noveau-riche*.

My ambulating precursor, Annraoi was, on the occasion of his walk, invited inside to join Henry Horace Holroyd-Smyth for a glass of beer. They spoke about the estate and the locality in which they had both grown up. Casting his eyes around the walls, Annraoi observed the portraits of Queen Elizabeth 1, Sir Walter Raleigh, Cromwell as well as those of Holroyd-Smiths who had served their monarch in foreign fields or brought embalmed specimens home to Ballynatray as testimony of their hunting exploits in Africa, South America and elsewhere. Amazingly, despite the passionate nationalistic attitudes that Annraoi expressed in his book *Cois Móire*, the republican and aristocratic royalist seemed to find one another's company convivial. Sadly, Henry Horace died tragically in 1969, and though Annraoi survived him for twelve more years, he died shortly after his retirement from the civil service in 1981.[14] The estate was bequeathed to the Ponsonby family of Kilcooley Abbey, Co. Tipperary who eventually sold it to the Boissevains.

Turning my back on the old Palladian mansion, I pass through a gate and from there I walk along the embankment that leads to Darinis (*Dair*

---

14 www.ainm.ie

Ballynatray Georgian mansion

Inis, 'Oak Island.') where the ruins of the Augustinian monastery still stand. The original monastic settlement was founded by St Molanfide (Molana) in 501 A.D.[15] During the Elizabethan era, the monastery passed into the ownership of Sir Walter Raleigh and later belonged to Richard Boyle, the first Earl of Cork. Since the early nineteenth century, the former island has been connected by a strong causeway from the Templemichael entrance and from the monastery to the site of the house. A stillness pervades these unstable ruins where, reputedly, the remains of Raymond le Gros, one of the first Norman invaders, are interred. Today, I can only peer through the security fence at the urn that commemorates the grave of *Le Gros* and at the fanciful statue of St Molanfide, bearing a plaque on which the inscription reads, 'Erected by Mrs Mary Broderick Smith, A.D. 1820.' Here in this monastery, the monks under the guidance of one of their elders, Rubin Mac Connaidh, compiled a collection of Church canon laws into a book named *Collectio Canonum Hibernensis.* 'At his death in 725, Rubin was described as the 'Scribe of Munster.' His compilation of Church laws was widely used throughout Europe and became an exemplar for clerics engaged in drawing up similar lists of ecclesiastical regulations.

15   Flanagan, J.R., p. 33.

Molana Abbey, Dairinis Island

We know that the Vikings plundered Darinis in the ninth century and that the Battle of Glendine was fought between two factions of Norse settlers, the Ravens of Munster and the Ravens of the West. Raymond le Gros had it reconstituted as an Augustinian foundation. For the next 300 years, the abbey seems to have prospered as it enjoyed the patronage of the Desmonds, the powerful feudal lords of Munster. The abbey was desecrated in 1588 prior to control of the Abbey passing from Raleigh to Sir Richard Boyle, whose sister married Smyth of Ballynatray.

Pausing for a short time, I envisage the Viking longboats hauled up close to the island shore, the savagery of the plunder and the pleading of the monks for mercy from the heedless heathens. We know that the Vikings sailed as far as Lismore where they pillaged the renowned school founded by St Carthage in 833.

Having left the ancient monastery, I follow the causeway to the point where it joins the road leading to the house. I turn towards the Templemichael gates with their twin lodges on either side. A short distance before the gates, the Glendine river passes beneath a restored bridge to join the Backwater. Back on the Youghal-Lismore road, I walk slowly towards the old cemetery, church and castle in Templemichael for the final part of the story of the Holroyd-Smyths. A passage leads past the cemetery, church and mausoleum where members of the family were interred. The moderate proportions of their crypt, in contrast to that of the Earls of Listowel in Ballyhooly cemetery, perhaps, indicates some awareness that Death the Leveller would find them out. At the steel door, I can just manage to glimpse through slits to see the outline of a coffin in the turgid darkness. Moving to the rear of the mausoleum, I discover a well-preserved limestone carving of the family coat of arms with their motto, *Vis unita fortior cum plena magis* ('Unity in strength,' *Ní neart go cur le chéile.*'). A thick coat of moss, flowering plants and even saplings carpet the stone roof with briars and taller bushes threatening to engulf the vaulted tomb of the Holroyd-Smyths from the ground. The lead coffins of various members of the family have been deposited within, the final coffin being that of Henry Horace Digby whose untimely and tragic death brought an end to 400 years of his lineage in Ballynatray. His funeral in September 1969 was the last service to be held in the adjacent church of St Michael's which had been the family place of worship since 1876. Sadly, the deconsecrated church has been deroofed and the casements have been blocked off. Nevertheless, contemporary pillagers have wrenched blocks clear and gained entrance to the interior of this desolate structure. No one now knows what has happened to the key of the vault. The loss of the key could be regarded as the final blow to the proud family that graced the Blackwater Valley for centuries.

The keeper of their story, Catherine Fleming, lives a short distance away in the Glebe house of Templemichael parish. Better known locally as Kitty, she has erected two memorials to the sons of Captain Rowland on the wall close to the entrance. The inscription to her friend and fiancé, Henry Horace, bears a poignant line from a poem by Thomas Campbell (1763-1854),

> To live in hearts we leave behind is not to die.

I cannot but notice the path worn to the memorial where a bunch of withered flowers lies on the ground.

Catherine Fleming's family had operated the Ardsallagh to Templemichael ferry for generations. Her granduncle, the handsome Patrick Fleming, caught the eye of Lady Harriette Smyth (1849-1928) who fell passionately in love with him at the young age of nineteen. The star-crossed lovers eloped during a hunt ball in Ballynatray and were ferried across the Blackwater to Ardsallagh. From there they made their way to Cobh where they boarded a ship bound for America. By then their elopement had been discovered and the frustrated couple were brought back to Ballynatray. Sometime later, Harriette married an English soldier,

John Henry Graham Holroyd who served in Egypt and Sudan. Hariette attempted to maintain the lifestyle she was accustomed to and Patrick often visited her, bringing her rabbits and fish to console her. Her brother Richard died in 1892, aged 28, and Harriette then became heir-apparent to Ballynatray. Subsequently, she and her husband assumed the surname and arms of Smyth in lieu of Holroyd.

A local versifier composed the following verse to commemorate their flight,

Miss Moore-Smyth who ran away,
With Patrick Fleming from Ballynatray,
One foot on the gravel,
And one foot on the grass,
Is to be the sound that my true love will pass.

The sound of the 'foot on the gravel' had been the pre-arranged signal for Harriette to emerge through a window to join her sweetheart. The episode must have given rise to great merriment among the army of estate workmen and local people. One comment relating to Harriette, 'She seems to have understood Ireland more than many of her peers,' provides a significant insight into her character and attitudes to the local people.

A century later, the hidden hand of fate caused the lives of the Smyth-Holroyds and the Flemings to become enmeshed once again in the relationship that grew between Catherine (Kitty) and Henry Horace. After his father's death in 1959, Catherine moved to the great house to assist Horace manage the administration of the large estate and household. He was a quiet unassuming man who dreaded the brown envelopes from the Irish government with their demands for rates and other charges. To meet such expenses, he was forced to sell land elsewhere. He had little interest in hunting but greatly enjoyed fishing on the Blackwater in the days when salmon were plentiful. The writer and journalist, Claud Cockburn, observed that such was their supply of fish that the Holyroyd-Smiths even gave salmon to their staff. They exported salmon packed in ice to Harrods in London up to 1940. In an earlier generation the estate had its own racecourse and even a distillery in the basement. [16]

Born in 1904, [Henry] Horace worked in Chile in the copper mining industry from 1939-1945. In 1944 his brother John was killed in action in Greece. Horace then became heir apparent and duly succeeded his father,

---

16 Morrow, Ann, *Picnic in a Foreign Land: The Eccentric Lives of the Anglo-Irish*, Grafton Books, London, 1989, p. 210-217

Captain Rowland, after his death in 1959. 'He was five foot eleven, clean-shaven and had a fondness for corduroy.' *Walking Man* can testify to his choice of wear as he [the author] often saw Horace driving through Youghal in his Land Rover Jeep.

In 1969 Horace proposed marriage to Kitty who accepted his offer despite their age difference as well as that of religion. Ann Morrow, an English journalist, later interviewed Kitty, and described all the events that transpired prior to their wedding in her book *Picnic in a Foreign Land*. Arrangements were duly made, the invitations were sent out and the cutlery was inscribed with their names. A short time before their wedding, Horace visited his younger brother Oliver in their summer house in Ardmore. According to Kitty, 'he returned to Ballynatray frustrated and angry.' 'What was said between the two men is unknown but it was certainly of an exceedingly black nature.' Horace left the house on the pretext of shooting deer despite the fact that he was not well known as a shooting man. His body was found soon after. The county coroner returned a verdict of accidental death.

Before departing Templemichael, I make my way through the nettles and thistles to the grave in which my own great-great-grandfather and great- grandfather are buried in the south-west corner of the cemetery. For years, this grave had been all but forgotten by our family until my brother Frank and I set out armed with a hedge clippers, a slasher and a chainsaw to locate the long-lost grave. The date was Saturday 27 September 1997, the eve of the Kerry v Mayo All Ireland football final. After two hours of cutting sapling sycamores, briars and other plants, we located the grave and succeeded in reading the inscription.

The older John Flynn (1786-1876) was born twelve years before the 1798 United Irishmen Rebellion. Having lived through the famine, he died at the ripe old age of ninety in the family home in Park where he had been born and lived all his life. The younger John (1820-1905) was evicted in 1887 along with his son John (1855-1947) when the National Land League organised the 'Plan of Campaign' strategy on the Ponsonby estate in east Cork. According to this plan, the tenants offered their landlords what they considered to be a fair rent. If the landlord refused to accept their offer, the money was then taken into safe-keeping by the organising committee in the hope that strap-cashed landlords would have no realistic option other than accepting the offer of their tenants. Ponsonby, a retired naval officer, lived in Park House for only six months in the year. Nevertheless, he had drawn up ambitious plans to refurbish his mansion.

His 10,600-acre property stretched for fourteen miles along the south-eastern coast from the mountainous moors bordering the Blackwater to the marshes at the western side of Youghal Bay.[17]

In targeting Ponsonby, the national committee had selected a landlord who, in their view, lacked the resources to hold out for long against the combined forces of a large number of small but determined tenants. Rev Canon Keller, at that time, the Parish Priest of Youghal, provided able and articulate leadership for the tenants. His arrest and imprisonment in Kilmainham in 1887 for his refusal to 'identify the trustees of the tenants' war chest, had given him the status of a national hero. Cork Corporation presented him with a laudatory address and the Archbishop of Cashel greeted him on his way to prison.[18] The beleaguered Ponsonby approached his fellow landlords in east Cork who intervened by providing him with the funds he needed to resist the demands of his tenants. Eviction notices were soon issued to the tenant farmers who, adhering to the Plan of Campaign, were evicted from their holdings. Four refuge-type villages were erected in the locality where the families had to endure severe deprivation that led to outbreaks of typhoid fever.

Canon Keller, demonstrating adroit leadership, wrote two tracts designed to influence liberal opinion in the English parliament. Referring to my great-grandfather John Flynn, he wrote that he had visited the Flynn family home and had seen the barriers of wood and stones erected on the approach to the house to bar the way of the sheriff and his enforcers. The slogan 'Plan of Campaign here' was written in large letters on the gable end of the house with the warning, 'Grabbers Beware.' Flynn had incurred considerable expense in draining and improving his land. 'If this man were a horse on the Ponsonby estate, he would receive fairer treatment,' Fr Keller concluded in his tract.

The Campaign, overtaken by national events, dragged on and the tenants were forced to settle individually with their intransigent landlord. The Flynns returned home and resumed their work on the farm. Ponsonby, having sold his land under the terms of the later Land Acts, retired to Hampshire where he owned a large tract of land.

My visit to Templemichael cemetery has aroused profound emotions deep within me. How ironic that landlords and tenants, who in their life

---

17 Donnelly, Jr. S., *The Land and People of Nineteenth-Century Cork: The Rural Economy and the Land Question,* London, p. 354
18 Donnelly, Jr, *The Land and the People of Nineteenth-Century Cork..,* p. 352-353

time frequently quarrelled over land, are consigned after death to the same patch of ground. Bidding farewell to the Holroyd-Smyths and the Flynns [my forebears], and to escape from the morbidity of the graveyard, I walk down to the very edge of the Blackwater where I find four anglers casting their lines in the hope that they can lure a large bass on to their baits. One of them, low-sized and burly with a peak cap and angler gear, proves to be more talkative than the others. In a strong Cork city accent, he tells me, 'We come here every September to fish for bass. They come in here from the sea. And there's a very deep hole just here.'

Indicating a point about thirty yards from the bank, 'They're down in there, and with a bit of luck you could land the finest bass you ever saw, up to fourteen-fifteen pounds weight.'

Then, taking off his baseball cap and growing thoughtful for a moment, he adds 'Look, I am not so sure about the day. I've a feeling that we should have waited a few days.'

Next, he scans me closely and asks, 'Where do you come from yourself? Are you just out for a stroll?'

I decide to come clean and tell him what I am up to, that I am walking the Blackwater from source to sea. He reacts dramatically, and turning to his three mates, he raises his voice to tell them, 'Did you hear that, lads? He's writing a book. Maybe he'll give us a good mention. Oh God! We'll be looking forward to that.'

Saying goodbye and wishing them good luck, I turn to retrace my steps. The anglers have distracted me from looking at the fine old quay, the Geraldine castle and the shell of the warehouse a short distance from where I now stand. The enduring quay structure and the presence of the old warehouse suggest that this was an important site for commercial activity. The ferry service from here to Ardsallagh (*Ard Saileach*, 'The Height of the Sallies) provided an alternative for travellers when stormy weather made the crossing of Youghal harbour unsafe. The story of an earlier ferryman, Garret Fitzgerald, who operated a weir at Templemichael is still recounted almost 300 years after his death. After his burial in Clashmore, the ferryman could hear a ghostly cry in Irish over the Blackwater at night, '*Bád do Ghearóid, Bád do Ghearóid.*'('A Ferry for Garret, a ferry for Garret.'). Fearing that his spirit was not at rest, his family had his body exhumed and reinterred in Templemichael.[19] Peace descended on the valley once again.

I glimpse the ruin of Templemichael Castle through the surrounding trees. While little is known about this castle, it is thought that it was another Geraldine fortification or may possibly have been erected by the Knights Templar. We do know, however, that the castle was subjected to cannon fire from the weapons of General Ireton during the Cromwellian campaign. The positioning of his cannon guns in Ardsallagh, directly across the Blackwater, made the castle an easy target. The Boissevains sealed off the old ruin with a strong wooden door but, unfortunately, that barrier has been wrenched open allowing access to intruders who have left their graffiti, beer cans and the remnants of their midnight fires after them. South of the castle, though largely screened by the trees that have invaded the site, lie the crumbling remains of an old warehouse which was intended to house imports and exports. The 6-inch ordnance survey map of 1840 records this as the site of Templemichael House. J. R. O'Flanagan noted this to be the 'handsome residence of Thomas Carpenter, Esq.'[20]

Before departing this forgotten world of graves, mausoleum, church, castle, warehouse and walls, it is worth noting that Ó Liatháin referred to the area as 'Rinn Mhíchil;' the word 'Rinn' clearly denoting the short headland, or spur that juts out into the Blackwater. Canon Patrick Power in his authoritative work, *Logainmneacha na nDéise: The Place-Names of the Decies*, writes that 'the name [Templemichael] of the parish suggests a Danish origin or...a

---

19   O'Brien, p. 128
20   O'Flanagan, p. 32, facsimile edition, Tower Books, 1975.

Templemichael Castle

Danish dedication.' Power refers to the devotion that the later Christianised Danes had to St Michael, adding that they erected churches 'under the Archangel's invocation' in their larger settlements.[21]

Back on the Glendine-Youghal road, I make steady progress at a comfortable pace. All the while I am observing and noting the significant features of the surroundings. On this three-mile stretch, *Walking Man* enjoys a superb view of the Blackwater. Looking across the river, he notes the cabin cruisers moored at intervals, the linear woods running between the water and the land on the Ardsallagh side and the fields sloping downhill to the water. Ardsallagh House, the residence of the Ronanyes has been demolished and a German family have bought the land where they now produce Ardsallagh goat cheese. The tolling of Youghal town bell was reserved for the death of a Ronanye. This privilege was conferred on the family as an expression of thanks for the intervention of Nicholas Ronanye in 1689 who succeeded in calming an angry crowd from setting fire to Tynte Castle where a crowd of local gentry had taken shelter.[22]

21 Power, Patrick Rev, *Logainmneacha na nDéise: The Place-Names of the Decies,* Cork University Press, 1952, p. 61
22 Hackett, Mike, p. 88-89

In this vicinity, a few years ago, I observed a seagull-like bird perched in the trees above the Backwater. Knowing that seagulls do not perch on trees, I contacted the wildlife ranger for east Cork who promptly informed me that little egrets had settled and hatched in the area. In a relatively short space of time, they have expanded their range considerably. Whether or not the arrival of a new member for our Irish avifauna is due to global warming, these new arrivals have exploited an ecological niche along our river valleys that had not been vigorously utilised by the long-settled waders. Their first appearance in significant numbers can be dated to 1997; since that year their numbers have grown exponentially, and that trend seems destined to continue. Rating myself as an L-plate ornithologist, the explanation for their dramatic expansion into England and Ireland may be linked to successful breeding in the Mediterranean countries which has triggered their expansion into north-west Europe.

A cul-de-sac road diverges to my left, marking the location of the small townland of *Stael* – a name that the scholarly Canon Power assumed to be of Viking origin or possibly derived from the Gaelic word *stiall* (strip or section).[23] The road to Youghal Bridge curves with the Blackwater and runs through a mixed woodland that slopes steeply to the water below me. Approaching the end of my walk, I am anxious to wring the last vestige of solace from *An Abhainn Mhór* but the river has turned restless tossing the boats anchored along the opposite shore. Again the ugly problem of litter disposal manifests itself along this scenic stretch. Consumers are dumping plastic containers, glass bottles, boxes, electrical equipment, runners and even items of clothing by throwing them over the low stone wall. High over the road are the remains of a preceptory of the Knights Templar in Rhincrew (*Rinn Chrú*, 'Point, headland of blood?'). Occupying a crucial site that provided a clear view of the harbour as well as the mouth of the river, the Templar Knights must have been empowered to control travel up and down the Blackwater.

Approaching the new Youghal Bridge, I pause to gaze at the five-arch structure that was completed in 1963 to replace the old metal bridge that spanned the river a short distance away where the Blackwater expands into Youghal Harbour. For many people this was the first mass-concrete and steel reinforced work of construction they had ever seen.

I can recall my science teacher in Youghal CBS, Br Sylvester Lennon (1960-63), explaining to us how the engineers left openings in the new bridge to allow for the expansion of metal during periods of warm weather.

---

23 Power Patrick, *The Place-Names of the Decies,* p.66

Youghal Bridge

Walking to the centre of the bridge to say goodbye to the river, I glance back at the Blackwater that has followed this course for millions of years. The ocean awaits its arrival.

The salmon fishermen of Ardsallagh feared that the construction of the bridge would affect their livelihood. Their fears were unjustified and they continued to cast their nets until the salmon run declined to such an extent that the government banned net fishing and compensated the fishermen for the loss of their traditional occupation. The decision by the county councillors of Waterford and Cork not to include a drawbridge or a swing-span in the new concrete bridge effectively ended the shipping and trade that had been an important part of the economic life of west Waterford and east Cork.

Here on the Rhincrew side of the bridge a steel plaque was inserted in the pier to commemorate the opening of the bridge on 23 January, 1963. On that very day, accompanied by a number of friends from the CBS, we cycled to hear the speeches and to witness the politicians in action. It was a bitterly cold day and our fingers were numbed around the handlebars. The official plaque names Niall Blaney as having opened the bridge but as he was indisposed, the then junior minister, Donagh O'Malley, substituted

for him. Standing well back from the assembly, we school boys stood with our bicycles, listening to the official speeches, until our lunch time began to run out. However, to this very day I can recall a phrase used by Donagh O'Malley. During the course of his speech, he thanked all the councillors who had contributed to the achievement, '...irrespective of their political affiliations.' The word 'affiliations' and 'irrespective' were new to me and, probably, for that reason, I have retained the memory of the phrase to the present day.

It was around this stage of my life that I consciously became fascinated by words for the first time. This fascination has stayed with me ever since. When I hear or come across a new word or phrase it resonates in my head emitting vibrations of connotation, derivation, sound, colour and feeling. No wonder then that when I heard, for the first time, Ludwig Wittgenstein's mind-boggling phrase 'The limits of my language are the limits of my world.' I knew then that my world would always be a world of words and wonder.

After walking a short distance from the bridge, I come to 'J.J's, All-Day Breakfast Café' roadside cafe, housed in a mobile cabin and painted blue and gold. Business is brisk here with motorists availing of the quick service, moderate prices and the convenience of parking at the door. The chef, a Londoner, recites the menu for me with an east-end accent that has not been affected by the intonation of the Waterford drawl or by the East Cork lilt. Selecting a hamburger, mushy peas, chips and tea, I pass the time glancing through the sports pages of the Sunday World tabloid newspaper in which the columnists are nearly all opting for a Kilkenny win over their arch-rivals, Tipperary, in the big match at Croke Park today. It's coming very close to throw-in time but our chef is keeping an eye on a premiership game between Villa and Spurs. Taking my courage in hand and employing all my limited diplomacy, I suggest that we would (another customer and myself) really like to see the hurling.

'Any chance we could watch the Tipp v Kilkenny game? It's due to start any moment...the biggest hurling game of the year.'

His response surprises and delights me, 'What channel is that on, mates?'

He replies while at the same time agitating the basket of chips in the cauldron of cooking oil. He immediately switches to RTE 2 where we can just about see Michael Lister along with the panellists Cyril Farrell, Ger Loughnane and Tomás Mulcahy through the snow storm of a poor quality reception and a barely audible commentary. It will have to do, after all we have seen enough hurling games to follow the action and understand the tactics without having the finer details relayed over the air. We're off to a flying start with the Tipp men racing into an early lead. And then Lar Corbett plucks a ball from the clouds, escapes the attention of the Kilkenny full-back and rifles the ball to the back of the net for the opening goal. Unfortunately, the reception deteriorates still

further as the action swings from one end of the field to the other. Mid-way through the first half, I am forced to resort to a tiny wind-up radio that Sean Radley gave me as a parting gift in Millstreet last Monday. I mange to tune quickly into Micheál Ó Muircheartaigh on Radio though later I switch to Seán Bán Breatnach on Raidio na Gaeltachta who keeps me enthralled with phrases such as *Tá an choimhlint fíochmhar; Tá an teannas damanta* (It's a ferocious contest and the tension is enormous). Not only is the All-Ireland title up for grabs today but Kilkenny are aiming to gain an unique slot in the history of the game by being the first team ever to win five titles in a row. By the twentieth minute Richie Power scores a goal for the 'Cats', so it seems that the onslaught of the men from the Premier County has been halted. Despite their early dominance, they have only a one-point lead to show for all their efforts: Tipperary 1-10 Kilkenny 1-9. Will it be enough to see them over the line?

Walking Man has to hit the road again, a road that curves away from the Blackwater to where it meets the estuary of the Tourig River (origin of name not known) – the last of all the tributary rivers. Having flowed from a hilly source near Tallow, the Tourig passes through the small hamlet of Inch and winds its way through a scenic wooded valley in Youghal Park. After Kilnatoora castle and below the Two Mile Bridge, the Tourig becomes a tidal river and delimits counties Waterford and Cork for a distance of two miles. Deep deposits of pottery clay lie along this tidal stretch of river. The ready availability of this raw material facilitated pottery making here where the ancient craft has been practised for centuries.

I am hooked up to my miniature radio and following the thrill of battle as I walk along this stretch of the N22. 'I am approaching my journey's end yet my mind has immersed itself in the titanic battle unfolding in Croke Park. After the restart, Kilkenny draw level and it looks as if it is going to be the same old story today, that the underdogs, while showing good form in the first half, will inevitably have to yield to the history-making team in the black and amber. Somewhere around the Stone Bridge and the Tallow roundabout, Lar Corbett, aided by Gearoid O Brien and Brendan Maher, strikes again, scoring a virtuoso goal to regain the lead for Tipperary.

The tall chimney stack (125') of the long-abandoned brickyard looms into view – a towering giant that stands as a memorial to another age when huge quantities of clay bricks were fired in the kiln chambers around the base of the chimney. Barges brought the fired bricks from the English Quay (*Cé an tSacsanaigh*) just above the Stone Bridge to ships in Youghal Harbour for export to the cities of England. At its peak the workforce numbered almost a thousand men who worked from 6.00 a.m to 6.00 p.m., six days a week. Many of these men walked long distances across the old metal bridge from Co. Waterford or elsewhere. A string of thirty Clydesdales was kept to transport the finished bricks to Youghal Railway Station, a journey of approximately four miles. The Youghal Brick Company went into liquidation in 1931 due to the growing popularity of the concrete block. The rising cost of fuel and the unsettled political situation from 1918 were another factors that led to the decline and eventually to the closure of the brickyard.[24]

I am now on the home straight with about two miles to walk. Meanwhile the fury of battle in Croke Park remains unabated. The two teams, locked in mortal combat, exchange points, keeping the outcome on a knife edge. During all this drama I ramble along past the closed pottery shop, past the closed factories where Eastman Kodak manufactured Compact Recordable Discs (C D-R's) and Avery Dennison made office archive material as well as ink-stamps. Occupying a 200,000 sq. feet facility, Kodak sold their business to Technicolour Home Entertainment in 2002. This latter company closed the manufacturing facility in 2003 with the loss of 243 jobs. Avery Dennison continued to produce products in the next-door plant until 2007 when they too shut their doors depriving 100 workers of their employment. Today both buildings are shut awaiting enquiries from other manufacturers who may be interested in starting production in Youghal. The usual reasons for closure have been cited by these giant American corporations such as 'market and competitive pressures' and 'the need to rationalise their

24 Breslin, Tony, *The Claymen of Youghal,* 2002

Chimney of the Youghal Brick Company

European facilities.' Globalisation has not been kind to the ancient and historic town of Youghal.

Turning left onto the approach road to the old metal Youghal Bridge, I pass the Eras Echo Ltd. waste treatment and industrial recycling plant for waste materials and sludge. Opened in 2004 on a 3.5 brown acre site with an initial work force of thirty, but now down to twelve, the firm has encountered quite an amount of opposition from people in Youghal. Though my ears are plugged, my nostrils cannot escape the pungent smell that pervades the immediate vicinity. The local management subsequently informed me that the treatment of the waste materials takes place inside a sealed building with odour-treatment equipment in place. *Walking Man*, however, is not prepared to linger here apart from reading the signage and security warning posted inside the high fence. The various operations that take place within the building are fully licensed by the Environmental Protection Agency (EPA).

Local residents are, however, particularly concerned about the discharge of hazardous waste into 'our beautiful Blackwater estuary.' Today, Sunday, 5th September, 2010, I am not aware that the Blackwater Estuary Action Group (BEAG) has just been formed to appeal the decision by An Bórd Pleanála to grant a license to Eras Eco to begin treating 30,000 tons of hazardous waste including pharmaceutical residue with a subsequent discharge of the treated effluent into the Blackwater. Something visceral begins to stir inside me. I am a nature-lover, an environmentalist and a member of *An Taisce* who strongly believes in the absolute importance of keeping clean the air we breathe, of preventing the pollution of rivers and the sea and conserving our fauna and flora for future generations.

Having passed the controversial facility and the landfill plus civic amenity site (recycling centre), the old paved road is engulfed by furze bushes and briars though explorers have managed to keep a path open.

I have just switched over to Micheál Ó Muirceartaigh for the final ten minutes of the All-Ireland. In fact, I have found a bench a short distance from the landfill where I decide to remain seated until the outcome has been decided. Tipperary enjoy a five-six point lead but Kilkenny have the time to erode that lead which they threaten to do but Tipp reply with their own points. Then comes the killer-goal from the hero of the day: Lar Corbett collects and evades his marker plus a 'thrown hurley' to finish the contest on the score of 4-17 to 1-18, leaving Tipperary victors with a margin of eight points to spare.

As the first drops of rain begin to fall, I don my rainproof anorak as cover from the weather that has been well flagged. Writing and walking are two different processes with the walker taking a direct route and the writer, in contrast, diverging from the route to follow linked topics. So before walking into the town of Youghal, I must say something about the old metal bridge that spanned the estuary of the Blackwater for 121 years. Designed by Alexander Nimmo, the government engineer, the metal structure was completed between 1829-1832. For 131 years it provided a convenient crossing for travellers journeying from Cork to Youghal until the county engineers of Waterford and Cork became seriously concerned when corrosion was detected in the bridge's metal piles. To reduce the risk of the bridge collapsing, restrictions were put in place from 1950: a speed-limit of 5 mph was imposed; a series of alternate barriers were placed in an alternate pattern across the bridge; buses, lorries and vehicles exceeding five tons were banned from crossing and a booth was built at either end for guards to open and close the barriers twenty-four hours a day. These restrictions caused considerable difficulties for lorry drivers who were forced to travel to Cappoquin and for bus passengers who had to disembark at the barrier and walk across the bridge carrying their luggage.

Sunday drives were not a prominent feature of our household when we were growing up in the early 1950s. However, I can recall my father Ned zig-zagging around the barrels to cross over to Clashmore or some other place. For a year or two after that frightening experience, the thought of having to repeat the same journey constituted the most enduring dread of my childhood. Even worse was my father's account of having brought a sow and a litter of bonhams across the bridge in a crib when the mare hauling the cart began to shy, forcing him to cover her head so that he could lead her across.

The threatening rain, driven by a gusty south-east wind, lashes me across the face. Here on the old slob bank I have no place to shelter. Below the bank the river, now being consummated by the sea, casts itself repeatedly and in vain at the stout barrier that prevents it from reclaiming the sloblands as its own once again. A retaining wall was built here in the first half of the nineteenth century that turned the former mud lands into grazing pastures that are still referred to as the 'slob.' Annual flapper races were held here up to the late 1950s. Now on the home straight, the buildings and houses of the quay area are beginning to emerge from their background, each assuming an individual shape. Nearing the end of the

The old Youghal bridge

slob bank walk, I turn right towards the town where I can see a parked car and three people glancing in my direction.

My old friend, school mate and fellow hurler, Sean De LaCour accompanied by his wife Anne and their daughter Gillian have arrived to meet me. Now I realise why Sean emphatically asked me what time would I arrive at Green's Quay. Sean and I are the same age, born in 1947, his birthday on the 12th July and mine on the 1st. Gillian jokes about my walking stick, 'I knew a walker was coming when I saw the stick. I go walking with a group in Cork and our guide is always telling us to use a walking stick.'

We talk briefly about the game, my walk and the broken weather. Sean is looking unwell; Ann is clearly concerned about him. Not wishing to detain them, we say goodbye to one another. Sean apologises for not being able to have a pint with me. They wave farewell and drive away. My old friend passed away a month later.

Anxious to keep my appointment at YCR, I walk along Catherine Street past the closed Youghal Carpets. Every street and lane are familiar to me and many of the houses as well. However, I do not intend to dwell on the history of this ancient town. After all, I am just a walker arriving after a journey into a town that teems with history. Arriving at the headquarters of YCR, the receptionist directs me to a waiting room where I begin to thaw out after the long walk. Within a short time, the presenter Mervyn Scott enters and extends a cordial welcome to me. Mervyn, a Dubliner, has put down roots here in Youghal. He then gives me a short summary of the questions he plans to ask me about the Blackwater. For my part, I am anxious to share the trip with the listeners as I feel that people should cherish the Blackwater and be more aware of the proud heritage that belongs to them. Mervyn, having introduced me, begins to ask questions: 'Why did you undertake the walk?' What were the highlights of the week for you? Any difficulties you encountered along the way? What places impressed you the most? Where does the Blackwater rise? What conclusions did you come to about the river?

Our conversation flows in a relaxed and pleasant way, and before I know it Mervyn is signing off and wishing me good luck with my plan to write a book about this very walk. Having said goodbye, I walk down the stairs but he follows me and presents me with a booklet about the religious community to which he belongs. Expressing my thanks, I casually ask him if there is anything about rivers in the publication. Glancing at the cover, I notice an illustration of the baptism of Christ in the River Jordan which turns my thoughts towards the symbolism of water and of rivers.

I had anticipated that arriving in Youghal would be a moment of elation but, on the contrary, a sense of anti-climax has affected me. The seven days have been filled with variety, sights, encounters, obstacles, castles, ruins, anglers, thoughts and feelings flitting in and out of the mind. Alas, the journey is over at a point where I have walked myself into fitness, knowing that I could endure another week exhilarating in the freedom and the contact with the primeval elements – air, water and earth. It is time to return home, but the fact that I have walked the Blackwater from source to sea, ó *Thriopall go caoin Eochaill*, leaves me with a quiet contentment.

Bibliography

Andrews, John Harwood, *A Paper Landscape: the Ordnance Survey in nineteenth-century Ireland* , Oxford Clarendon Press, 1975

An Introduction to the Architectural Heritage of North Cork, Government of Ireland, Department of the Environment, Heritage and Local Government, Dublin, 2009

Barry, Patrick (Patsy), *By Bride and Blackwater: Local History and Traditions,*

Donal de Barra, Miltown Malbay, Co. Clare, 2003

Baylor, Robert J. (ed.), *Fermoy and District Anglers Association: 60 Years a Growing, 1935 -1995*, (Fermoy, 1995)

Barry Connolly, Tom Barker, Kevin O'Farrell and Tom Tobin, *Walking in Fermoy, The Galtees and Surroundings*, Blackwater Development Group, 1999

Billensteiner, Friedrich & Heffernan, Kieran, *The History of Strancally Castle and the Valley between Lismore and Youghal*, 1999

Bowen, Elizabeth, *Bowen's Court*, Collins Press, 1998

Clifford, Brendan, *Duhallow: Notes Towards a History*, 1986

Cronin, Dan, *In the Shadow of the Paps*, Sliabh Luachra Heritage Group

Culloty, Anthony, *Ballydesmond: A Rural Parish in its Historical Setting*, Elo Press, Dublin, 1986

Deakin, Roger, *Wildwood: A Journey through Trees*, Penguin Books, 2007.

Dennis, Eugene F., *Lismore*, 2011

Denham Jephson, Maurice, *An Anglo-Irish Miscellany: Some Records of the Jephsons of Mallow*, Allen Figgis & Co, Dublin, 1964

Dickson, David, *Old World Colony: Cork and South Munster 1630-1830*, Cork University Press, 2005

Donnelly, James S., *The Land and People of Nineteenth-Century Cork: The Rural Economy and the Land Question*, Routledge and Kegan Paul, 1975.

Duffy, Patrick J., *Exploring the History and Heritage of Irish Landscapes*, Four Courts Press, 2007

Feehan & O'Donovan, *The Bogs of Ireland*, University College Dublin, 1996

Foster, John Wilson, *Nature in Ireland: A Scientific and Cultural History*, Lilliput, 2001

The Cambridge Companion to the Irish Novel

Goodwillie, Roger, *Areas of Scientific Interest*, An Foras Forbartha, 1986.

Eoghan Rua Ó Súilleabháin: Dánta, Poems with translations by Pat Muldowney, Aubane Historical Society, 2009.

Hadfield, Andrew, *Edmund Spenser: A Life*, Oxford University Press, 2012

Hackett, Mike, *Echoes over the Blackwater*, 1997

Hajba Anna-Maria, *Houses of Cork, Vol. I, North*, Ballinakella Press, 2002

Hall, Mr & Mrs Samuel, *Hall's Ireland: Mr & Mrs Hall's Tour of 1840*, Sphere Books

Healy, James, *The Castles of County Cork*, Mercier press, 1988

Hennessy Pope, *Sir Walter Raleigh*

Hepburn, Alan (Ed.), *People, Places, Things: Essays by Elizabeth Bowen*, Edinburgh University Press, 2008

Hickey, Donal, *Stone Mad for Music: The Sliabh Luachra Story*, Marino, 1999

Journal(s) of Cumann Luachra, Vol. 1, 14 December 2010. 'Time of the Fishing,' Padraig O Duinnín, p. 81 & 'A Night to Remember,' Fr Padraig Cox

Memories of Kilconey & Rathcoole¸ n.d.

Laing, Olivia, *To the River: A Journey Beneath the Surface*, Canongate Books, 2011

Lane, Jack, *250 Years of the Butter Road*, Aubane Historical Society

Leland, Mary, *The Lie of the Land: Journeys through Literary Cork*, Cork University Press, 1999

Mabey, Richard, *Nature Cure*, Chatto & Windus, London, 2005

Mac Greagóir Art, *Stair na nDéise*, Foillseacháin Rialtais, 1938

McCormack, Anthony M., *The Earldom of Desmond 1463-1583: The Decline and Crisis of a Feudal Lordship*, Four Courts Press, Dublin, 2005

Milner, Liam, *From the Kingdom to the Sea: The River Blackwater in History and Legend*, 1976.

Morrow, Ann, *Picnic in a Foreign Land*, Grafton Books, London, 1989

Moylan, Seán, *In His Own Words: His Memoir of the Irish War of Independence*, Aubane   Historical Society, Millstreet, 2004

O' Brien, Niall, *Blackwater and Bride: Navigation and Trade, 7000B.C to 2007*, Niall O Brien Publishing, Ballyduff Upr, Co. Waterford, 2008.

O' Brien, George, *The Village of Longing*, Viking & Lilliput Press, 1987.

Ó Cadhla, Diarmaid, Seanchas Duthalla, 1976-77; *Duarrigle Castle*, p. 16-17

Ó Conchúir, Breandán (Eag), *Eoghan Rua Ó Súileabháin*, Field Day Publications, BaileÁtha Cliath, 2009

Ó Conluain, Proinsias agus Ó Céilleachair, Donncha, *An Duinníneach: An tAthair Pádraig Ó Duinnín, a shaothar agus an Ré inar Mhair sé*, Sáirséal agus Dill, Baile Átha Cliath, 1958

O'Connor, Kevin, *The Ironing of the Landscape: the Coming of the Railways to Ireland*, Gill & Macmillan, 1999.

O'Flanagan, J. R., *The River Blackwater in Munster: Historical and Picturesque Guide to the River Blackwater in Munster*, facsimile edition, Tower Books, 1975, first edition 1844

Ó hÓgáin, Daithí, *The Lore of Ireland: An Encyclopedia of Myth, Legend and Romance*

O'Keeffe, Peter & Simmington Bob, *Irish Stone Bridges, History and Heritage*, Academic Press, 1991

O'Keeffe, Tadhg, *An Anglo-Irish Monastery (Bridgetown)*, Cork County Council, 1999

Ó Liatháin, Annraoi, *Cois Móire*, Sairséal agus Dill, 1964

O' Mahony, Tony, *The Wild Flowers of Cork City and County*, The Collins Press, 2009.

Ó Muirthille, Liam, *An Teanga Bheo, Abhainn Mhór*, Irish Times

O Regan, Edward, *In Irish Waterways*, Currach Press, Blackrock, Co. Dublin, 2005

Top of Form

Ó Ríordáin, John J., *Where Araglen so Gently Flows: A Story of Munster and of*

Ireland through life around Kiskeam in Duhallow, Co. Cork, 2007.

O Riordan, John J., *A Tragic Troubadour: Life and Collected Works of Folklorist, Poet and Translator, Edward Walsh 1805-1850*

Pochin Mould, *Discovering Cork*, Brandon, 1999.

Power, Bill, *Fermoy on the Blackwater*, Brogown Press, Mitchelstown, 2009

Power, Patrick, Rev, *Logainmneacha na nDéise: The Place-Names of the Decies*, Cork University Press, 1952

Radley, Seán (ed.), *Picture Millstreet: A Photographic Profile of Millstreet 1880 – 1980*, Millstreet Museum Society, 1997

Roche, Christy, *The Ford of the Apples: A History of Ballyhooly, earliest times to 2008*, Éigse Books & Ballyhooly GAA, 1998 & 2008

Solnit, Rebecca, *Wanderlust: A History of Walking*, Verso, London & New

York, paperback edition, 2002

Spenser, Edmund, *A View of the Present state of Ireland* (Ed. W.L. Renwick), Oxford, Clarendon Press, 1970

Twomey, Michael, *Irish Heart & English Blood: The Making of Youghal*, The History Press Ireland, Dublin, 2014

Tucker, Fr Sean, *The Origin and the Development of the Parish of Millstreet*, Aubane Historical Society, 2003.

Whelan, David A., *The Big Houses of the Blackwater Valley*, thesis, NUIM

WEBSITES

www.ainm.ie|Irish –language biographies

www.buildingsofireland.ie

http://irishwaterwayshistory.com

www.logainm.ie|Placenames Database of Ireland

www.ose|Ordnance Survey Ireland

Index